IMAGES
of America

Portland's Goose Hollow

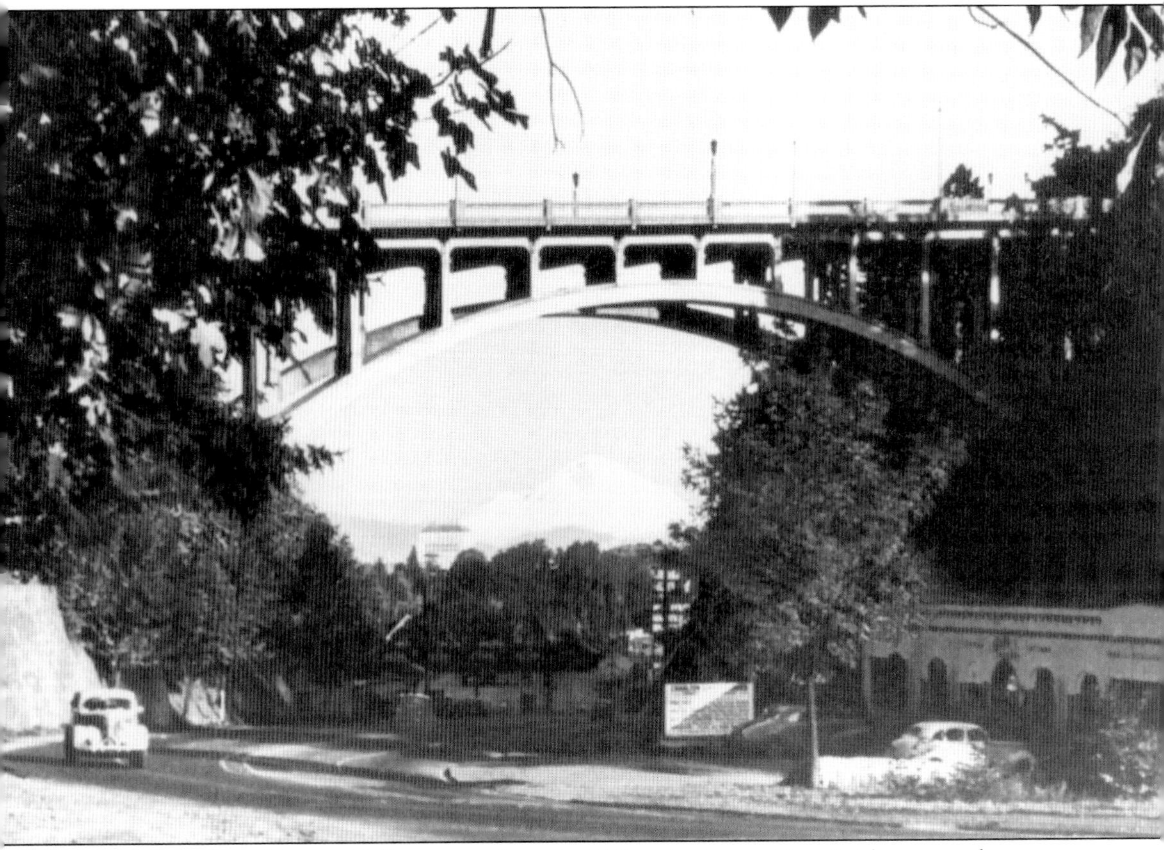

A quintessential Goose Hollow scene from the 1930s, the iconic Vista Bridge spans the canyon, the only remaining part of "the hollow" carved out by Tanner Creek that is now Jefferson/Canyon Road. King's Hill is on the left, with Vista Ridge on the right—both are in Goose Hollow. Nowadays downtown buildings block this perspective of Mount Hood. The MAX light rail runs through the Robertson Tunnel near where the Charlton Laboratories once stood. (Janice Ahl.)

On the Cover: From 1902 until 1960, Multnomah Field hosted Rose Carnival activities (changed to Rose Festival in 1907). Generations of Oregonians visited Goose Hollow, participating in and viewing pageantries of athletic exhibitions, acrobatic displays, parades, and fireworks. This gymnastics-inspired act performed for the 1936 Rose Festival, with the next act waiting on the stage. The garage advertising "Machine Work" in the upper left was on Southwest Eighteenth Avenue. (OrHi bb007430.)

IMAGES
of America

Portland's Goose Hollow

Tracy J. Prince

ARCADIA
PUBLISHING

ISBN 978-0-7385-7472-1

Published by Arcadia Publishing
Charleston, South Carolina

Printed in the United States of America

Library of Congress Control Number: 2010938532

For all general information, please contact Arcadia Publishing:
Telephone 843-853-2070
Fax 843-853-0044
E-mail sales@arcadiapublishing.com
For customer service and orders:
Toll-Free 1-888-313-2665

Visit us on the Internet at www.arcadiapublishing.com

To my wonderful husband, Scott Schaffer, my fellow Goose Hollow booster and technical advisor, for your patience, encouragement, and mad organizational skills during my many months of research.

Contents

FOREWORD

It is wonderful to see how this book preserves Goose Hollow's history, a topic close to my heart. The Goose Hollow neighborhood has given me a lifetime of memories of good times, friends, and landmarks like the Blue Baboon Tavern (located at Fourteenth and Jefferson) and, of course, the original Goose Hollow Inn that was on Sixteenth and Jefferson when I was growing up.

When I was six years old, in 1938, my family moved to the Imperial Arms Apartments at Fourteenth and Clay Streets in Goose Hollow. I loved racing my scooter down Clay Street to the bottom of the hill, where my friends and I built forts and made tunnels under the blackberry bushes on a vacant lot. We kids roamed freely—climbing the public stairways on Market Street, picking and eating wild sweet pea blossoms as we climbed to Vista Avenue and crossed the Vista Bridge. On my way to Washington Park, I always admired the magnificent homes on Park Place, wondering who lived there.

When we moved to Northwest Portland a few years later, I watched my old neighborhood and saw that within a few decades almost no one knew that there was a neighborhood called Goose Hollow. The old Goose Hollow Inn was torn down in 1948, and a car dealer calling himself "the Mayor of Goose Hollow" in his advertisements was long gone too. I remembered my old "homestead playground" and wanted that identity and sense of place back. So in 1967, forty-six years after I left Goose Hollow, I bought Ann's Tavern and changed the name to the Goose Hollow Inn. "The Goose" became a neighborhood gathering place. And by the time the Goose Hollow neighborhood association was formed in the mid-1970s, the identity of the neighborhood was no longer uncertain.

Besides having my business in Goose Hollow for more than four decades, in 2010 I decided that I wanted to move back. I now live high in an apartment building overlooking my neighborhood and its beautiful surroundings. I agree with *Money Magazine* when, in 2007, it named Goose Hollow a top neighborhood to retire to.

Whoop! Whoop!!

—Mayor Bud Clark

ACNOWLEDGMENTS

Living in a 100-year-old house in Goose Hollow and having countless Portlanders tell me that in the 1960s they broke in and smoked pot in the basement, I've always known that Goose Hollow has a lot of stories to tell. (For a decade, architectural salvage preservationist Eric Ladd used the house to store his treasures.) While researching those stories, I met historians Norm Gholston, William Hawkins, Don Nelson, and Mike Ryerson whose knowledge of local history is astounding and who graciously lent many images for this book. Thank you to Margaret Parypa and Janice Ahl for the use of images. For lovely times spent discussing the good ol' days, thank you to Albert Gentner (whose family owned the Mallory Hotel from 1943 to 2005); Jane Kendall (who grew up next door to the C. E. S. Wood family, when the house on the northwest corner of St. Clair Avenue and Kings Court was next door to what is now the Portland Garden Club); and Eloise Durkheimer Spiegel (whose grandparents and great aunt and uncle built mirror-image homes at 2220 and 2226 Southwest Main Street, leaving the windows open between the houses and chatting with each other throughout the day). I am much obliged to Drew Vattiat at the *Oregonian* and Geoff Wexler at the Oregon Historical Society, without whose help many dynamic images would not have been included. (Oregon Historical Society images are identified by OrHi with the image number). The City of Portland Archives (CoPA) is appreciated for making its images available online—an incredible resource. Hugs to my children, Zadie and Price—they wondered why the house exploded with piles of pictures. My gratitude is extended to Aaron Johanson, a talented neighbor who contributed his photography, and to neighbors Jean Auel, George Johanson, and Ken Shores who patiently posed around the neighborhood. Uncredited images are from my collection. I am grateful to Arcadia Publishing editors Sarah Higginbotham, Devon Weston, and Donna Libert who graciously shepherded me through the book-making process. And I am deeply indebted to Bud Clark who lent photographs from the walls at the Goose Hollow Inn and paved the way for preserving Goose Hollow's identity.

—Tracy J. Prince, Ph.D.

Introduction

One of the oldest neighborhoods in Portland, once on the far western edge of town, Goose Hollow is now a close-in neighborhood. The Goose Hollow boundaries include King's Hill, Vista Ridge, and Gander Ridge in the heights and the original boundaries of Goose Hollow in the flats. The first use of the Goose Hollow name in the 1870s referred only to the lower elevations around the path of Tanner Creek. However, since the 1970s the Goose Hollow name has applied to the larger neighborhood of flats and adjacent heights and canyons. (See map on page 126.) Today's Goose Hollow is beloved for its quirky character, historic residences, and spectacular views of the Portland skyline, Mount Hood, Mount Adams, Mount St. Helens, and even Mount Rainer on a clear day.

When the first settlers came to Portland, the region had few remaining indigenous people. In 1805, Lewis and Clark estimated that there were 2,400 Chinook-speaking Native Americans living on nearby Sauvie Island and another 1,800 along the shore. West of Goose Hollow, across the Tualatin Mountains, the Atfalati tribe, also called the Tualatin (of the Kalapuya people), lived in the Tualatin Valley and periodically burned brush to corral deer and make food gathering easier. Interaction with European explorers and traders brought outbreaks of malaria, smallpox, and influenza, almost wiping out entire tribes. When settlers traversed the Oregon Trail in the 1840s, they found large areas around the Willamette Valley, which includes the Tualatin Valley, almost completely empty of native people. However, historically, Native American travelers had set up temporary camps along the river in "the clearing" now known as Portland, and the Atfalati hunted, gathered, and did periodic burns in the Tualatin Mountains (known locally as the West Hills).

The first pioneer resident of Goose Hollow, Daniel Lownsdale, established a land claim near a creek in 1845. He opened a tannery where Civic Stadium now stands and chose the spot because of its abundant water supply (which was later named Tanner Creek) and the proximity of hemlock trees. Ground hemlock bark is an astringent used to tan leather. According to Joseph Gaston's 1911 history of Portland, Lownsdale's was the only tannery north of Mexico and west of the Rockies. As the only regional commercial source for tanned skins drew a stream of customers, the tannery played a significant role in boosting commerce for the young frontier town, which was incorporated in 1851 with approximately 800 residents. Daniel Lownsdale went on to become an important, though not well-remembered, city father. He sold his tannery and land in 1848 to a Mr. Apperson and Mr. Balance, though they quickly sold out to Amos King and headed to the California gold rush. Using $5,000 worth of leather goods, Lownsdale bought out Francis Pettygrove's land claim beside the Willamette River. Pettygrove won the famous coin toss with Asa Lovejoy, thus the right to name the town after Portland, a city in his home state of Maine. Like Lovejoy, who sold his interests in 1845, Pettygrove sold his stake, moving on to other prospects.

Even as Daniel Lownsdale was helping convince Portland to tax itself and build the Great Plank Road, the area around Canyon Road (the road he wanted to plank) was thought of as the seedy side of town, with a deep gulch and creek cutting through a "no man's land." At a time when Portland's Chinese residents faced the Chinese Exclusion Act (1882) and routine abuse, Chinese farmers rented land in the gulch from Amos King, for truck farms alongside the flood-prone Tanner Creek. Mostly forgotten in Portland's collective memory, Chinese Vegetable Gardens and shanties once covered 21 acres of Goose Hollow, including on the slope and in the gulch where the Multnomah Amateur Athletic Club and stadium were built. (Amateur was dropped from the name, and the club is often called "the MAC.")

According to Joseph Gaston, Goose Hollow was a place where "a miscellaneous lot of people got in there who did not really go in the 'upper ten' class of 1862." An *Oregonian* reader, quoted on April 12, 1914, remembered it as a "gulch" filled with "shabby" houses and people: "Some years ago, when the gulch at the base of the Heights Terrace was known as Goose Hollow and was bordered by small shanties with shabby inhabitants, the hillside was covered with dense undergrowth and dotted with tall fir trees. A favorite promenade, even then, was Heights Terrace, despite the steep climb and the fact that the old boardwalk was in bad repair. The commanding elevation revealed a superb view, the shacks below being hidden by a fringe of fir trees." The referenced shacks were the Chinese shanties and small cottages housing mostly Irish and German immigrants. Today's residents are intrigued by the blue-collar origins of the neighborhood and the little-known history of the Chinese Vegetable Gardens. Like many American place names with the word "hollow," Goose Hollow was a name with negative connotations, though a name now adored by its residents.

Tanner Creek was once an important part of Portland. The creek meandered through Goose Hollow and Northwest Portland, flowing into Couch Lake (covering parts of today's Old Town/ Chinatown and Pearl District neighborhoods, largely wetlands at the time). To put the Tanner Creek Gulch into perspective, Weinhard's Brewery (now the Brewery Blocks Development) was once on the edge of the gulch, which was several blocks wide and 50 feet deep at that point. A July 14, 1921, *Oregonian* article pointed out back in the day when the best place to catch catfish was in the lake where Union Station now stands. Generations of Portlanders learned to swim in the creek's swimming holes and caught trout in the creek. In the March 21, 1922, issue of the *Oregonian*, a man remembered when he and his friends caught 60 trout "one fine afternoon . . . between Sixteenth and [Burnside] streets and the Willamette River." According to the July 29, 1921, issue, one reader remembered catching crawfish "in the springs along the bottoms," while another remembered it in the August 26, 1921, issue as "the beautiful trout stream up what is now Jefferson street, ran through what is now Multnomah field, crossed [Burnside] . . . and reached the river at about what is now Quimby street." Another fascinating story from the January 24, 1922, issue recalled when children used old boards to raft the creek's currents underneath the trestle at today's Burnside Street.

Diverted underground from the 1870s to the early 1900s, with extensive use of Chinese and Irish laborers, Tanner Creek still drains the surrounding hills via storm drains, though it runs to the Willamette River as a shadow of its former self in a deeply buried culvert. Even on a dry summer day, the creek can be heard rushing by under manhole covers near its historic course. One of the best spots to hear the creek is at a manhole cover on the west end of the Goose Hollow MAX Station.

For a short time from the 1860s to the 1870s, Tanner Creek was called "Canyon Creek," and the neighborhood was also briefly referred to by this name. For example, a Dr. McLennan advertised in the *Oregonian* from 1878 to 1879 about his ability to cure by "vital magnetism," including a patient testimonial with the patient's address listed as "Canyon Creek, Portland, Oregon." Possibly this name became confusing since newspaper reports were coming back from gold strikes near a Canyon Creek in Oregon and silver strikes near a Canyon Creek in Idaho. If this neighborhood name had stuck it would be difficult to explain today since the creek has been buried for more than a century. It is likely that when the Goose Hollow nickname was first applied to the area in the 1870s (see page 18), the quirkier name quickly gained traction over one only intermittently used.

Except for the Tanner Creek Canyon, all of the gullies, cuts, gulches, and swampy lowlands created by the creek over centuries have long since been filled in. The most notable example is the infill that occurred around Eighteenth Street and on the land where the stadium now stands where once stood several tall trestles for crossing the Tanner Creek Gulch. The intersection at Eighteenth Avenue and Salmon Street runs across 50 feet of infill where a block-long trestle bridge once spanned the gulch. Most of the Lincoln High School field was part of the gulch and home to another group of Chinese farmers. Houses one block north of Lincoln High School's field on Taylor Street were once on pilings, hanging over the edge of the gulch.

An enormous amount of infill was required to level Tanner Creek's 50-foot-deep gulch. This was partially obtained when new streets were cut through what was once a more rolling terrain in northwest Portland. An August 17, 1873, article from the *Oregonian* describes the grading of B Street (later called Washington, then Burnside Street) west of the gulch as a monumental task with cuts sometimes 25 feet deep. The dirt was hauled to the edge of Tanner Creek Gulch and dumped in. Throughout the northwest Portland neighborhoods of Nob Hill and Slabtown, it is easy to see how much dirt was hauled away to create streets and sidewalks since yards in this area are often several feet higher than the road. An excellent example can be seen at Temple Beth Israel between Flanders and Glisan Streets on Nineteenth Avenue where the property is high rolling terrain with the street cut through many feet below. When the deeply buried Tanner Creek Culvert was repaired in 2001, workers reported finding infill made up of rock, dirt, garbage, bricks, boulders, concrete, wood, tree stumps, old streetcar tracks, and old planked roads. This is not surprising since the trestle bridge across the Alder Street Gulch even had a trap door for street cleaners to dump refuse into the ravine.

Though most of the creek's hollow has been topped up and smoothed over, Tanner Creek's presence is still felt in this neighborhood's identity and in the hollow it carved out of the West Hills, spanned by the Vista Bridge. However, even the remaining hollow, Canyon Road (now part of Highway 26), was once in a deeper ravine. (Jefferson Road becomes Canyon Road as it enters the ravine.) When the Foothills and Stadium Freeways were cut through Goose Hollow in the 1960s, the excavated dirt was dumped into the ravine, thus raising the old Canyon Road so that it could more easily meet up with the tunnel drilled through Vista Ridge.

By the early years of the 20th century, with the heights accessible by streetcar, preceded by a cable car, Goose Hollow followed similar patterns of other neighborhoods around the city, with middle- and upper-class folks heading to the higher elevations and "foreigners" and lower income people occupying the lower elevations. Goose Hollow's lower elevations were known for its many "workingmen's cottages." According to a 1930 map, which carefully detailed where black and foreign-born residents lived in Portland, there were many foreign-born and a few African American residents in Goose Hollow.

With the advent of the automobile culture, Goose Hollow came to be known briefly as a hub for automobile dealers, service stations, and repair shops, often located where horse stables and streetcar barns once stood. One resident reminisced about how quiet it was before automobiles came along. Orvaleta Dodd, as recorded in the fall 1984 issue of *Oregon Historical Quarterly*, remembered Goose Hollow's streets lined with fragrant roses, and the streets were so empty she roller skated down Clay Street using a broom handle as a brake. It was so quiet she could hear the lion roar at the zoo, then located near today's Rose Garden in Washington Park. The western boundary of the neighborhood, City Park/Washington Park was and is an important part of life in Goose Hollow, so this book briefly details its history.

By the late 1960s, Goose Hollow faced the bulldozers of urban "renewal," and the neighborhood name had fallen out of common usage for several decades. Bud Clark's strategy, to rename a tavern he purchased in the hollow as the Goose Hollow Inn to help rekindle civic regard for the neighborhood, prevented the neighborhood name from fading away. Today neighborhood spirit is strong. Geese now flap once again throughout the neighborhood, as many residents and businesses fly Goose Hollow banners with pride. Now Goose Hollow is a well-situated neighborhood, just steps from downtown. It is graced with diverse and interesting architecture, a lovely park next door, and excellent light rail access. It is the kind of place where residents walk to their destinations and greet neighbors along the way. It is dense urban living done well.

One

A Tannery, a Creek, and "A War About Geese"

1845–1879

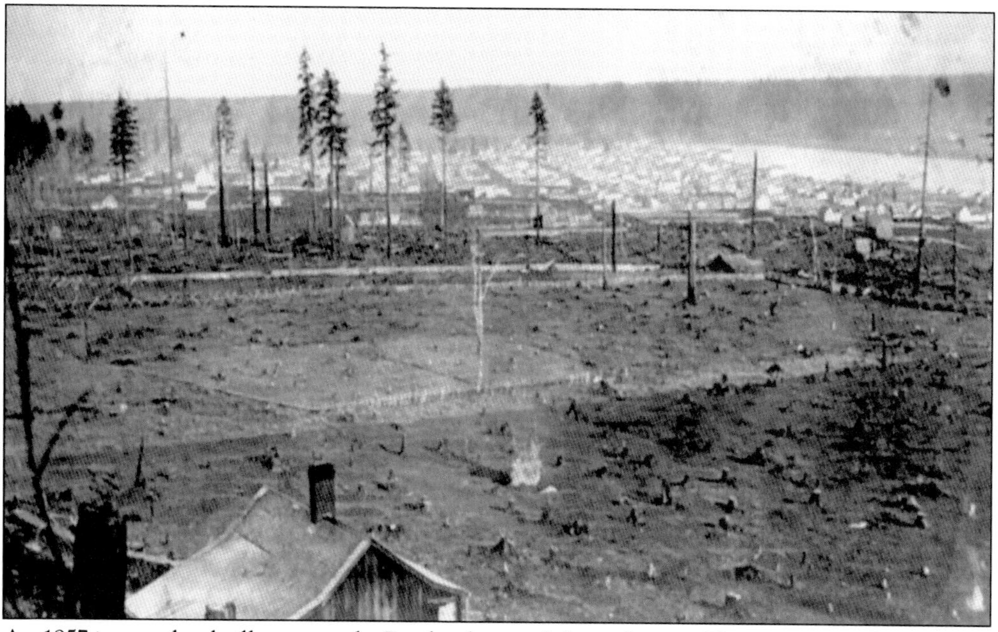

An 1857 image clearly illustrates why Portland earned the nickname "Stumptown"—from stumps left after thick forests were cleared for the new town. Jefferson Street is at the lower end of the platted section and extends to the far left, where today's Goose Hollow begins. The tannery (out of the frame, near the grove of trees to the far left) was in operation at this time and owned by Amos King. (OrHi-5487.)

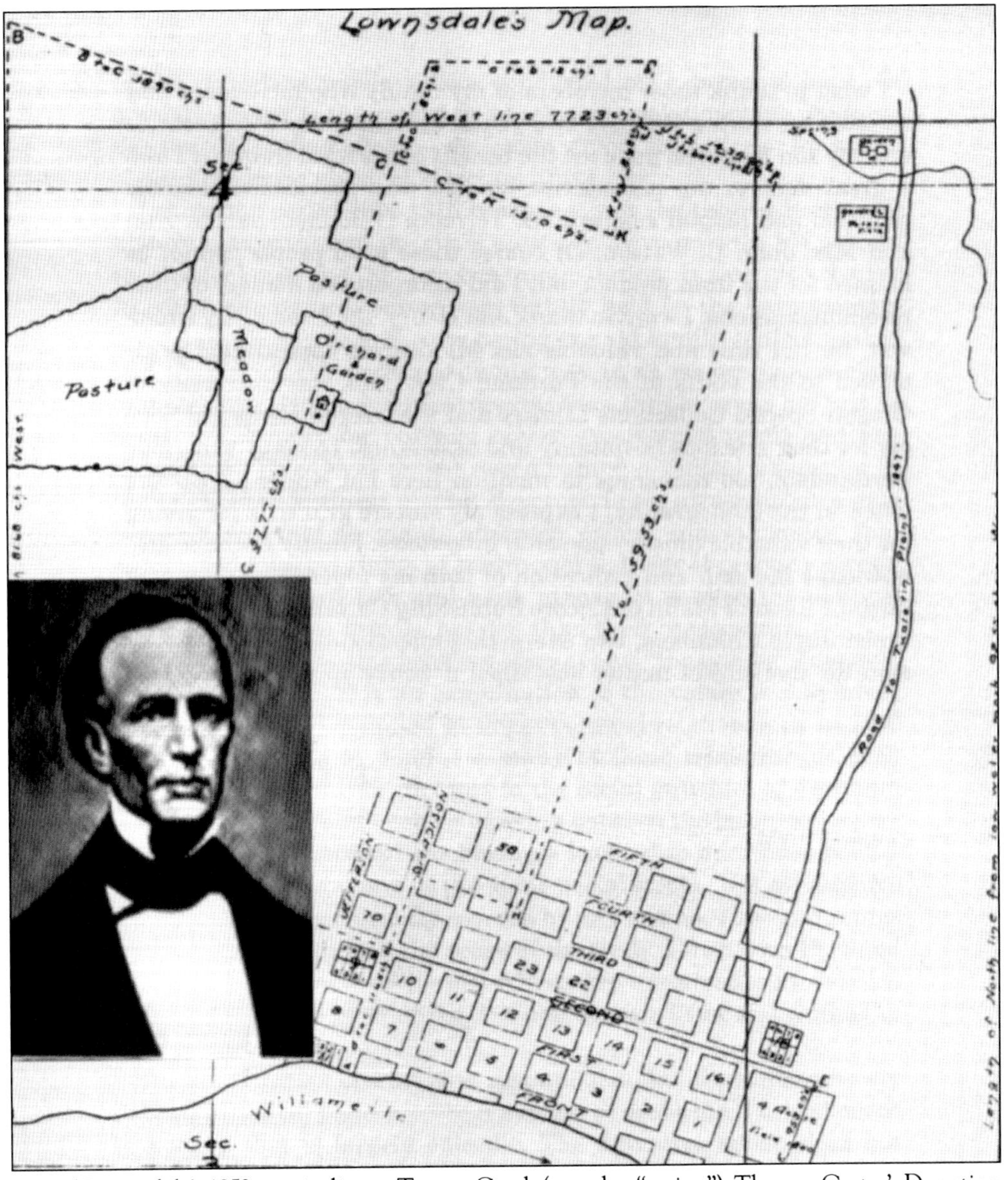

Daniel Lownsdale's 1852 map indicates Tanner Creek (noted as "spring"). Thomas Carter's Donation Land Claim, filed in 1850, was in the upper left with Amos King in the house above the spring and the tannery buildings below depicted in the upper right. The indicated "road to Tualatin Plains—1847" was known as Tuality Road and passed over the hill through today's Washington Park. This planked road (created by Francis Pettygrove in 1845) was more useful than the mucky unplanked Canyon Road because it followed the well-drained crests of the hill. Today's Burnside Street partially follows the path of the old Tuality Road. Sometimes called Portland's first suburb, the area that later became Goose Hollow was described by Joseph Gaston in 1911 as "a sort of 'no man's land,' being too far out to be salable for city lots, and not worth grubbing out to put in potatoes." (CoPA.)

According to H. W. Scott in 1890, Canyon Road passed "through woods so deep that the mud dried only by virtue of the longest droughts." Despite being the shortest route across the Tualatin Mountains, before it was planked it was a hard slog through a muddy ravine. Though water is visible on the left in this c. 1900 image, Tanner Creek is likely on the right where a depression and denser vegetation can be seen. (OrHi-bb005723.)

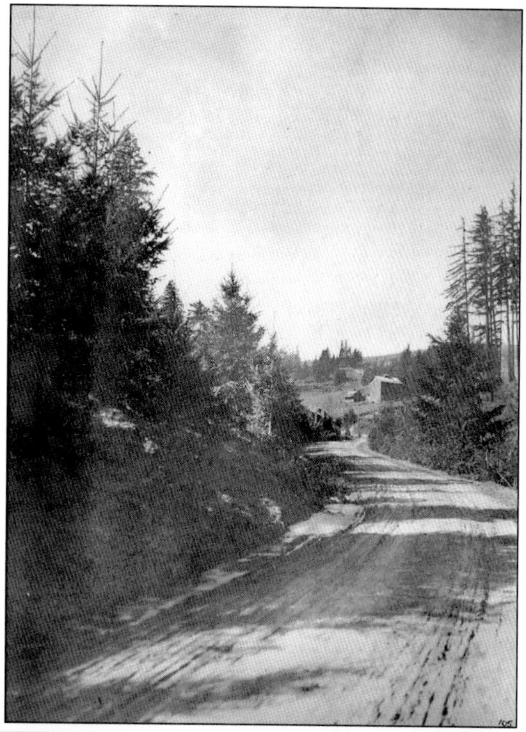

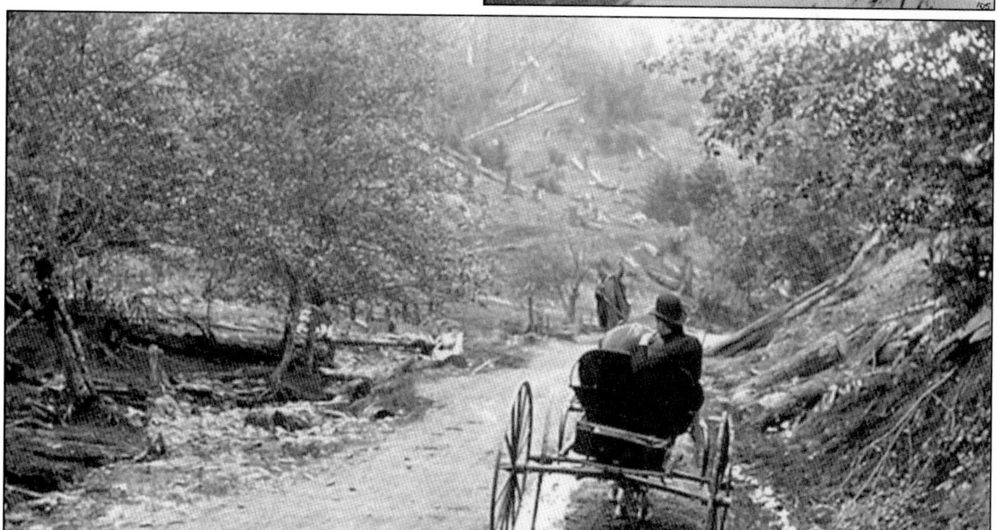

Opened in 1856, the Great Plank Road (now Jefferson/Canyon Road), pictured here in 1896, was the arms race of its day because whichever city could provide Tualatin Valley farmers the best access to a harbor would win the race to be the biggest and best port city in the area. The Willamette Valley, which includes the Tualatin Valley, has produced bumper crops of wheat, hops, fruit, nuts, and vegetables since the 1840s. (CoPA.)

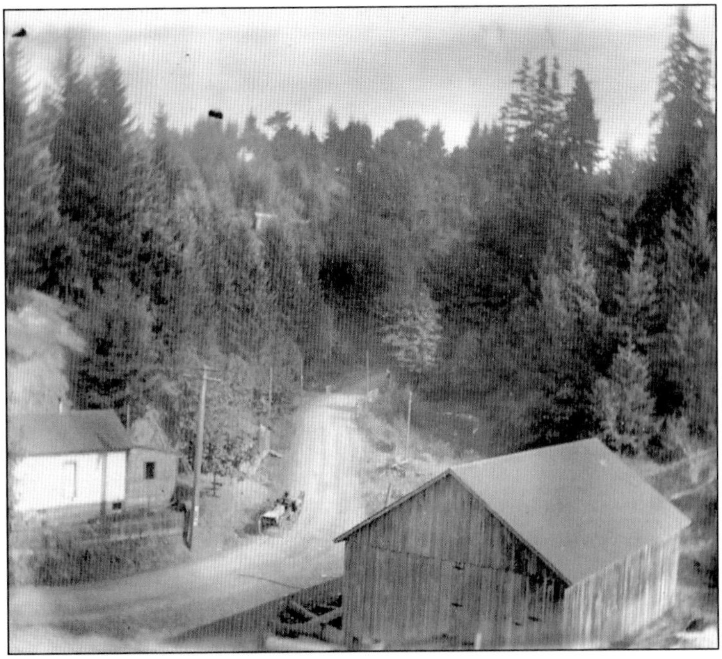

Daniel Lownsdale believed that Portland's role as the primary harbor—contending against Oregon City, Milwaukee, and St. Helens—could be secured by investing in a planked road through the hollow. St. Helens gave Portland a run for its money by building Cornelius Pass Road, but in the end the planked Canyon Road, pictured here around 1903, proved more expeditious and Portland's harbor deeper. (OrHi-bb006775.)

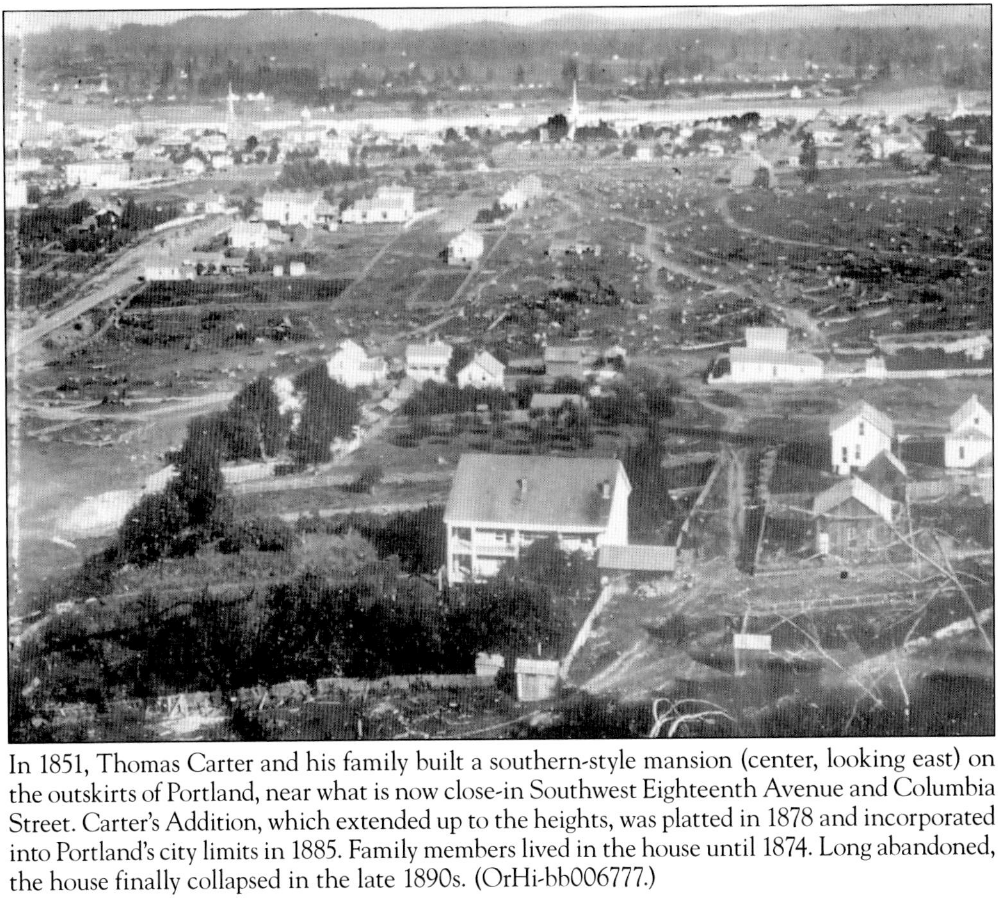

In 1851, Thomas Carter and his family built a southern-style mansion (center, looking east) on the outskirts of Portland, near what is now close-in Southwest Eighteenth Avenue and Columbia Street. Carter's Addition, which extended up to the heights, was platted in 1878 and incorporated into Portland's city limits in 1885. Family members lived in the house until 1874. Long abandoned, the house finally collapsed in the late 1890s. (OrHi-bb006777.)

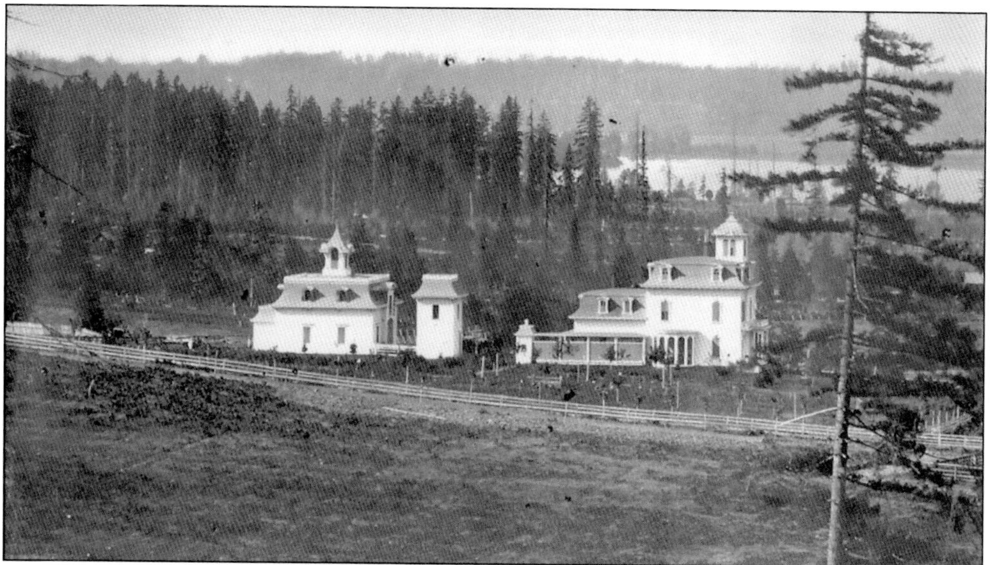

Arthur Johnson's home, pictured here around 1870, extended from today's Southwest St. Clair Street to Vista Avenue. Johnson owned a slaughterhouse beside a small stream near Twenty-third and Flanders Streets. He married Cordelia St. Clair in 1853, bought the land from Amos King, and platted out Johnson's Addition in 1871 (naming a street after his wife). Burnside Street passes through a canyon carved out by Johnson Creek (buried in 1889), named after Arthur, which headed north around Northwest Twentieth Avenue. (OrHi-bb007442.)

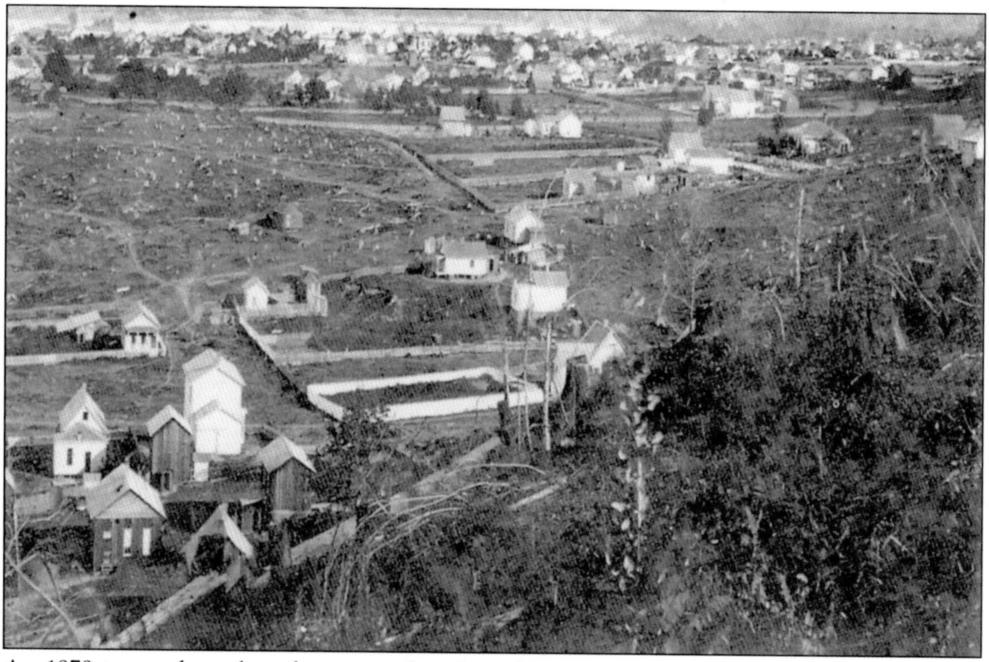

An 1878 image shows how far out on the edge of "stumptown" Goose Hollow once was. This photograph was taken from Vista Ridge, at the time called Mr. Carter's Hill, looking south toward Gander Ridge. By this time, the tannery (to the north of this area) was no longer in operation and Amos King's profession was listed in the 1873 city directory as "speculator." (King's Addition was platted in 1871.) (OrHi-bb007447.)

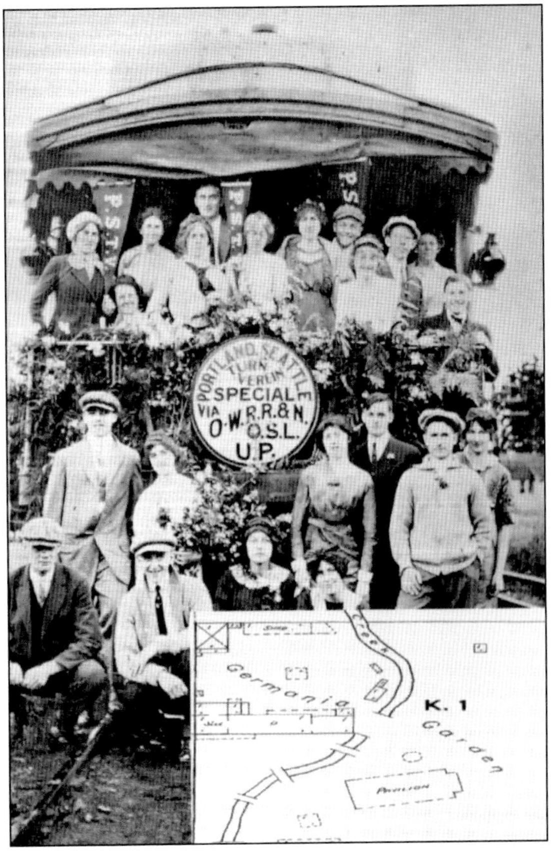

From 1868 to the 1910s, German immigrants, such as members of the Turn-Verein (which translates as "gymnastics club")—a German-American gymnastics, civic, and social association pictured on a 1913 trip (left) and around 1910 at their Thirteenth Street gymnasium (below)—enjoyed picnics, concerts, athletic events, and dances at Canyon Gardens. Located at the northwest corner of today's Eighteenth and Jefferson Streets and extending across the site of today's Goose Hollow Inn, over the years Canyon Gardens was also known as Germania Gardens and Brussels Gardens. Henry Miller, a German immigrant known as an avid horticulturist, sold flowers nearby. (Left, OrHi-ba018167 and 1889 Sanborn map database; below, Norm Gholston.)

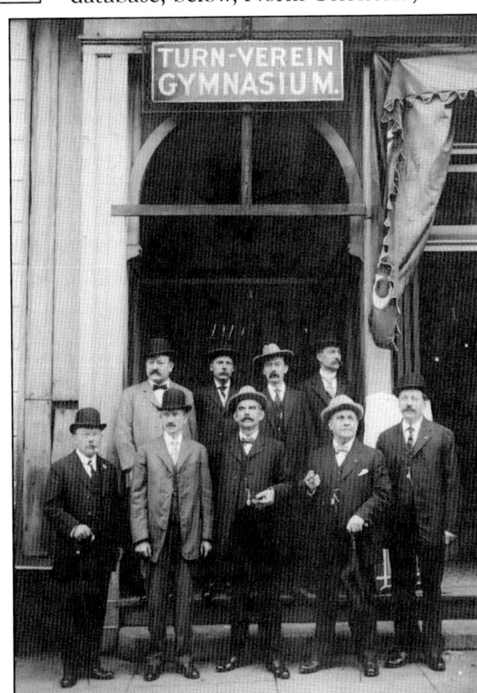

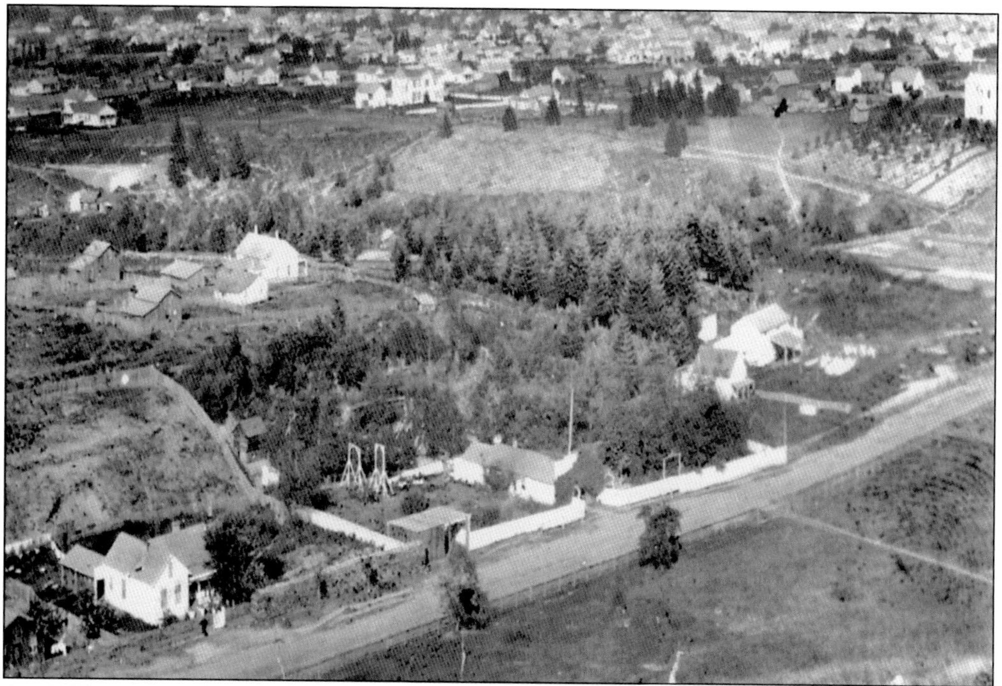

An 1875 view north from the heights shows developing activity surrounding Jefferson/Canyon Road. The white fenced enclosure in the foreground is Canyon Garden, with its wooden gymnastics equipment visible. Tanner Creek flowed through the garden. Water can be seen in the creek bed as it runs alongside Jefferson Street at the right, then slants toward Tanner Creek Gulch. This is a rare sighting of water flowing in the banks of Tanner Creek. (OrHi-bb007427.)

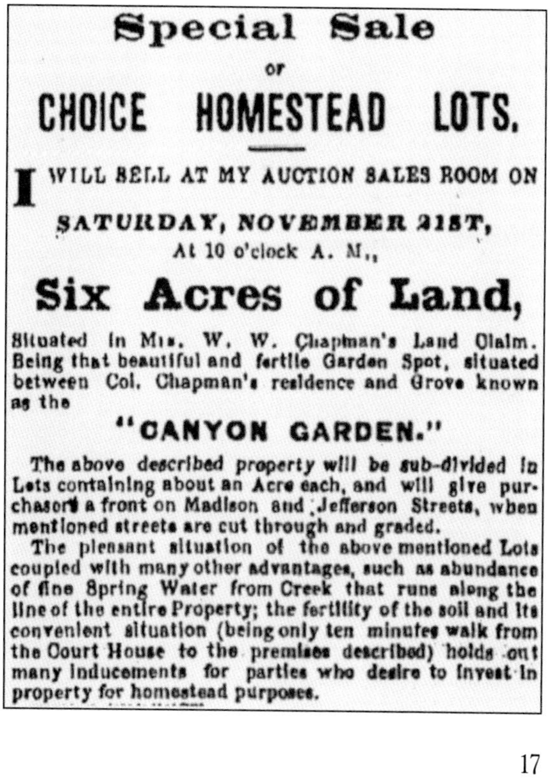

Special Sale

OF

CHOICE HOMESTEAD LOTS.

I WILL SELL AT MY AUCTION SALES ROOM ON

SATURDAY, NOVEMBER 21ST,

At 10 o'clock A. M.,

Six Acres of Land,

Situated in Mrs. W. W. Chapman's Land Claim. Being that beautiful and fertile Garden Spot, situated between Col. Chapman's residence and Grove known as the

"CANYON GARDEN."

The above described property will be sub-divided in Lots containing about an Acre each, and will give purchasers a front on Madison and Jefferson Streets, when mentioned streets are cut through and graded.

The pleasant situation of the above mentioned Lots coupled with many other advantages, such as abundance of fine Spring Water from Creek that runs along the line of the entire Property; the fertility of the soil and its convenient situation (being only ten minutes walk from the Court House to the premises described) holds out many inducements for parties who desire to invest in property for homestead purposes.

A November 13, 1868, *Oregonian* advertisement offers land for sale out near Canyon Garden, a "pleasant situation" with an "abundance of fine Spring Water from Creek that runs along the entire property" (Tanner Creek) and "only ten minutes walk" to the courthouse. (*Oregonian.*)

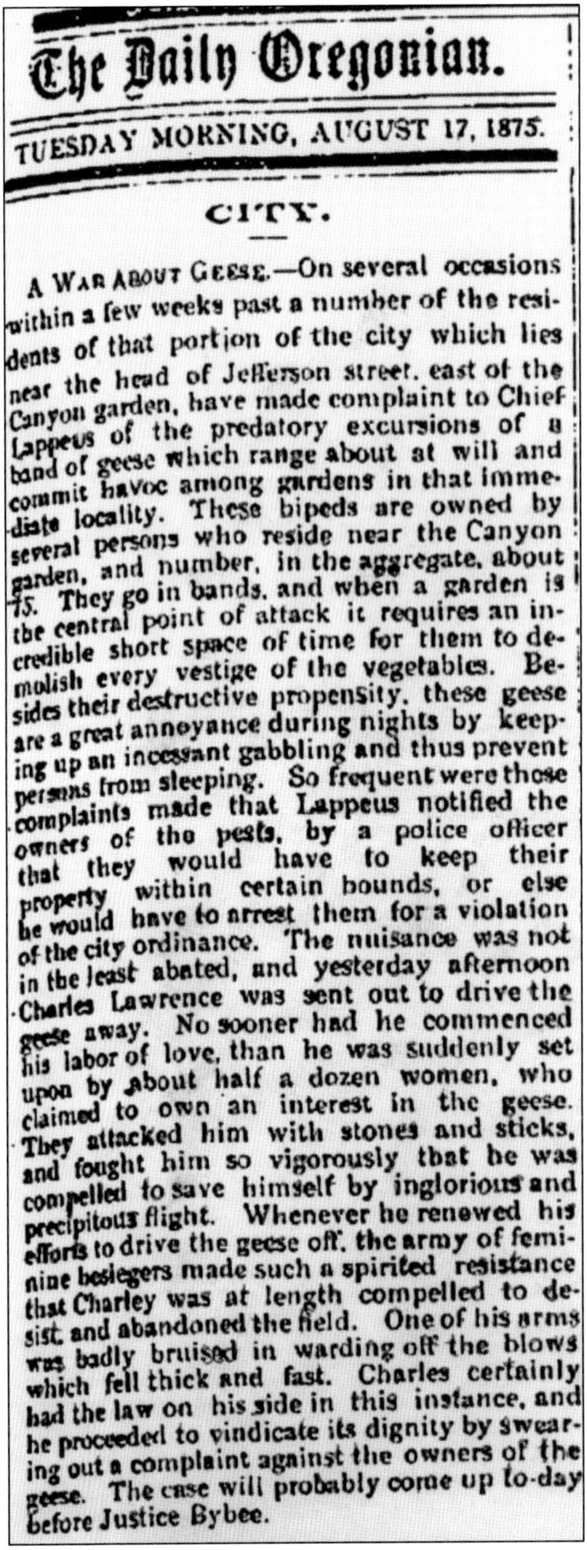

The Daily Oregonian.

TUESDAY MORNING, AUGUST 17, 1875.

CITY.

A WAR ABOUT GEESE.—On several occasions within a few weeks past a number of the residents of that portion of the city which lies near the head of Jefferson street, east of the Canyon garden, have made complaint to Chief Lappeus of the predatory excursions of a band of geese which range about at will and commit havoc among gardens in that immediate locality. These bipeds are owned by several persons who reside near the Canyon garden, and number, in the aggregate, about 75. They go in bands, and when a garden is the central point of attack it requires an incredible short space of time for them to demolish every vestige of the vegetables. Besides their destructive propensity, these geese are a great annoyance during nights by keeping up an incessant gabbling and thus prevent persons from sleeping. So frequent were these complaints made that Lappeus notified the owners of the pests, by a police officer that they would have to keep their property within certain bounds, or else he would have to arrest them for a violation of the city ordinance. The nuisance was not in the least abated, and yesterday afternoon Charles Lawrence was sent out to drive the geese away. No sooner had he commenced his labor of love, than he was suddenly set upon by about half a dozen women, who claimed to own an interest in the geese. They attacked him with stones and sticks, and fought him so vigorously that he was compelled to save himself by inglorious and precipitous flight. Whenever he renewed his efforts to drive the geese off, the army of feminine besiegers made such a spirited resistance that Charley was at length compelled to desist and abandoned the field. One of his arms was badly bruised in warding off the blows which fell thick and fast. Charles certainly had the law on his side in this instance, and he proceeded to vindicate its dignity by swearing out a complaint against the owners of the geese. The case will probably come up to-day before Justice Bybee.

In 1875, a neighborhood argument over geese made big news in Portland. This *Oregonian* article from August 17, 1875, written somewhat tongue-in-cheek, tells of squabbles requiring police intervention. A Works Progress Administration–commissioned history of Portland from 1940 describes the judge's "Solomonic decision" to "round up all the flocks and divide the geese equally." He also threatened to jail "the first woman to start another ruckus over geese." Thereafter the neighborhood's identity captured the city's imagination as a gulch (hollow) with women squabbling over geese. Portland historians H. W. Scott and Joseph Gaston credit police chief James Lappeus with naming the neighborhood Goose Hollow after this incident, though this has not been confirmed with primary sources. The first use of Goose Hollow appeared in the *Oregonian* in 1879. In 1889, there was a brief attempt to change the name to Paradise Valley; nevertheless, the more colorful Goose Hollow prevailed. Though at times a pejorative term, the name is now celebrated by its residents. (*Oregonian*.)

Two

Tanner Creek Gulch, Chinese Vegetable Gardens, and Cable Cars 1879–1910

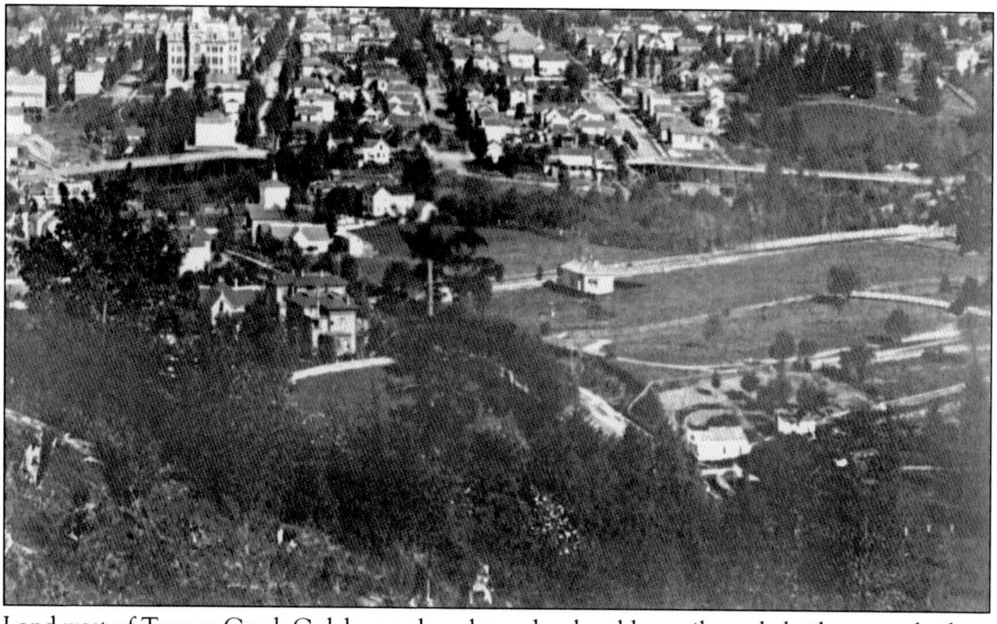

Land west of Tanner Creek Gulch was thought undevelopable until trestle bridges were built to span the gulch. This 1887 image shows how anomalous "the flats" of Goose Hollow are today since bridges spanned several blocks of a 50-foot-deep gulch. All of today's Morrison Street west of Eighteenth Avenue, most of Alder Street in Goose Hollow, and several blocks around Eighteenth Avenue and Salmon Street (right trestle) were infilled. (Don Nelson.)

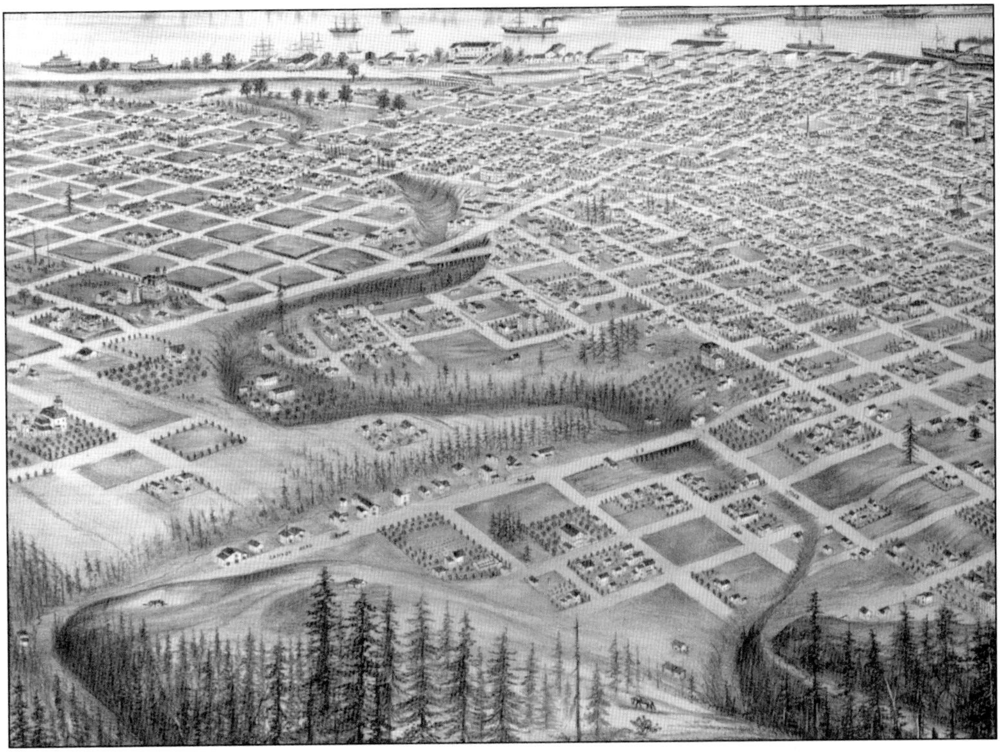

An 1881 map details Tanner Creek meandering in a gulch from Canyon/Jefferson Road to Couch Lake. From left to right, trestle bridges cross the gulch at Everett, Burnside, Alder, and Jefferson Streets. The old tannery buildings are at the base of the "U." The incredible 1887 photograph below shows Burnside Street before the Exposition Building was built. Trestles cross the gulch at today's Burnside Street and at Nineteenth Avenue, with Amos King's white house on the right near the edge of the gulch. (Above; Library of Congress; below, Norm Gholston.)

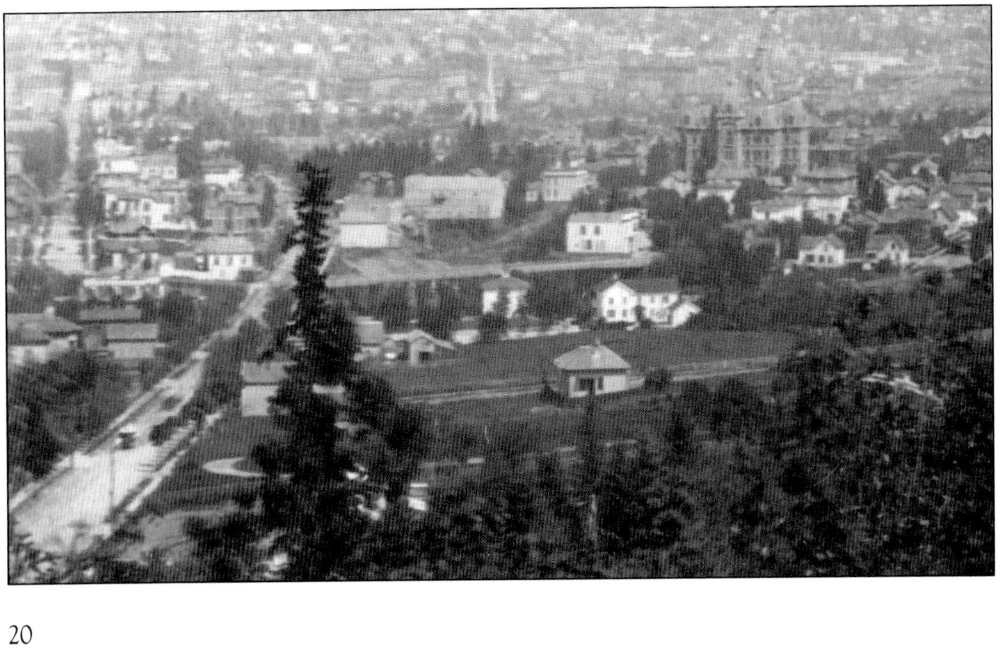

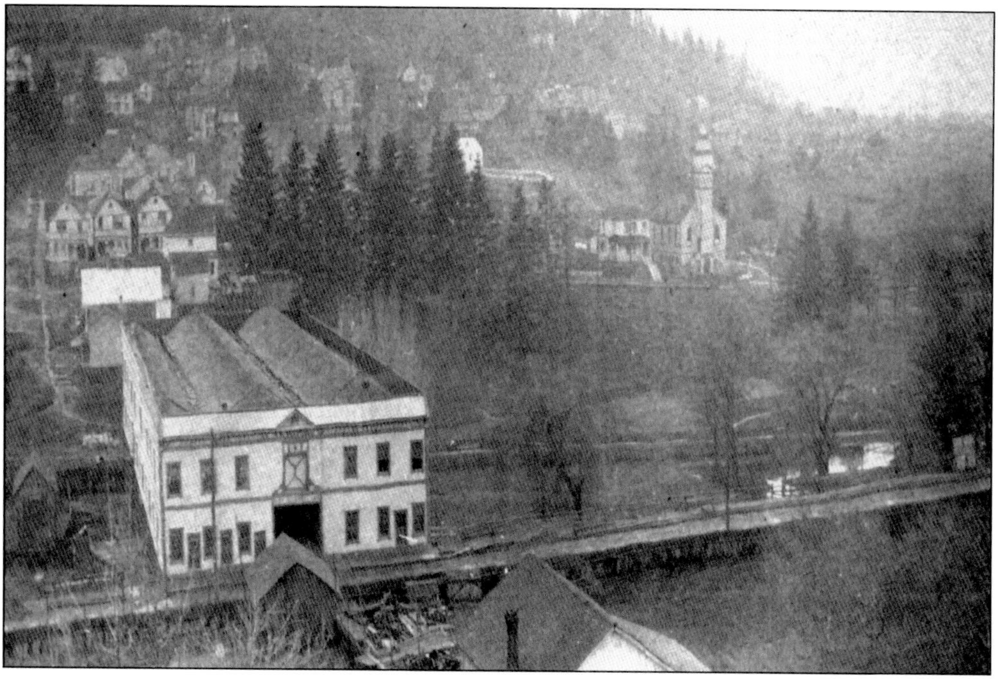

An 1890s photograph offers another rare glimpse of Tanner Creek's water actually running in its banks (zoom below). The building in the foreground fronted Sixteenth Avenue on pilings, near Jefferson Street. The creek appears to run under the street, then head northwesterly toward a trestle, crossing what is now Eighteenth Avenue and Salmon Street (far right). Note the sizable gulch between Zion Lutheran Church and Sixteenth Avenue, a fairly flat area today. (Both, Norm Gholston.)

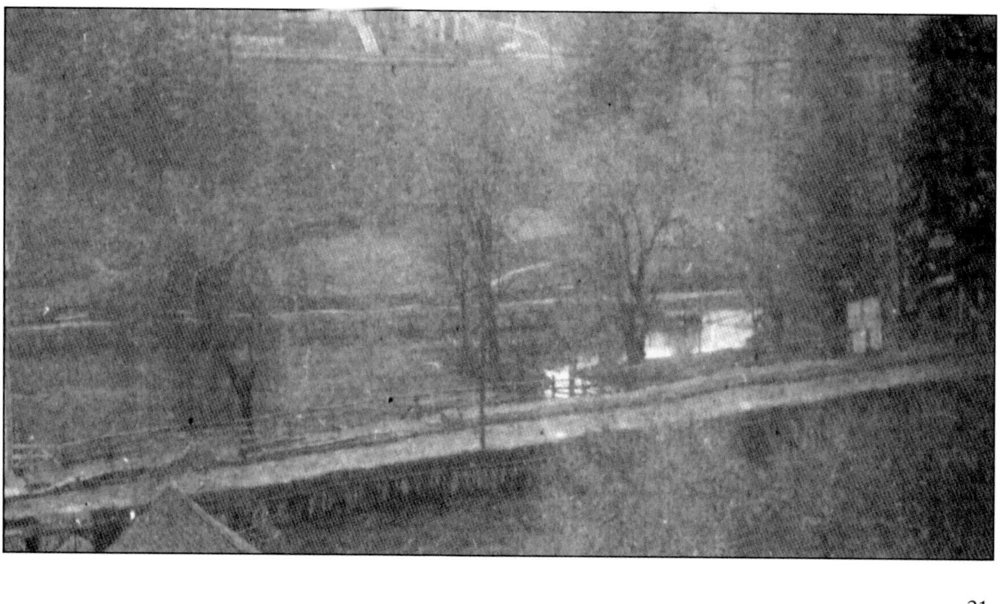

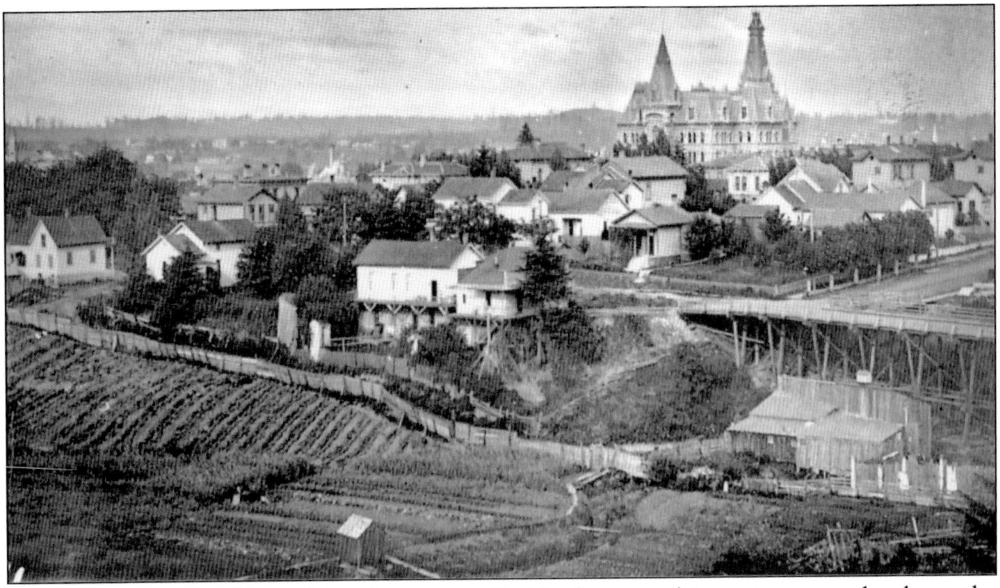

Every winter, Portland braced for what were called freshets—rushing rain waters that burst the banks of creeks and caused flooding and lost property from collapsing embankments. This flood-prone, undesirable land was rented to Chinese laborers for truck farms. Pictured around 1890, a trestle bridge crossed what is now Eighteenth Avenue from just south of Salmon Street to Taylor Street. (OrHi-bb007389.)

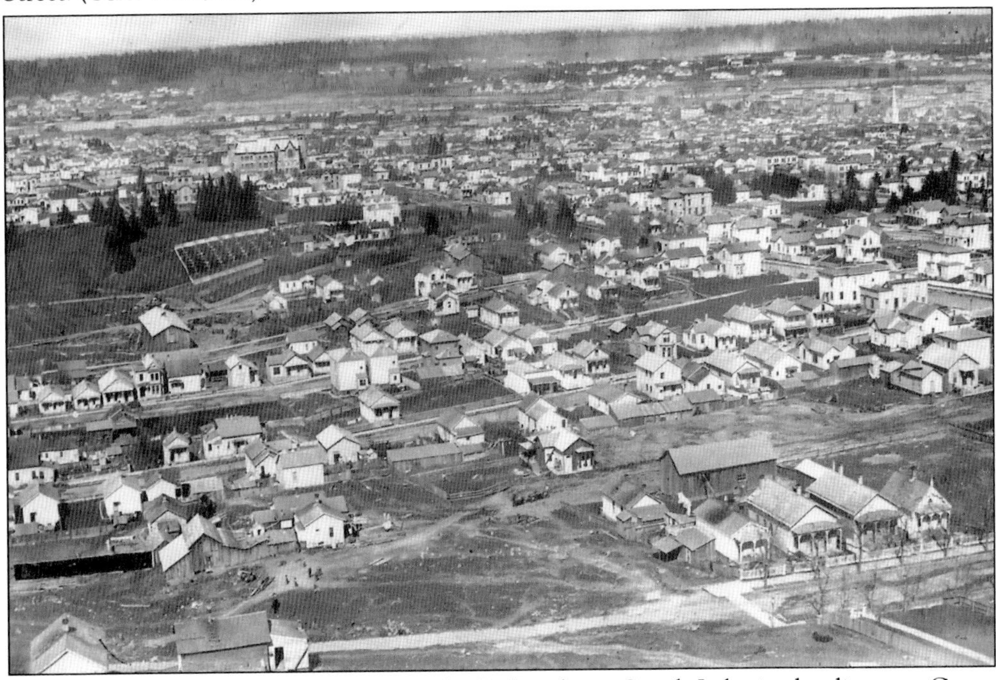

An 1888 image, looking north from Gander Ridge, shows Couch Lake in the distance. Goose Hollow's "working men's cottages," the homes of predominantly Irish and German immigrants, were constructed in the vernacular Queen Anne style. In the distance (and in the upper photograph) is Portland High School on Fourteenth and Morrison Streets. From 1885 until 1912, this served as Portland's high school. The building was demolished in 1929. (OrHi-bb006774.)

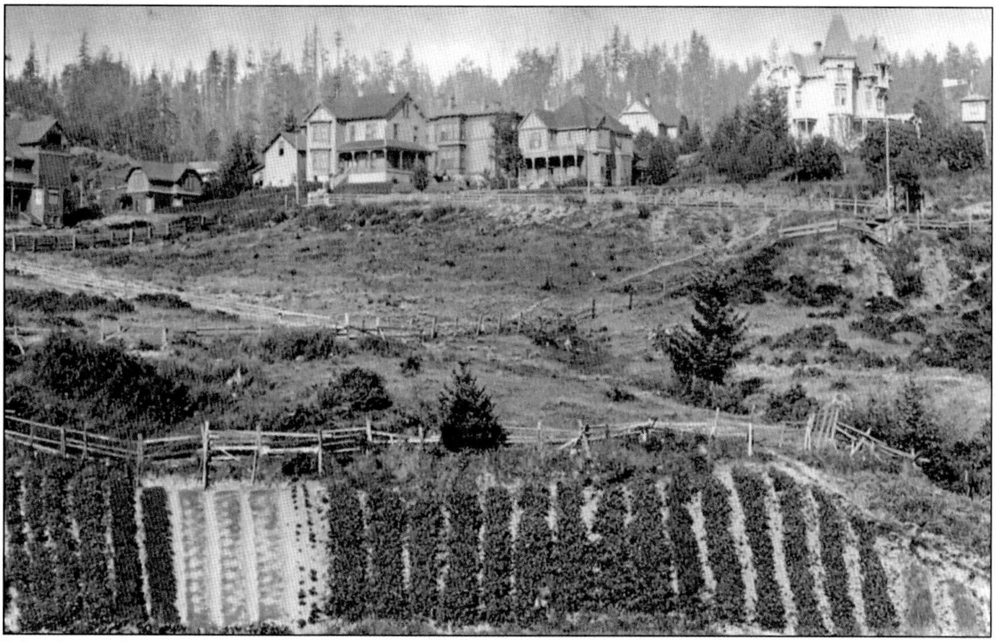

The first Chinese Vegetable Gardens were recorded around 1879, and by 1889 they covered 21 acres in Goose Hollow. These rows of vegetables, pictured in the 1880s, are at the current site of the Multnomah Athletic Club (MAC) on King's Hill, looking west. From 1856 to 1926, Amos King's mansion stood nearby on what is now Twentieth Avenue near Morrison Street. Wealthy merchants and capitalists built mansions nearby. (OrHi-bb007396.)

For more than three decades, Portlanders relied on produce grown by Chinese farmers in Goose Hollow, as seen in this image from 1880. A Portland resident was quoted in the June 13, 1921, issue of the *Oregonian* as remembering "when vegetables were brought to your door in huge baskets carried by a Chinaman, who balanced one at each end of a pole across his shoulder." (OrHi-bb007429.)

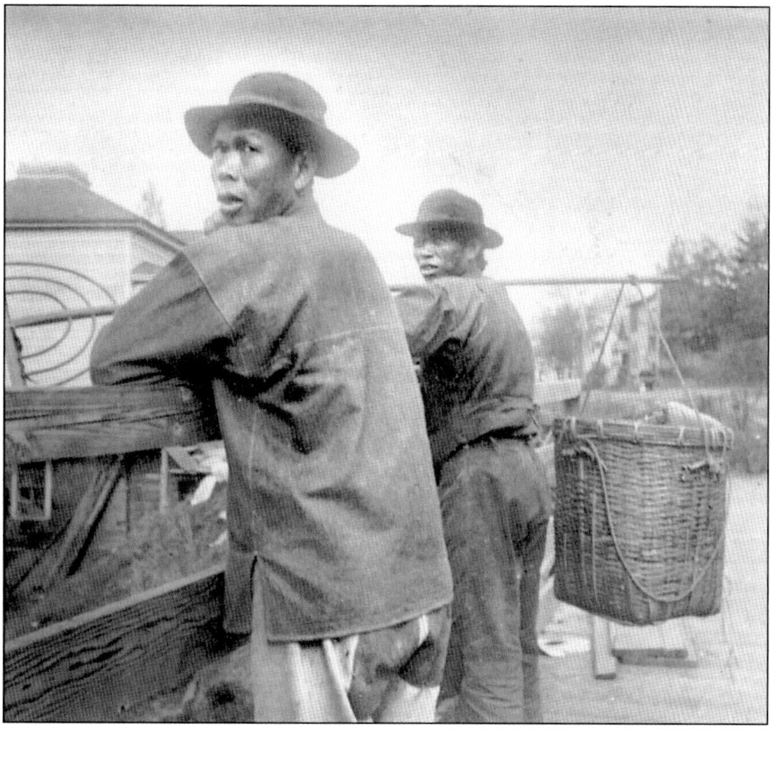

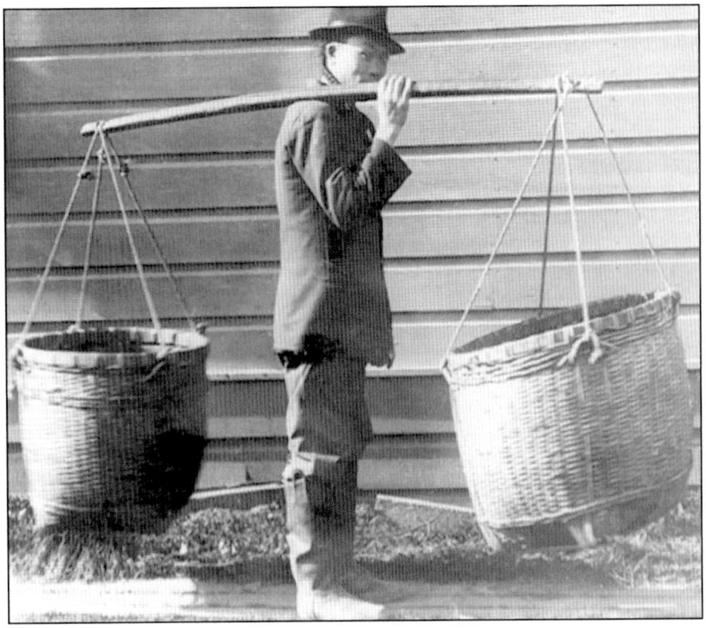

This was a common sight in Old Portland, frequently commented on by visitors to the city: a Chinese peddler, pictured here around 1888, transporting laundry in baskets or carrying vegetables he had grown or wood he had chopped. These men were tormented by gangs of boys, "young toughs," who "thought it a fine sport to assault inoffensive Chinese laundrymen, and the season was always open," as recalled in the July 17, 1921, issue of the *Oregonian*. (OrHi-13128.)

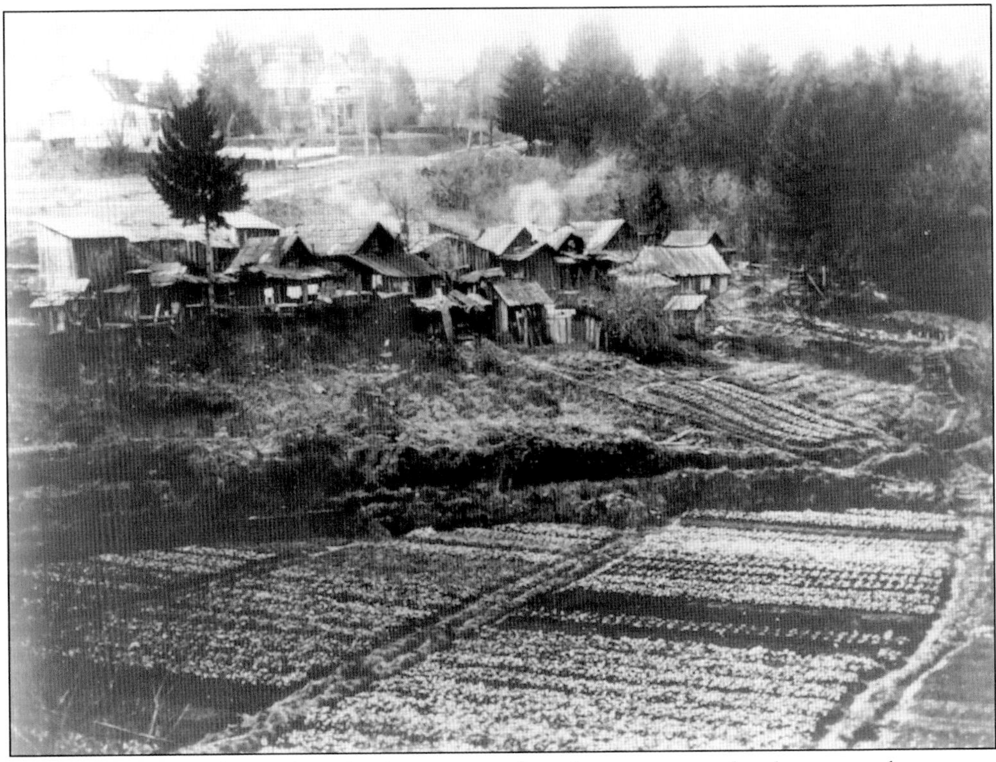

Noted as Chinese "shanties" on Sanborn maps, these houses are on the slope near the current intersection of Twentieth Avenue and Salmon Street. In 1890, H. W. Scott wrote, "the creek forms a sunken valley, with little meadows on either side, which have been . . . occupied by the Chinese for garden purposes." The line cutting diagonally through the center of this 1890 photograph is Tanner Creek. (CoPA.)

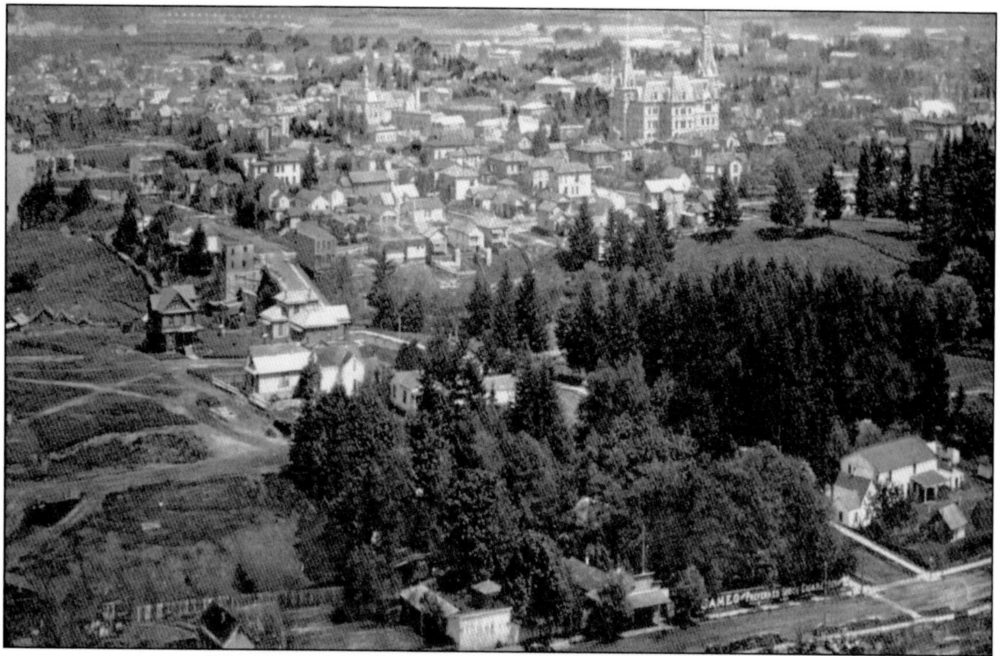

Looking north in this 1890 image, with Jefferson and Eighteenth Streets in the foreground at the right, the Tanner Creek Gulch begins just out of frame, around Sixteenth and Jefferson Streets, going diagonally back toward the trestle (left center at Salmon Street) and extending to where the Multnomah Athletic Club and Civic Stadium are today. Some houses fronting Taylor Street are on stilts with the slope dropping off precipitously. (Norm Gholston.)

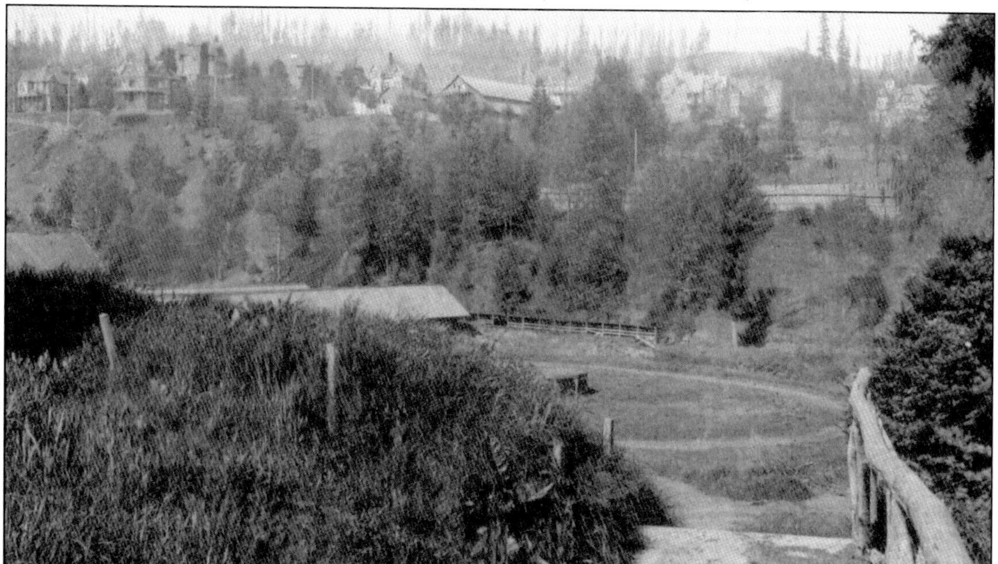

In 1892, the MAC leased the gulch behind the Exposition Building (the Chinese Vegetable Gardens are visible in the upper left). Once the tannery site, historians describe an acre of either stone vats or giant wooden hewn vats used to soak hides. Perhaps an urban legend, though repeated by a century of Portland history books, the vats were said to have been filled and buried under Multnomah Field because they were too heavy to move. (Norm Gholston.)

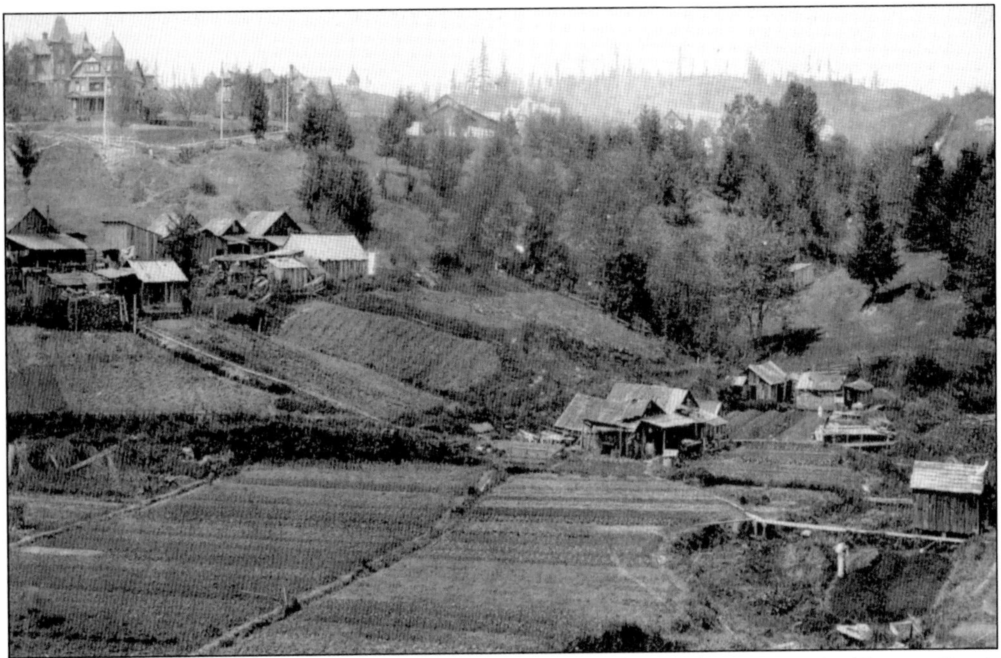

Taken around 1893, this photograph looks west from atop the trestle crossing the Tanner Creek Gulch at Eighteenth and Salmon Streets (see page 22). At the far right, the Multnomah Athletic Club fence is visible. At the base of the hill, Tanner Creek curves behind the lower shanties, then heads east at the lower right where a Chinese gardener is faintly visible. (Norm Gholston.)

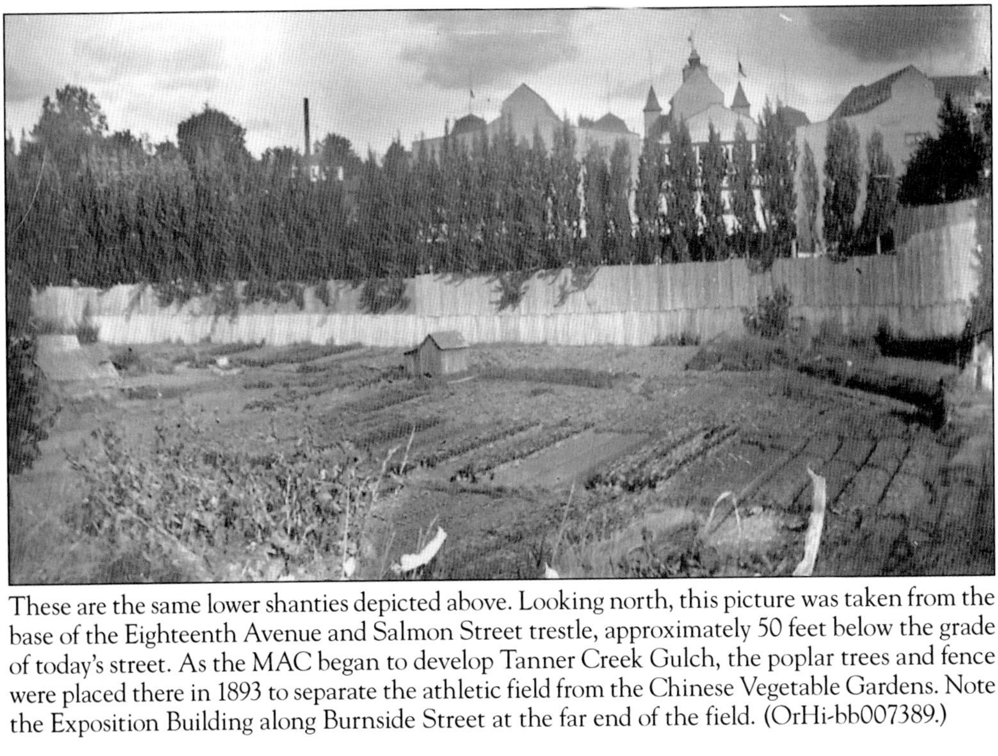

These are the same lower shanties depicted above. Looking north, this picture was taken from the base of the Eighteenth Avenue and Salmon Street trestle, approximately 50 feet below the grade of today's street. As the MAC began to develop Tanner Creek Gulch, the poplar trees and fence were placed there in 1893 to separate the athletic field from the Chinese Vegetable Gardens. Note the Exposition Building along Burnside Street at the far end of the field. (OrHi-bb007389.)

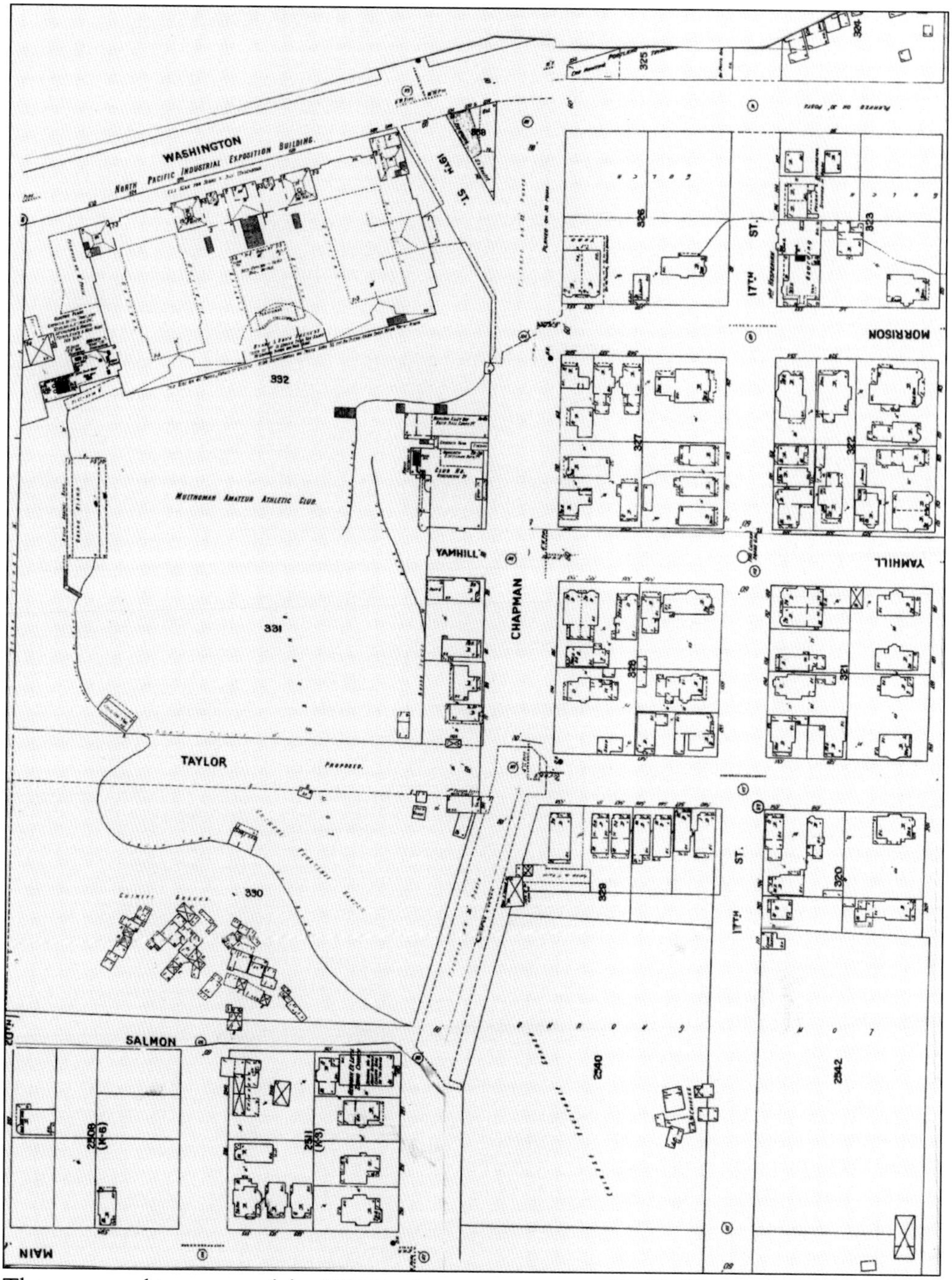

This map combines parts of the 1901 Sanborn maps, sections 30, 32, 36, and 37. Jefferson Street crosses the bottom, while Burnside (then called Washington) Street crosses the top. Eighteenth Avenue was then known as Chapman Street. Sections of this 1901 map show Chinese Vegetable Gardens and shanties as far out as the south side of Jefferson between Southwest Eighteenth and Twentieth Avenues at the site of the First United Methodist Church, in the gulch at Salmon Street, and across what is now the football field for Lincoln High School. Buildings on Morrison and Alder Streets are shown on stilts hanging over a ravine.

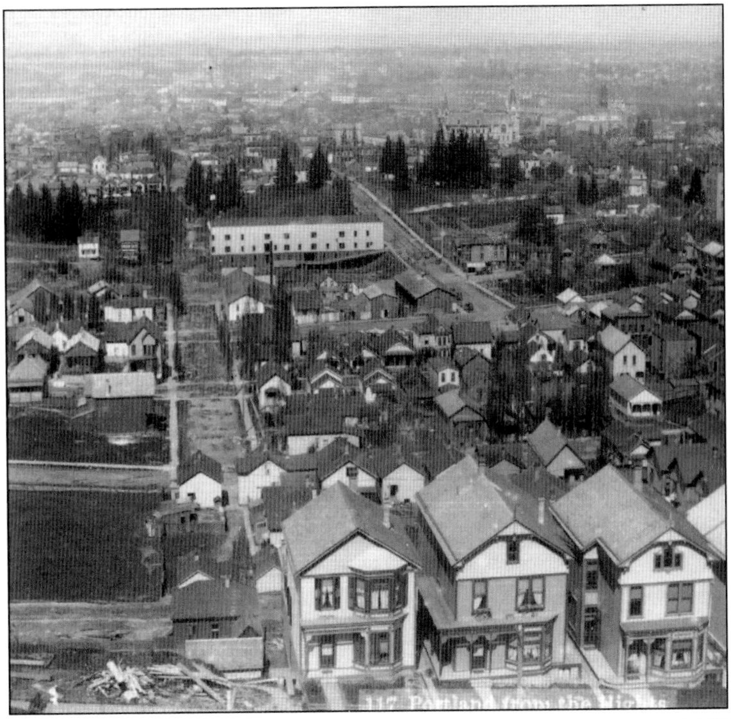

A photograph taken from Gander Ridge in 1891 shows Mill Street in the foreground with Eighteenth Street heading north at the left. In the 1960s, all of Mill Street in Goose Hollow was destroyed to make way for the Stadium and Foothills Freeways. (Don Nelson.)

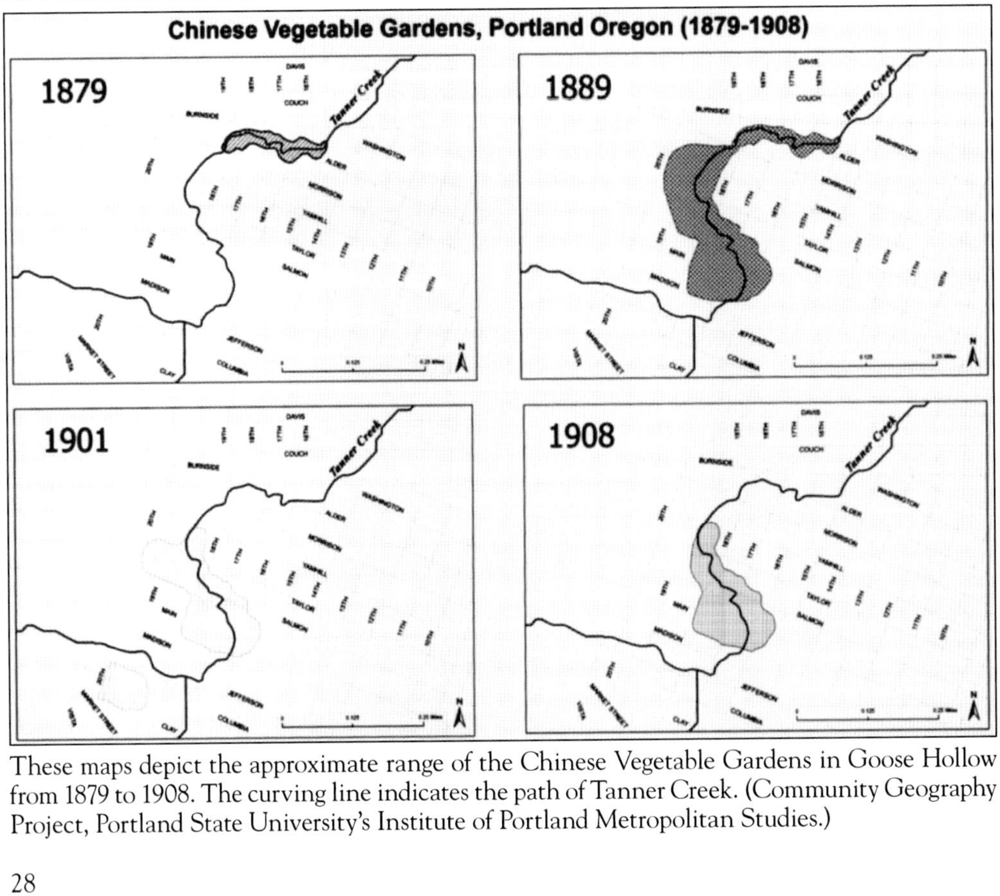

These maps depict the approximate range of the Chinese Vegetable Gardens in Goose Hollow from 1879 to 1908. The curving line indicates the path of Tanner Creek. (Community Geography Project, Portland State University's Institute of Portland Metropolitan Studies.)

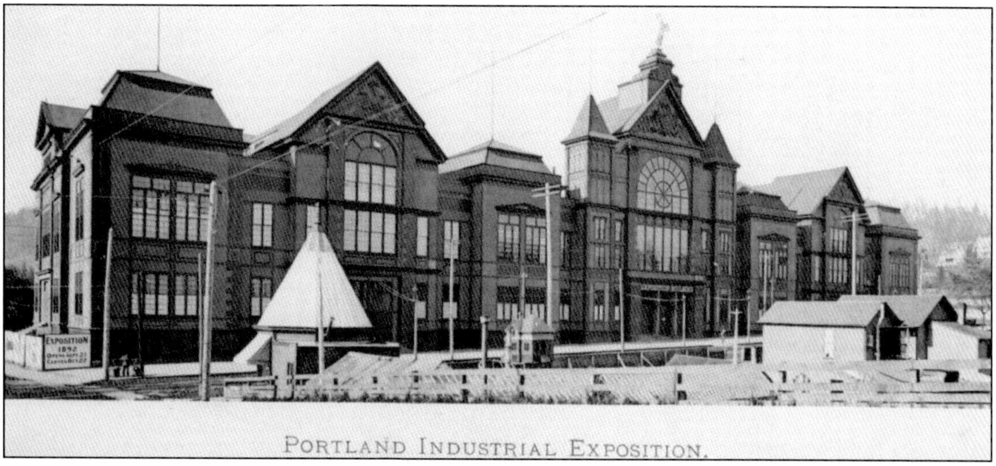

The North Pacific Exposition Building was built in and alongside Tanner Creek Gulch in 1888. Note the deep gulch visible on the left side of the top image. The building fronted the south side of Burnside Street, from Nineteenth to Twentieth Avenues, and was used for basketball, roller skating, dances, meetings for civic and social organizations, livestock shows, flower shows, and presidential visits. The image below was published in *West Shore* magazine in 1888. Crowds enjoyed concerts from the balcony above, with a zoological garden below. The clamshell bandstand was a glamorous setting for many orchestral performances. Mount Hood was painted as a fetching backdrop. The building was destroyed by fire in 1910. (Both, Norm Gholston.)

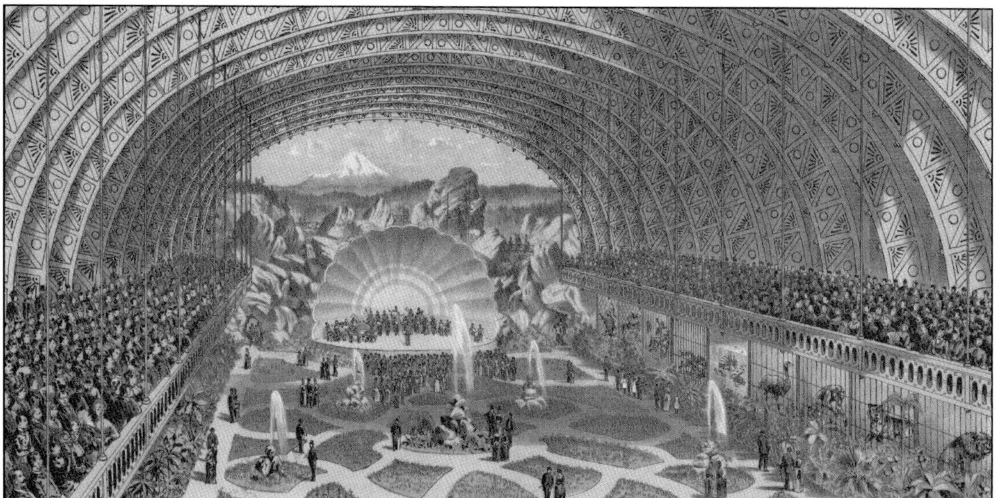

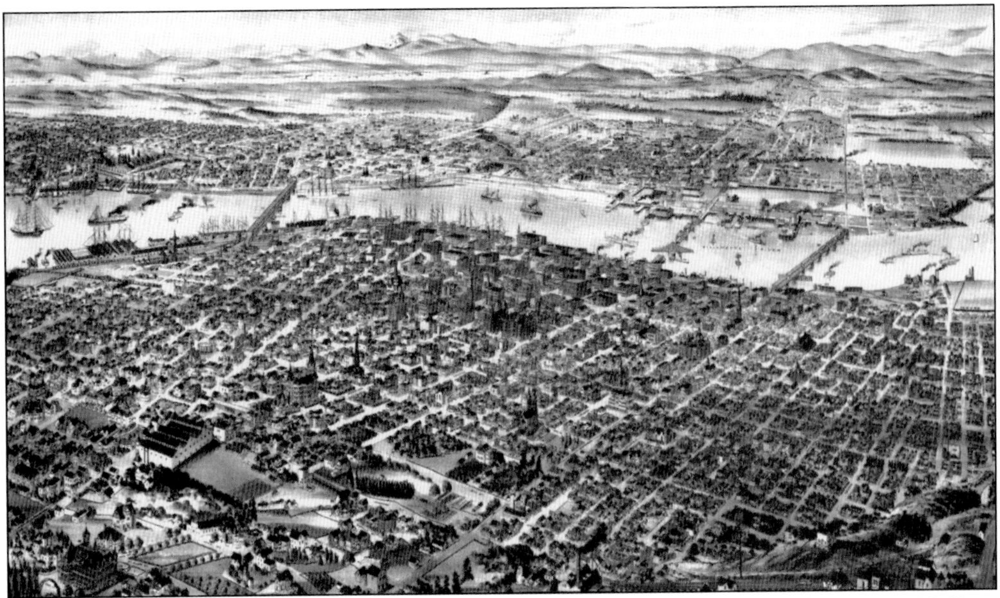

An 1890 bird's-eye sketch of Portland shows large sections of undeveloped land in Goose Hollow. The Exposition Building is visible at the base of King's Hill on the left. Chinese Vegetable Gardens are visible on the slopes behind the Exposition Building and along Jefferson Street. The cable car trestle heads up to the heights on the right. (CoPA.)

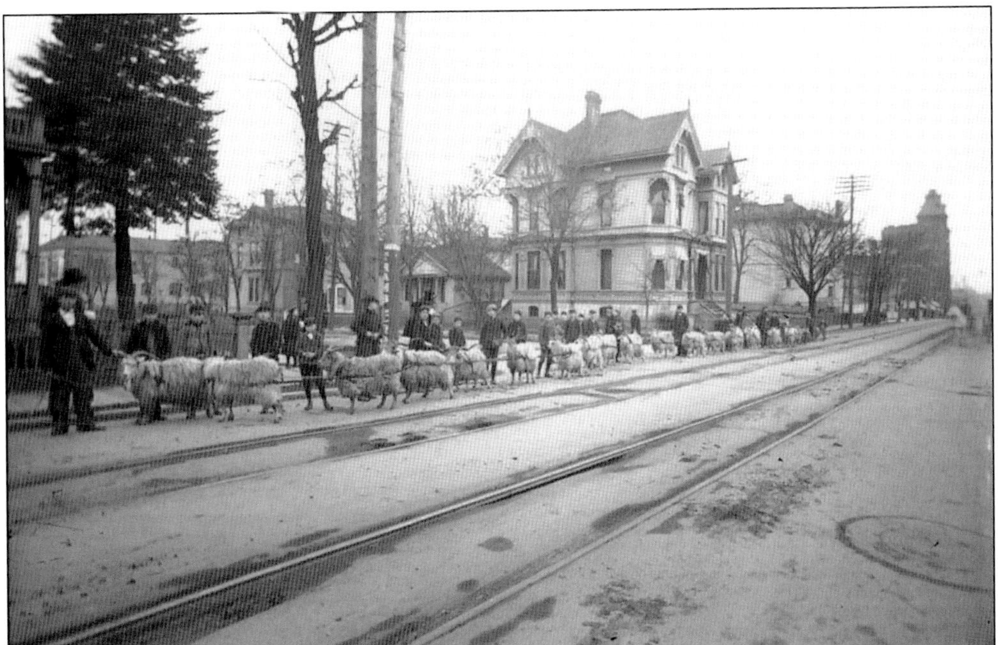

Just outside of Goose Hollow, at Twelfth and Morrison Streets, boys are training teams of goats. Photographed in 1898, the boys hope to sell these goats to prospectors heading to Alaska for the Klondike gold rush. (CoPA.)

In the early days of Portland, Native Americans lived in the area around the Alder Street Gulch. Portland residents recalled in the July 2 and October 11, 1921, issues of the *Oregonian* that Native American women once sold kindling and wild berries to households in Portland. Portland photographer Lily E. White (1866–1944) took this photograph in 1902, probably in Portland, of an elderly Native American woman holding an infant in a cradleboard ornamented with beadwork. (Library of Congress.)

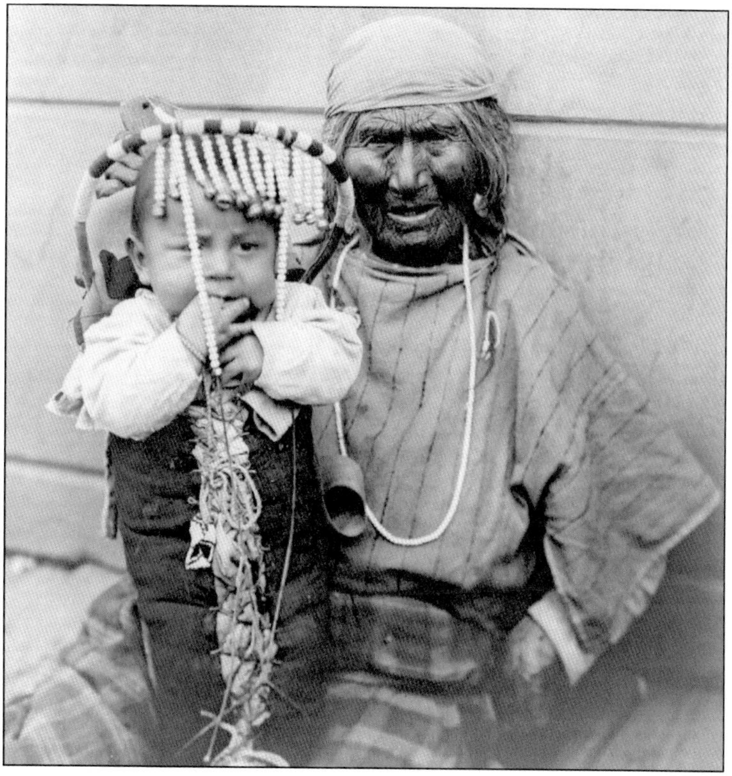

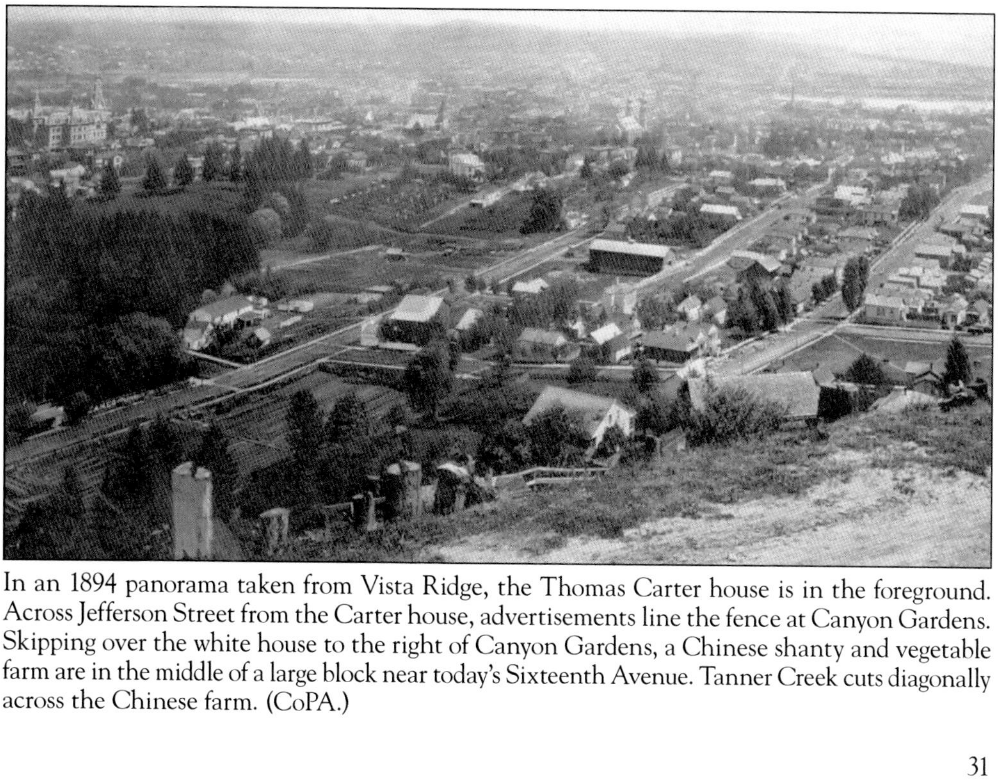

In an 1894 panorama taken from Vista Ridge, the Thomas Carter house is in the foreground. Across Jefferson Street from the Carter house, advertisements line the fence at Canyon Gardens. Skipping over the white house to the right of Canyon Gardens, a Chinese shanty and vegetable farm are in the middle of a large block near today's Sixteenth Avenue. Tanner Creek cuts diagonally across the Chinese farm. (CoPA.)

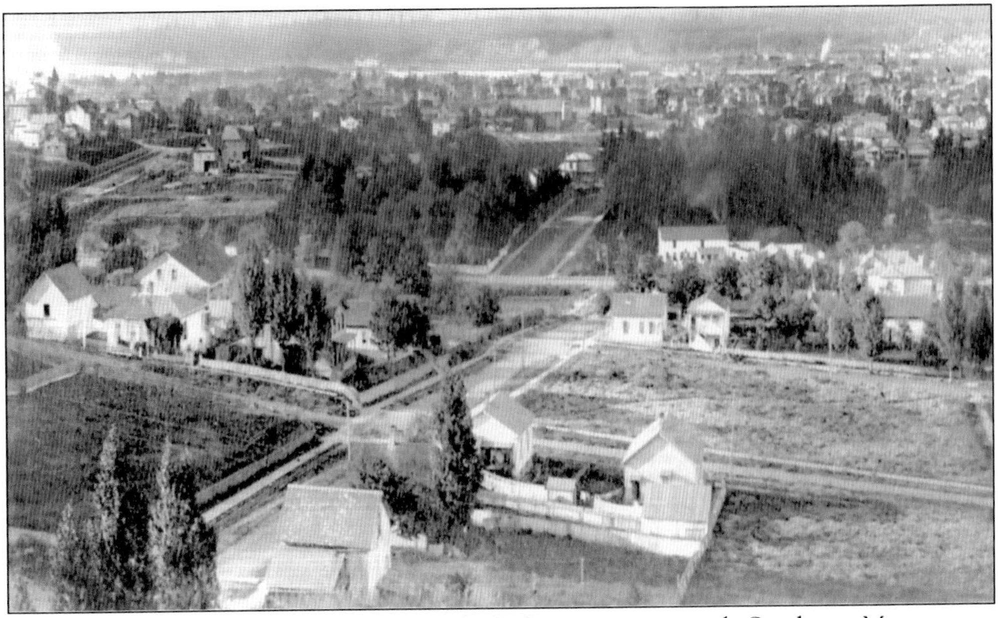

In an 1880s image looking north from Gander Ridge, at approximately Southwest Montgomery Street and Seventeenth Avenue, the Carter house is on the left with today's Eighteenth Avenue fronting the property. Canyon Gardens is the fenced-in property across Jefferson Street with the thick grove of trees. King's Hill is up the slope from Canyon Gardens. (OrHi-bb007438.)

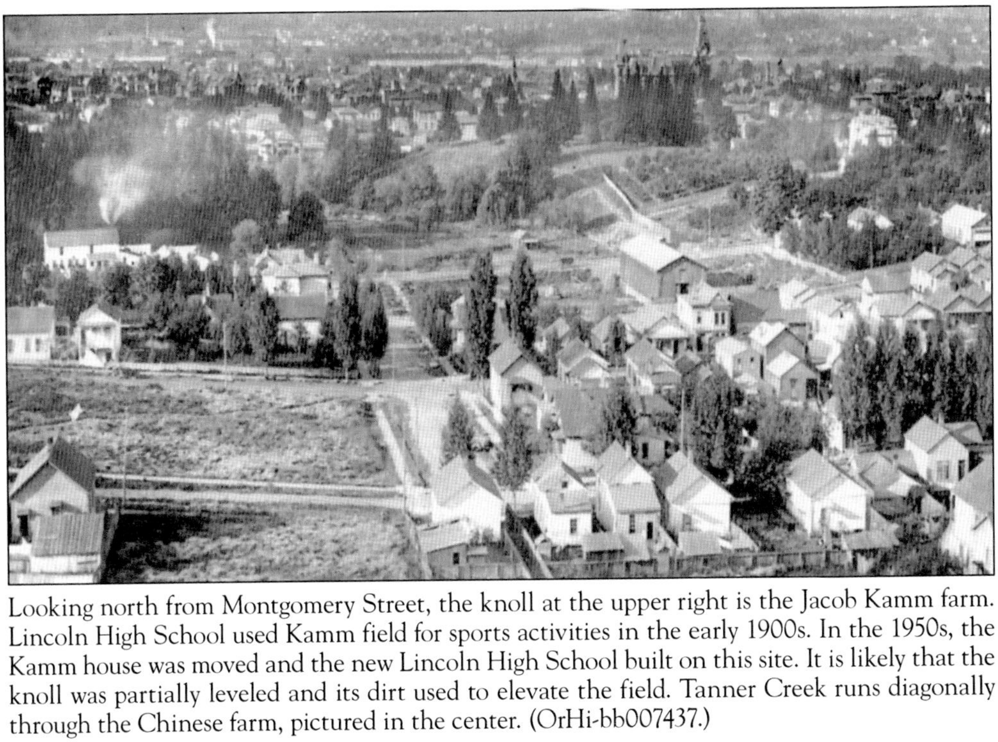

Looking north from Montgomery Street, the knoll at the upper right is the Jacob Kamm farm. Lincoln High School used Kamm field for sports activities in the early 1900s. In the 1950s, the Kamm house was moved and the new Lincoln High School built on this site. It is likely that the knoll was partially leveled and its dirt used to elevate the field. Tanner Creek runs diagonally through the Chinese farm, pictured in the center. (OrHi-bb007437.)

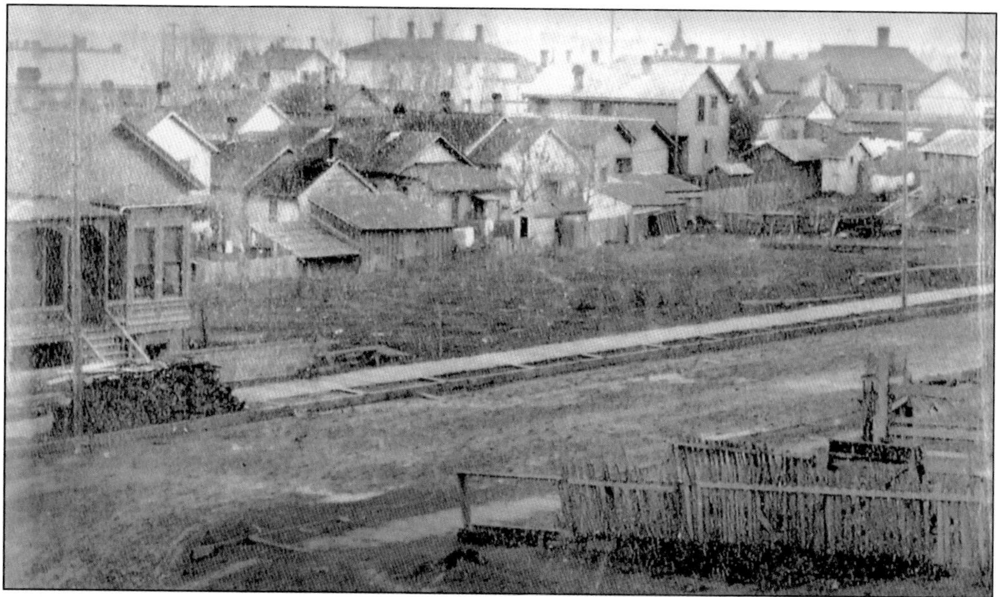

Although a section of town was called "Slabtown" for its copious stacks of slab wood remnants from lumber mills, all of Portland was known for its many cordwood piles in front of residences. During her time photographing in the region, Dorothea Lange commented that "woodpiles along the street are characteristic of Portland." Note the wood stacked by the planked sidewalk along Mill Street near Seventeenth Avenue in 1890. (OrHi-bb007393.)

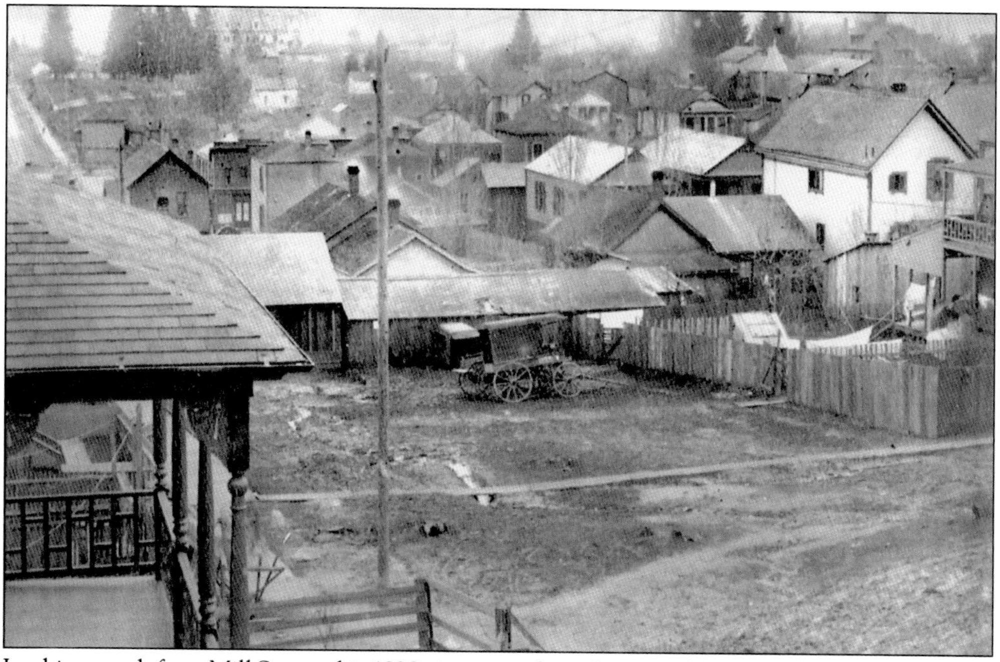

Looking north from Mill Street, this 1890 view provides a close-up of Goose Hollow's workingmen's cottages. In the 1870s, Irish laborers migrated to Portland to work on docks, railways, sewers, and roads, and many lived in this section of Goose Hollow. Two Irish families had such dramatic disputes over property boundaries and were so litigious that their antics were known as the "Goose Hollow War" in the newspaper. (OrHi-bb007395.)

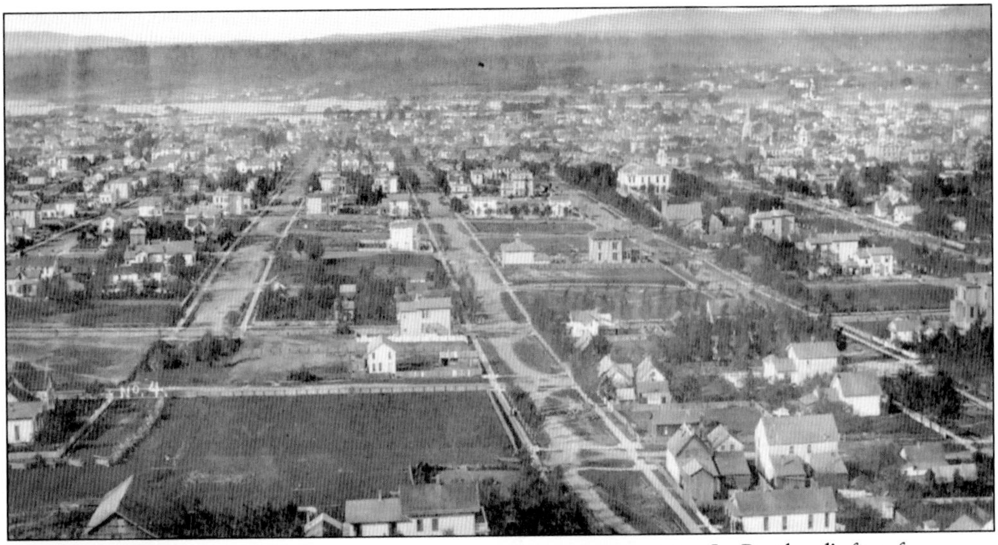

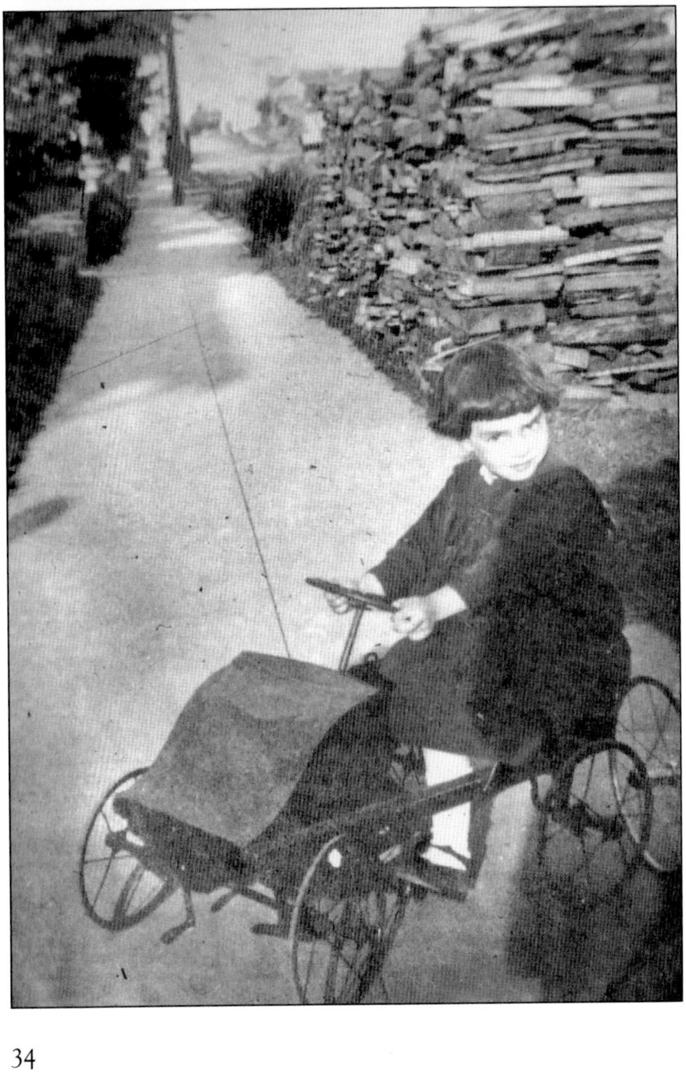

In Portland's first few decades, Burnside Street (then Washington Street) divided the city into North Portland and South Portland. In later years, only the area on the lower right of the top image toward the river was called South Portland, which was home to many Jewish and Italian immigrants. Before Interstate 405 divided Goose Hollow and South Portland, the neighborhoods were not so clearly separated. Couch Lake is visible in the distance, with Fourteenth and Fifteenth Avenues in the center. In the bottom image, taken around 1900, a Jewish girl rides a toy pedal car in South Portland in front of a curb stacked with slabwood. (Above, OrHi-bb007409; left, OrHi-bb007424.)

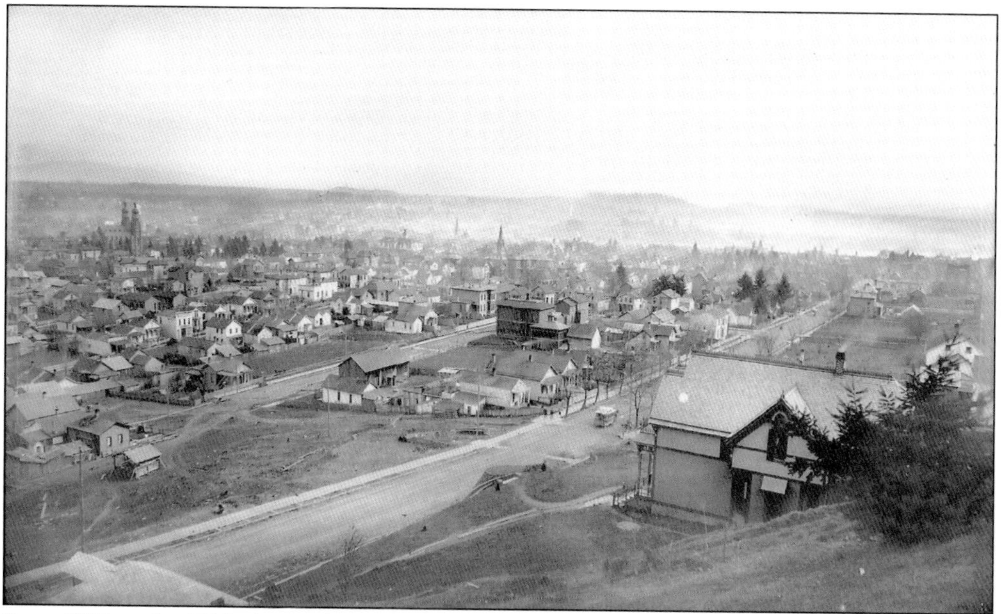

From 1871 to the 1890s, horse-drawn streetcars were a common sight on Portland streets. In this c. 1890s photograph, a horse-drawn streetcar winds its way down the hill. The streetcar passes a house at the lower right that is still standing near public stairs leading up the hill in the 1900 block of Market Street Drive. Temple Beth Israel is visible in the upper left. (OrHi-bb006776.)

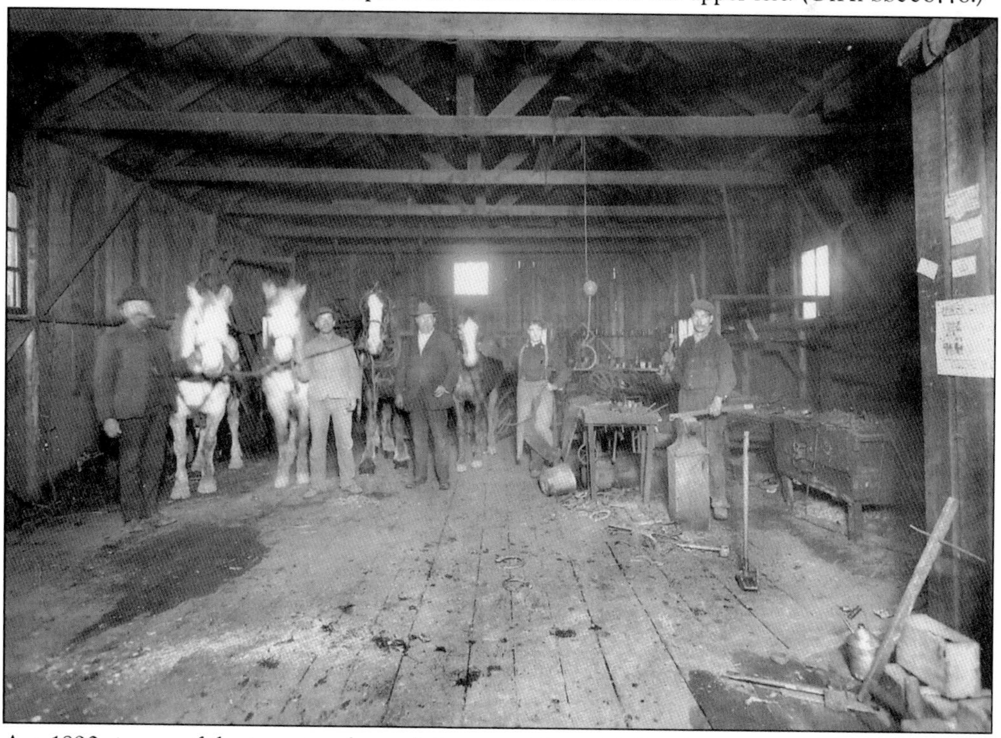

A c. 1890s image of the interior of one of the many Goose Hollow businesses dealing with horses and streetcars is shown. The Hutcheon Blacksmith Shop was located at Fourteenth Avenue and Alder Street. (OrHi-bb007425.)

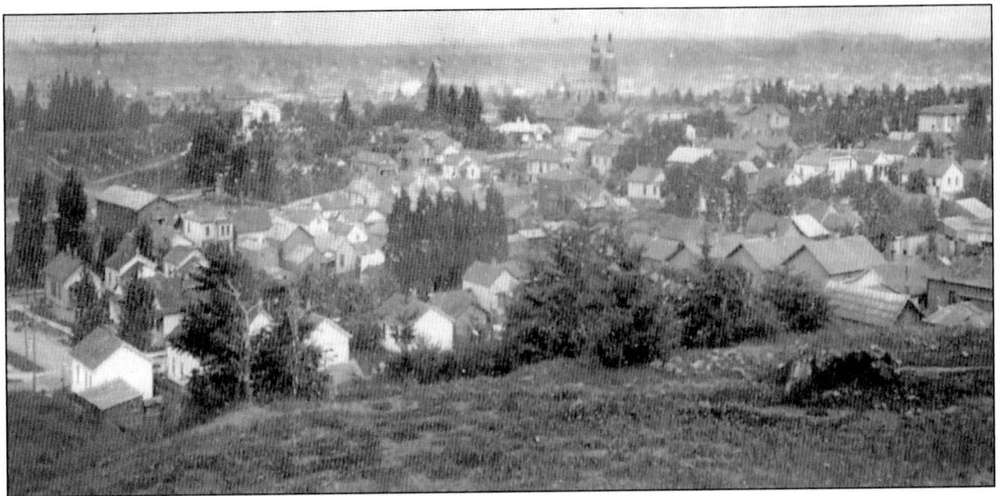

This photograph, taken around 1890, is from Gander Ridge looking northeast from Montgomery Street. Portland High School is at the upper left. In many pictures of Portland, the twin spires of Temple Beth Israel (background center), located at Twelfth and Main Streets, clearly rise above the city. The spires were an iconic Portland image from 1889 until 1923 when the temple was destroyed in a fire of suspicious origin. (OrHi-bb007392.)

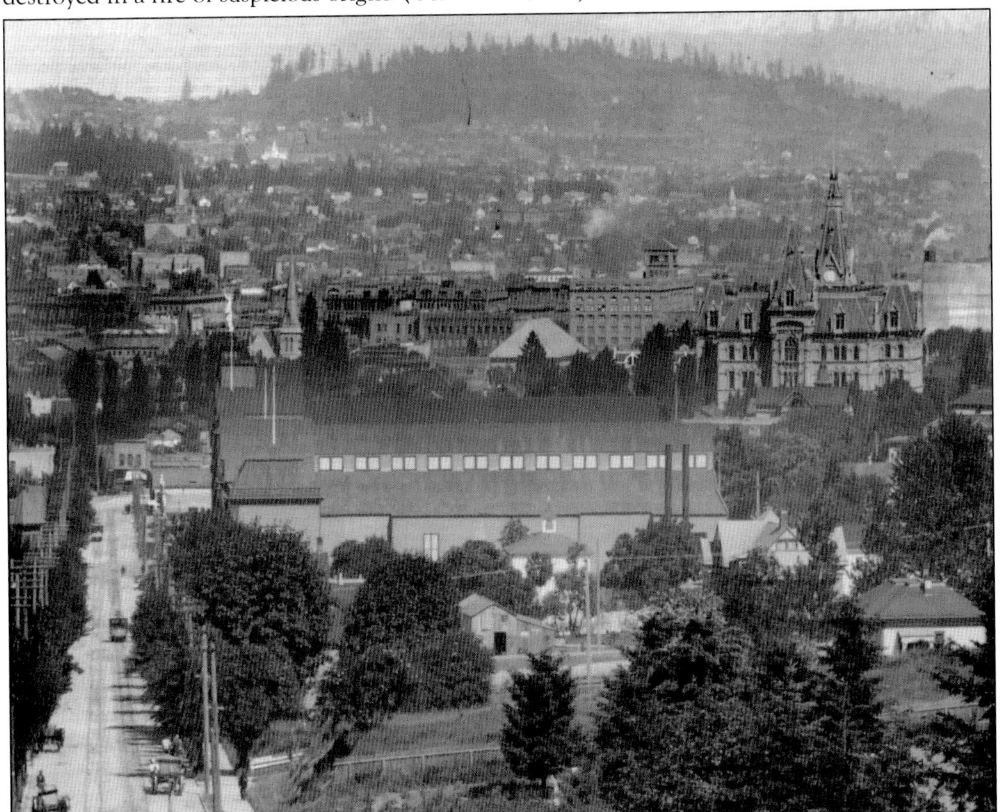

An 1890s view of Portland, looking east, shows lively activity on Burnside Street, where streetcars, horse-drawn carts, and people pass by the Exposition Building. Portland High School is on the right. (Norm Gholston.)

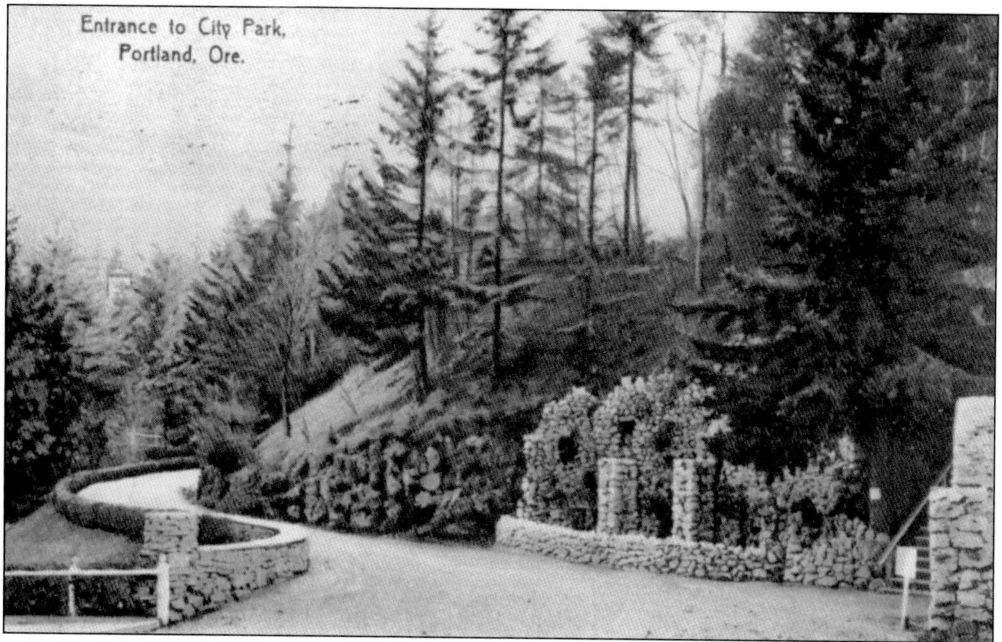

Portland's oldest park was first called City Park, later Washington Park. In 1871, Portland purchased 40.78 acres from Amos N. King for $32,624. Though this was an excellent deal, many grumbled since the location was thought of as the outskirts of town. There was once literally a gate to the city near this park entrance. In 1922, the County Poor Farm, totaling 160 acres, was added to the park. The former poor farm is now home to the Oregon Zoo, the Hoyt Arboretum, the Vietnam Veteran's Memorial, the World Forestry Center, and the Portland Children's Museum. These *c.* 1900 images depict the first entrance to City Park on today's Burnside Street across from Northwest Twenty-fourth Place. In the lower image, note the enormous pile of slabwood across the street. The rustic bridge over the pond was frequently depicted in postcards of this era. (Below, Norm Gholston.)

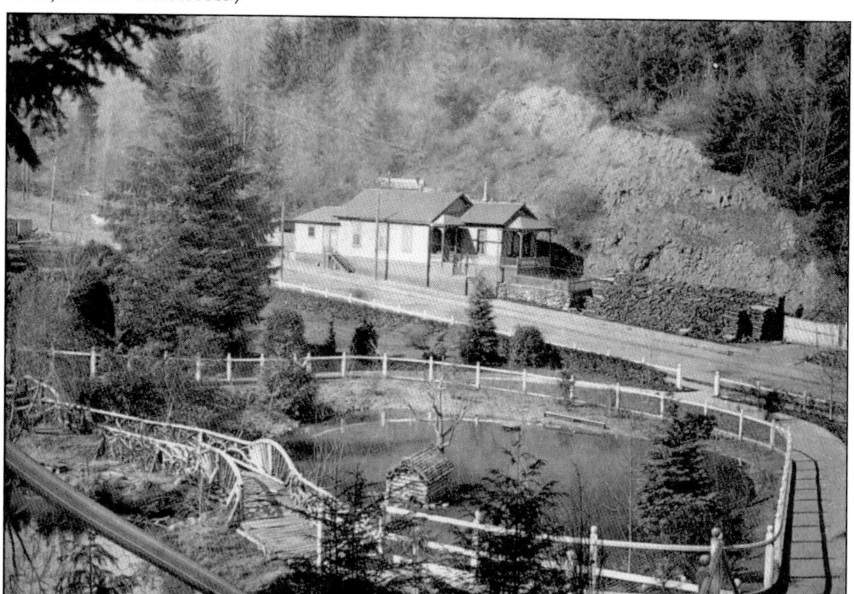

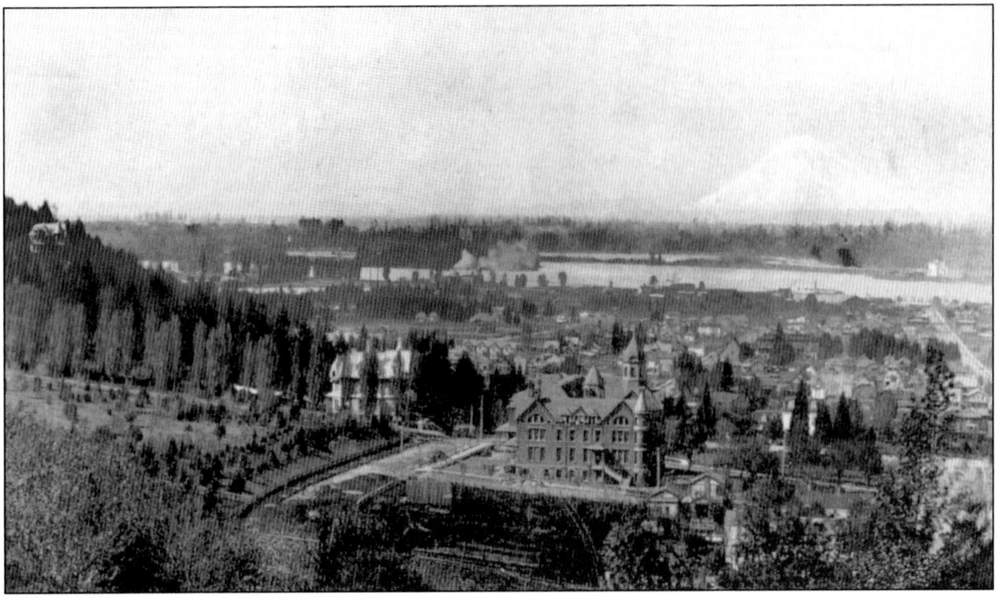

A postcard titled "From the Heights Above Canyon Road—North," the top image, taken around 1892, is of the Goose Hollow heights called King's Hill. At times called Park Hill, the heights, and Portland Heights, during the 1880s and 1890s it was also called Gander Ridge, though the name shifted to refer only to the ridge at the south end of the bowl that makes up today's Goose Hollow. In the center of the image is St. Helen's Hall, a girls' school located at St. Clair Avenue and Park Place from 1890 until 1914 when it was destroyed by fire. In the upper right, Guild's Lake and Mount St. Helens can be seen. The C. M. Forbes house is near the school and the Henry Green house can be seen on the far left. In the lower image, St. Helen's Hall students perform a can-can dance at the Civic Theater for a 1940 spring festival. (Above, Norm Gholston; below, OrHi-bb007411.)

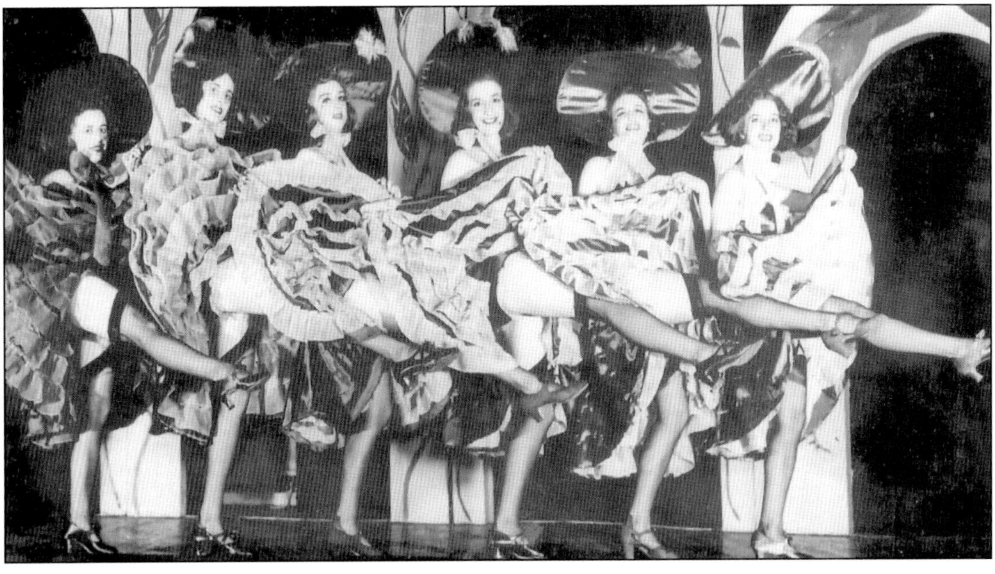

A photograph from 1900 looks north from today's Gander Ridge. Gander Ridge was so named by "young toughs" in the lower elevations. These boys, the Goose Hollow Gang, resented what they saw as a derisive name given to their blue-collar neighborhood. By naming the heights Gander Ridge, the boys were possibly attempting to subordinate the heights, which were known for expensive mansions, as merely a subsection of Goose Hollow. The city now defines Gander Ridge's boundaries as Montgomery Drive to Cardinell Drive, extending south to Lincoln Street. (OrHi-bb007439.)

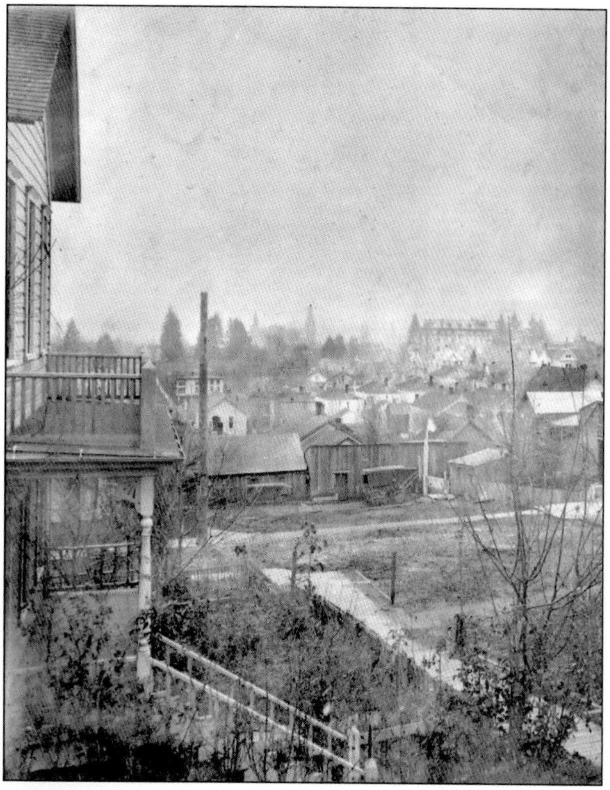

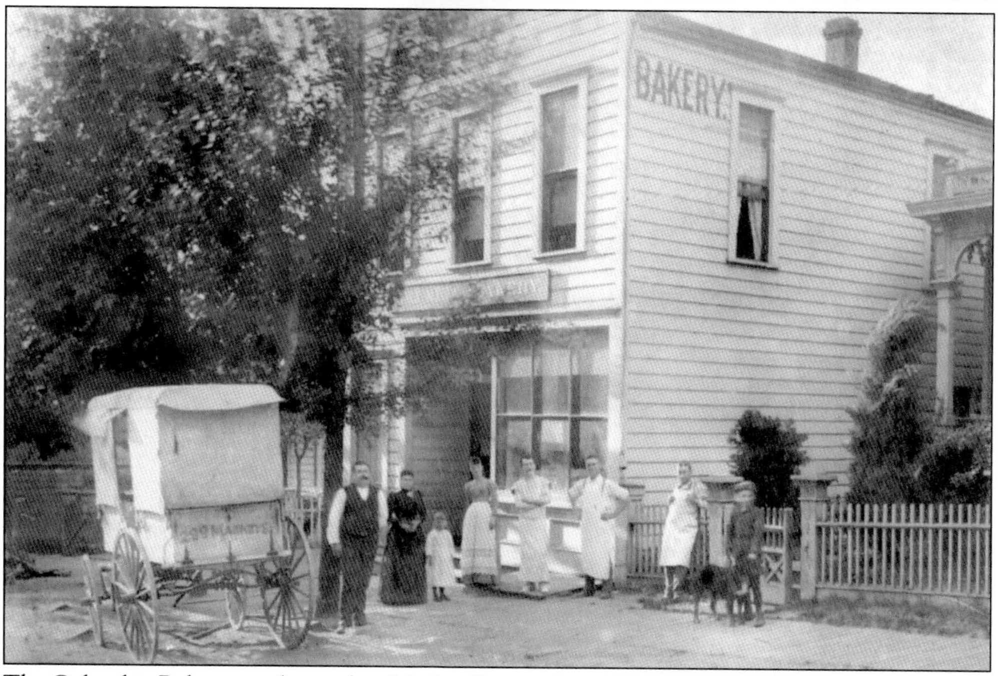

The Columbia Bakery was located on Market Street where the building still stands. This image is from around 1890. Streets have been renamed and houses renumbered several times since then, so the number for this building was variously 299, 499, and 1501 Market Street. (OrHi-bb007414.)

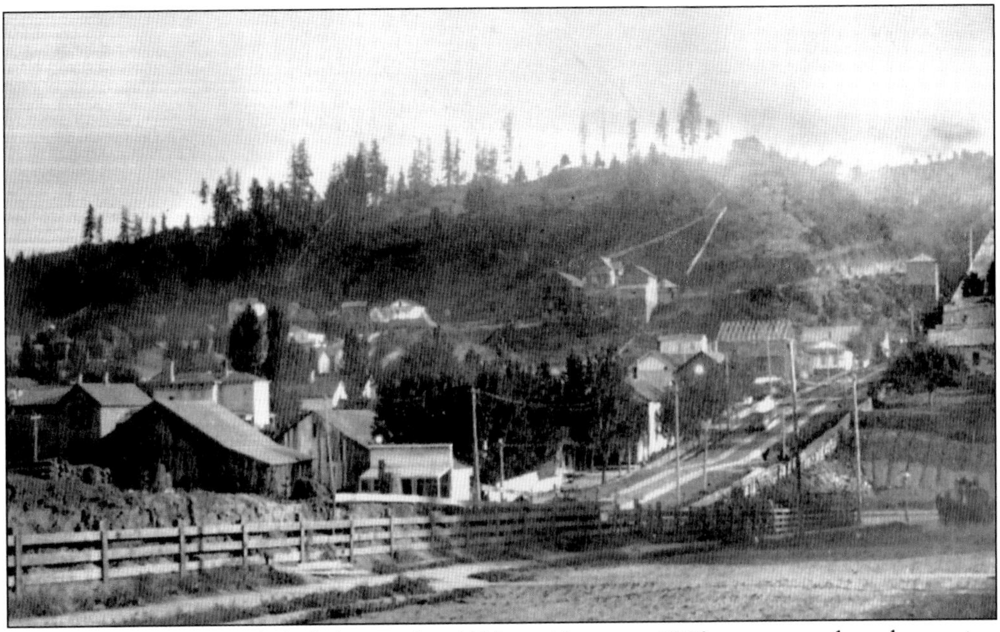

Before the cable car trestle (right) opened in 1890—with a steep 20.93 percent grade and spanning 1,000 feet—lots on these heights were cheap. After the cable car eased access, residential lots there were in high demand. Using the same cable car system as the one used in San Francisco, Portland's cable car ran from Union Depot to Jefferson Street, then headed uphill at Chapman (now Eighteenth) Street to Spring Street. The ravine where the cable car once charged up the hill is now thought of as Cable Car Canyon, with Vista Ridge to the west and Gander Ridge to the east. Historically the heights at thc south end of Goose Hollow have been referred to as Carter's Hill (west), Robinson's Hill (east), and briefly as Paradise Hill but most often as Portland Heights or the West Hills. (OrHi-bb007390.)

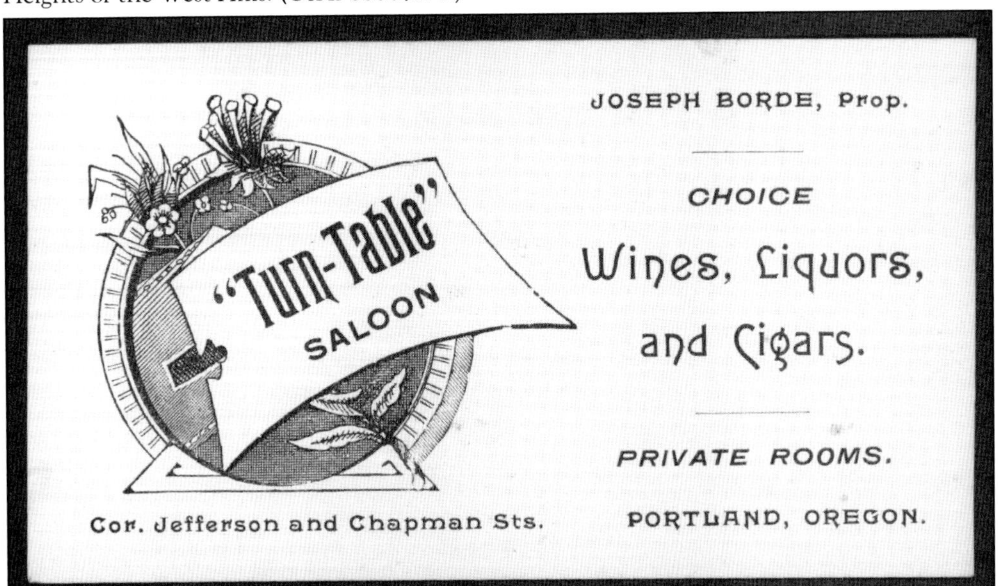

The Turn-Table Saloon at the base of the cable car incline provided respite for passengers. It was on the southeast corner of Jefferson and Chapman Streets. (Norm Gholston.)

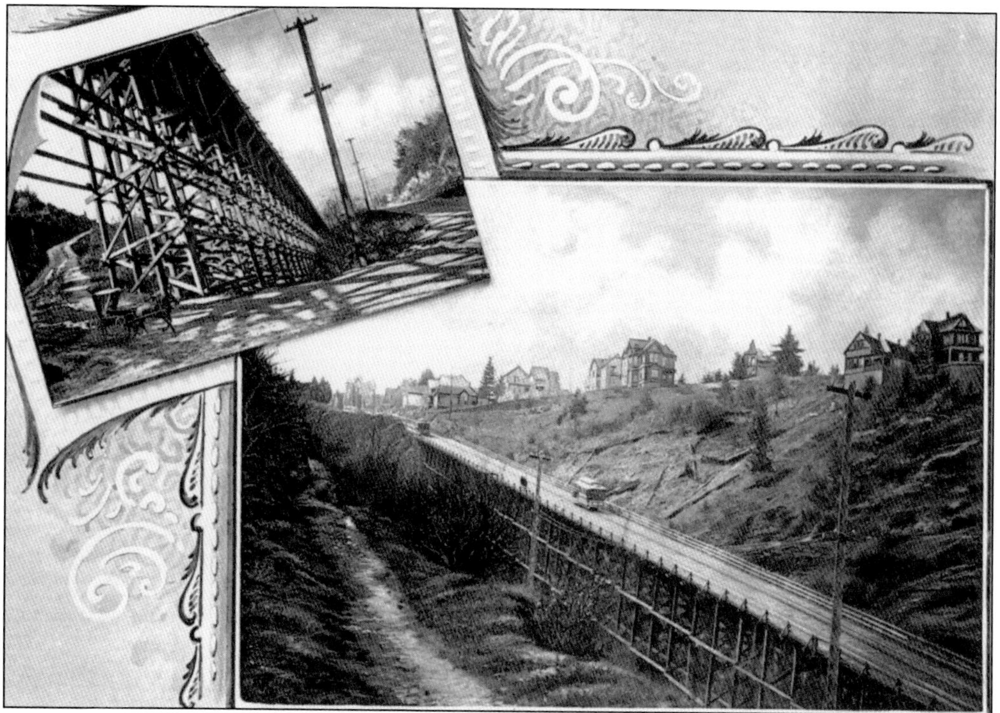

In this 1890 postcard, a horse-drawn carriage passes under the steep trestle at the upper left on a road that connected to Montgomery Drive. Pedestrians are on the ramp with cable cars passing nearby. According to the January 14, 1922, issue of the *Oregonian*, the climb was a slow and creaky process for the cable cars, but the views were terrific! (Norm Gholston.)

An 1891 image shows cable cars passing each other on the trestle, giving a sense of the steepness of the incline. The house visible behind the trestle still stands at 1903 Southwest Cable Street. It is the Alice Druhot House, built in 1891. Like many buildings in Goose Hollow, it is listed on the National Register of Historic Places. (CoPA.)

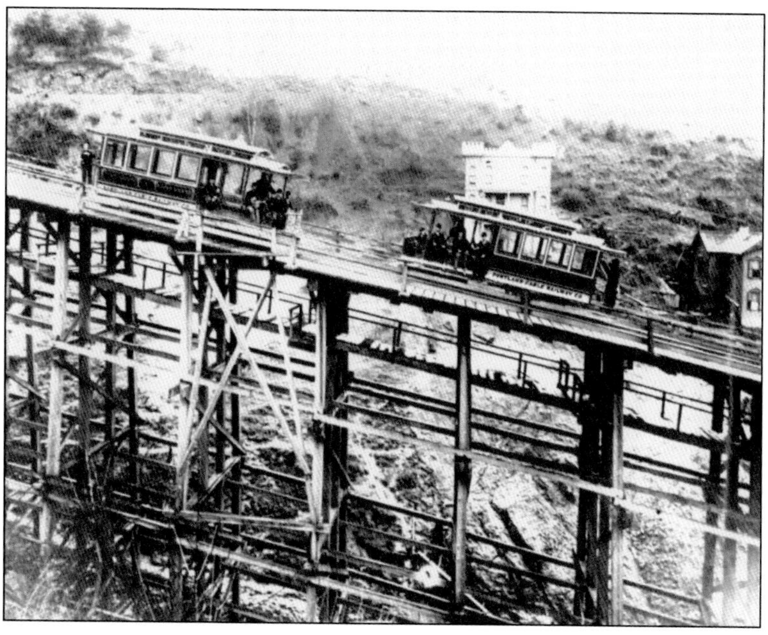

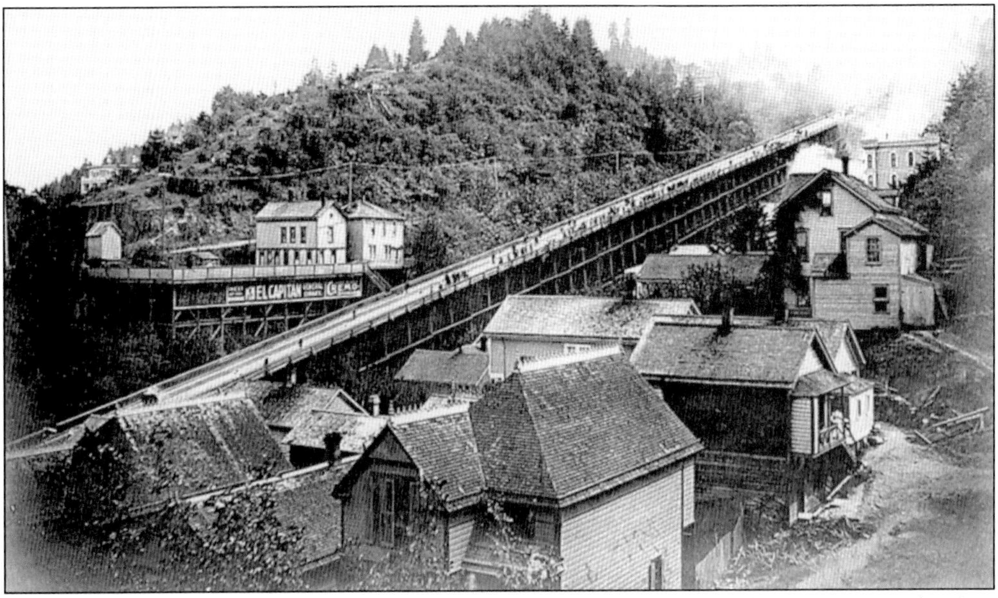

Though a monumental structure, the cable car trestle was only in use for 14 years. In this late 1890s image, a common postcard of the era, Goose Hollow houses crowd around the trestle as more of the ravine, now called Cable Car Canyon, is developed.

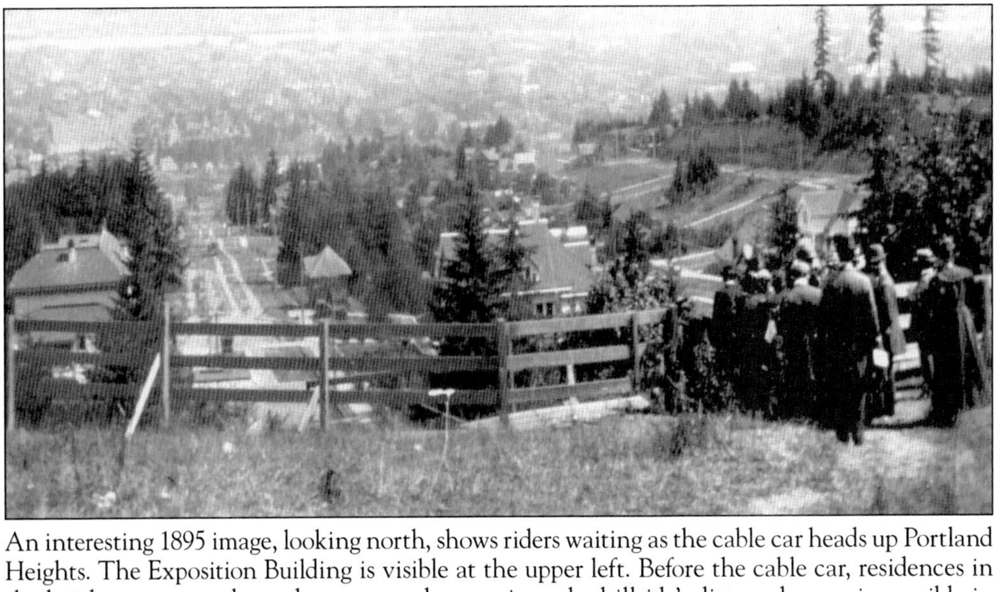

An interesting 1895 image, looking north, shows riders waiting as the cable car heads up Portland Heights. The Exposition Building is visible at the upper left. Before the cable car, residences in the heights were mostly used as summer homes since the hillside's dirt roads were impassible in Portland's rainy winters. (Norm Gholston.)

Three

Streetcars, Automobiles, and Progress 1889–1949

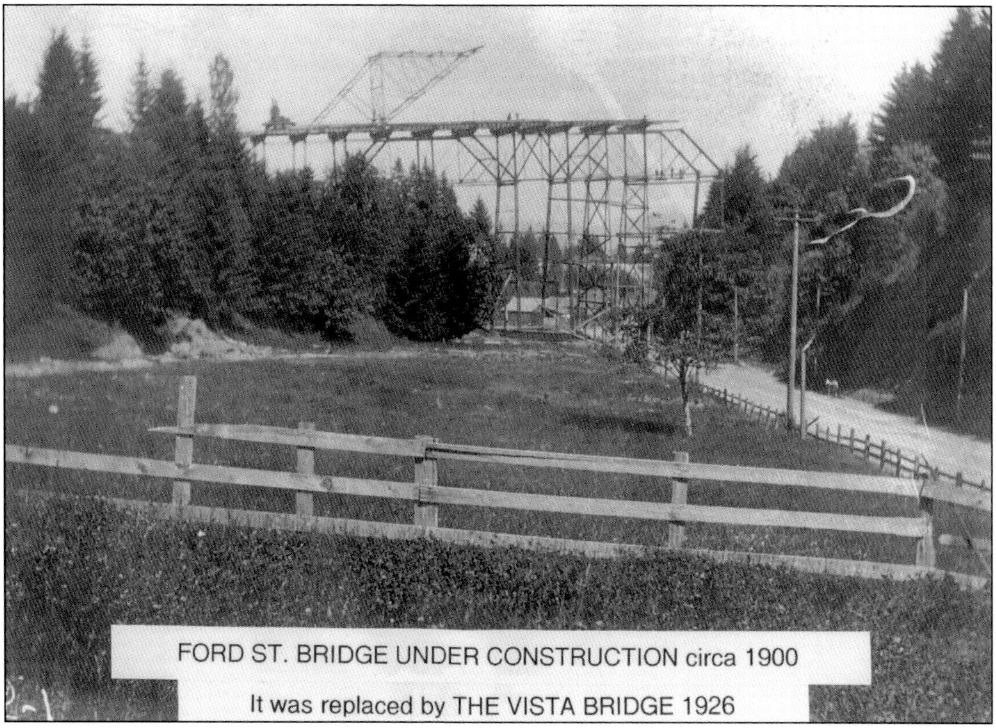

In 1903, a wooden bridge was built across the Tanner Creek Canyon. Crossing over Jefferson/Canyon Road, the Ford Street Bridge was used by electric streetcars, which began running in 1889. With this easier access to the heights, the cable car line began to decline. The nearby cable car trestle was demolished in 1904. (Bud Clark.)

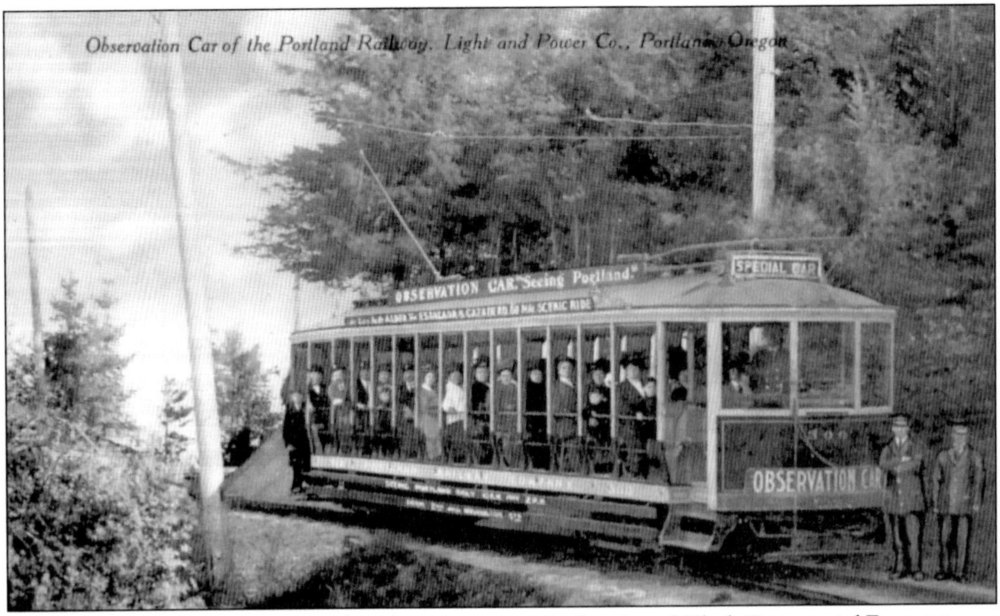

In 1905, a million passengers a week rode streetcars to the Lewis and Clark Centennial Exposition at Guild's Lake, with the entrance near Twenty-sixth Avenue and Upshur Street. This tourism boom led to a boom in observation cars touring around Portland, including the lovely neighborhoods of King's Hill and Portland Heights and up to the views of City Park and Council Crest. A 1910 postcard depicts the Council Crest observation car. (Norm Gholston.)

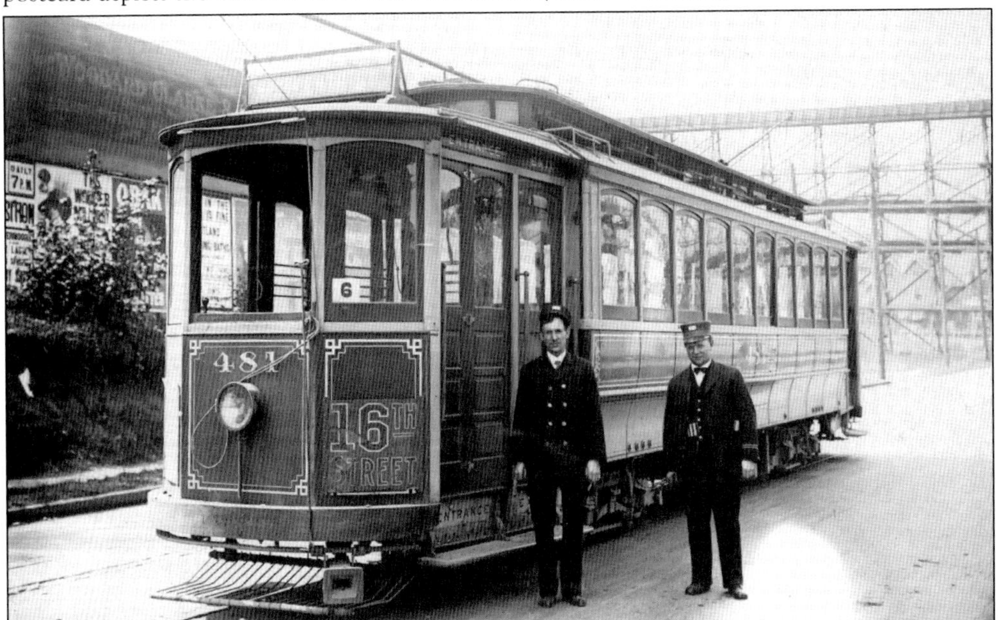

An extension of the cable car line ran to the end of Jefferson Street and up the slopes of City Park. Completed in 1891, the line was abandoned in a few years because a slow-moving landslide in City Park warped the rails and made maintaining the line costly. This early 1900s image looks east with the cable car on the west side of the Ford Street Bridge, near where it terminated at the reservoir. (Norm Gholston.)

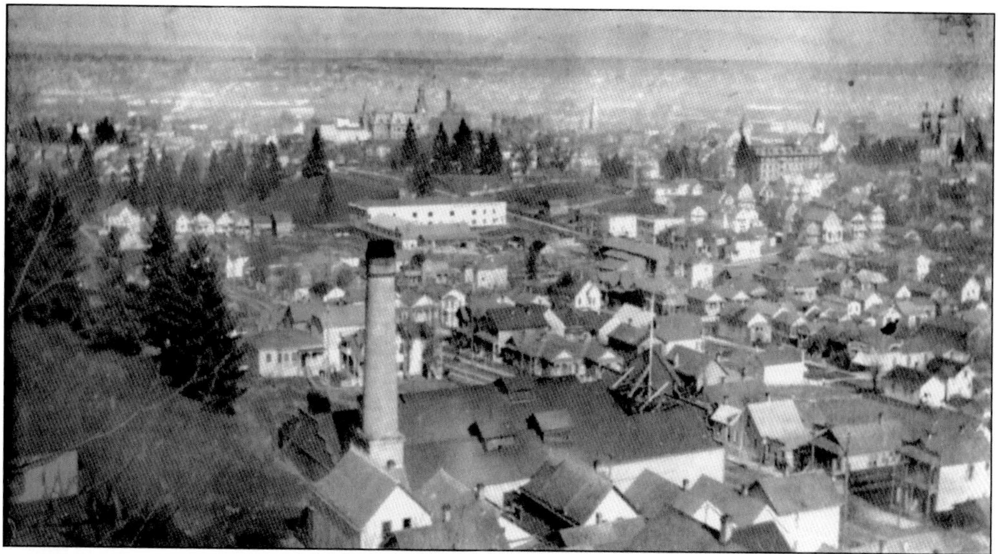

In this 1905 photograph looking northwest from Gander Ridge, the cable car powerhouse and car barn are in the foreground at Eighteenth Avenue and Mill Street. When the Vista Ridge tunnels and the Foothills Freeway were cut through the hillside in the 1960s, the powerhouse was buried under approaches to the tunnel. (OrHi-bb007410.)

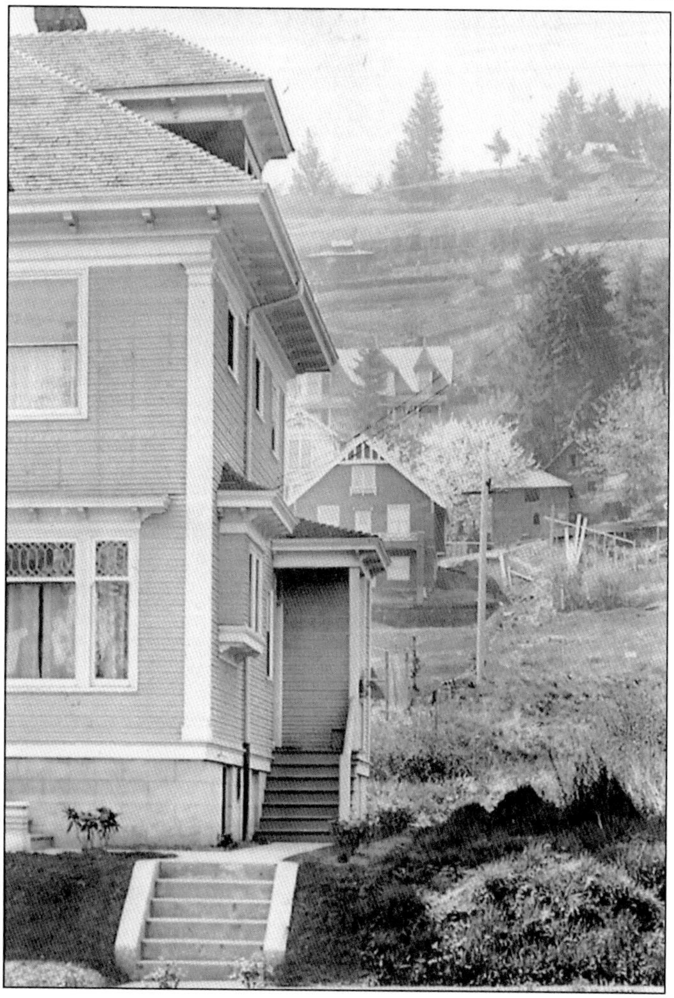

A 1907 photograph of a house at 1416 Southwest Montgomery Street shows increasing development on Gander Ridge. (OrHi-b007399.)

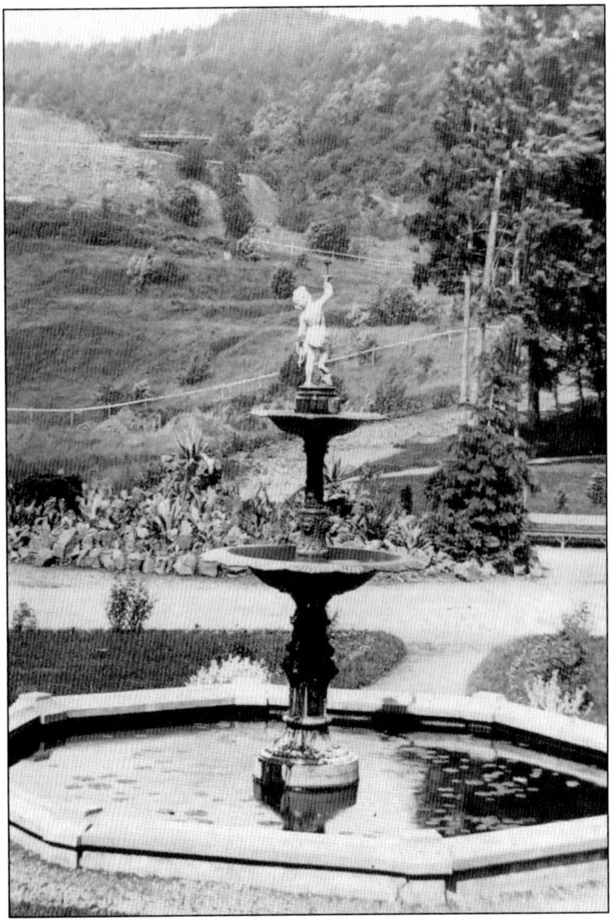

In 1894, two water reservoirs were built by damming a ravine in City Park, but soon cracks started appearing, leading engineers to discover a slow-moving landslide on the hill behind the fountain, shown at left. This "phenomenal land slide" was happening deep underground with movement increasing during winter rains and diminishing during dry summer months. Thirty-three boring holes, 22 wide shafts, and 2,507 linear feet of 5-foot, four-inch tunnels were dug to drain the hillside, and they continue to drain the hills today. To control liability, the city bought out 60 acres west of the reservoirs. Where private residences once stood now stands the Rose Garden and a sports field. The image below shows the entrance to the park, which was changed to Park Place. In 1903, John Olmsted proposed changing City Park's name and moving the entrance, among other suggestions. The name was changed to Washington Park in 1909. (Left, CoPA.)

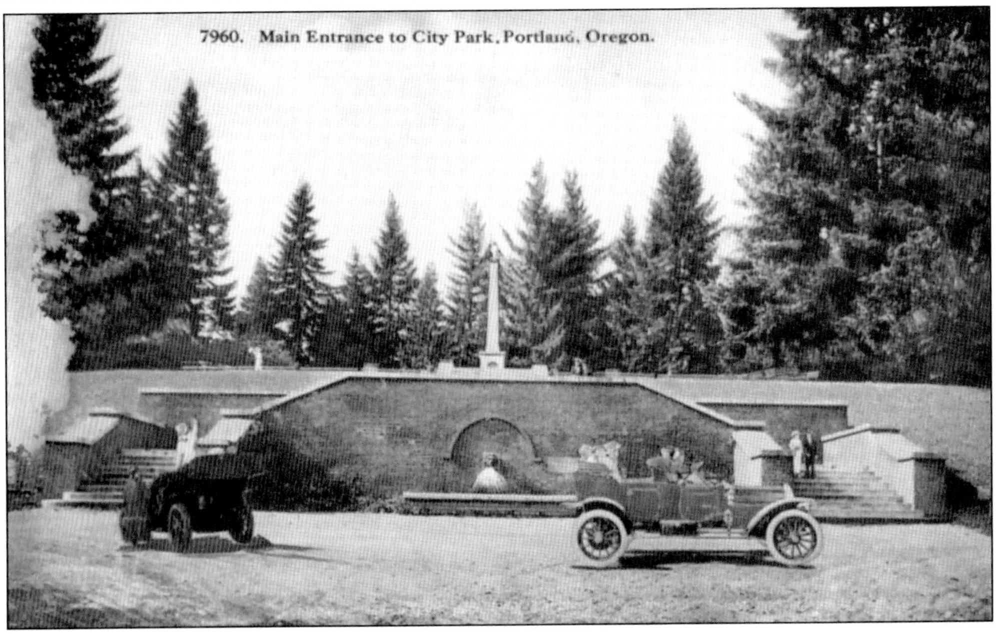

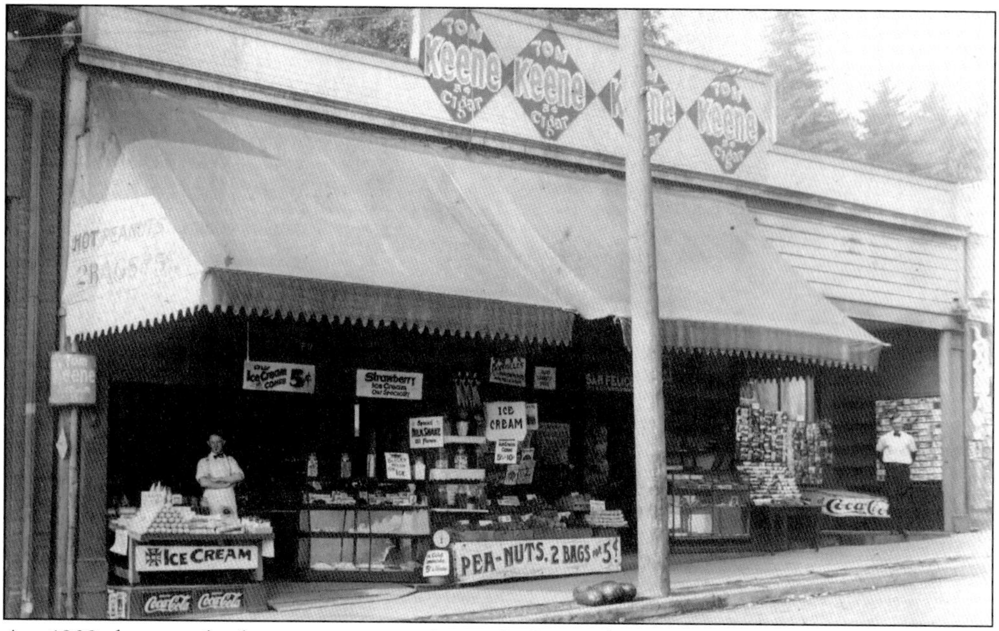

A c. 1909 photograph of a concession stand near the Burnside Street entrance to the park is shown. The concession sells hot peanuts, two bags for 5¢, and ice cream cones for 5¢. Also available is sliced melon on ice, and customers are invited to "leave laundry here." The shop to the right is likely City Park Gallery, and the man in front of the shop is possibly the proprietor, Cal Calvert. (Norm Gholston.)

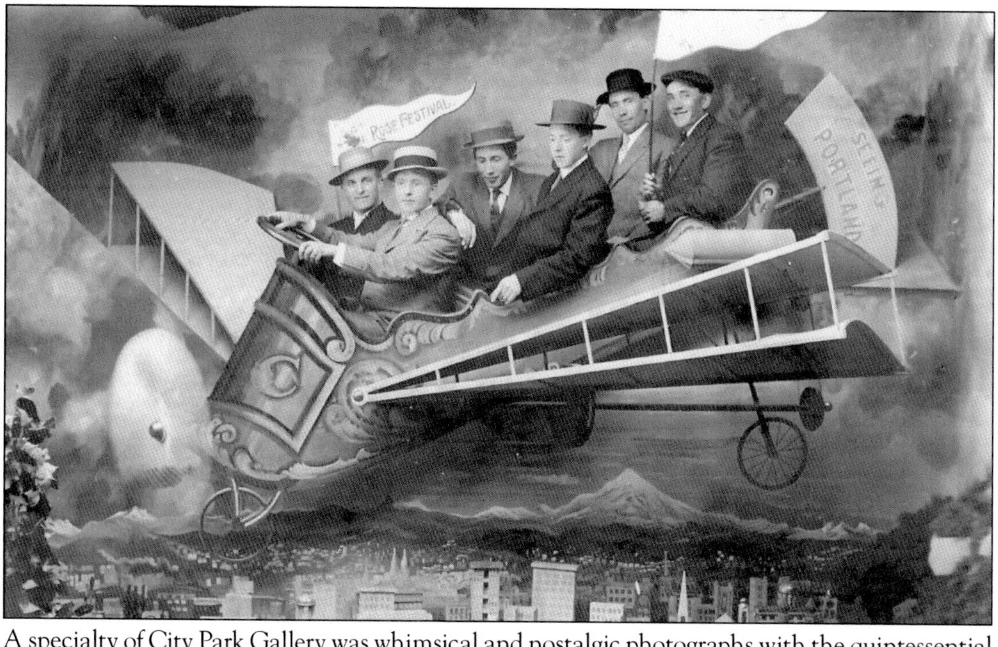

A specialty of City Park Gallery was whimsical and nostalgic photographs with the quintessential view of Portland's skyline as the painted backdrop. This group photograph was taken during the Rose Festival, as indicated by the banner toward the front of the prop plane. The banner held by the man in the last row reads "The Rose City" and at the back of the plane "Seeing Portland." (Margaret Parypa.)

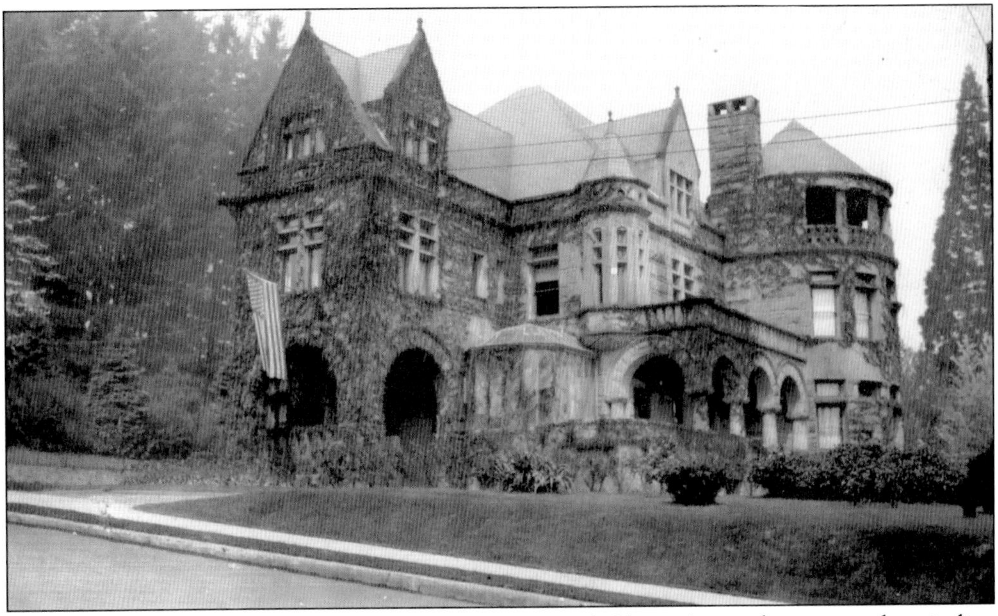

The Julius Loewenberg house (built in 1891) was on Park Place. A merchant turned capitalist, Loewenberg lost his fortune in the financial panic of 1893. The Loewenbergs called their estate Cedar Hill, a name also applied to the Henry Green house next door (page 122) and to this hillside, from Park Place to Burnside Street (platted as Cedar Hill Addition in 1890). Later owned by the Leadbetters, the house was demolished in 1960, replaced by the 2393 Park Place apartments (see page 101). (Norm Gholston.)

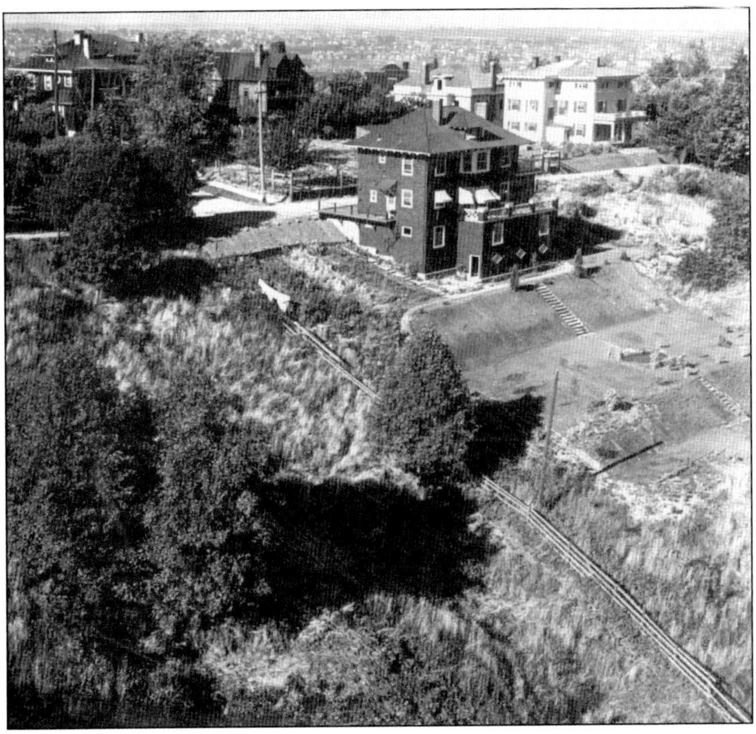

A c. 1905 image gives a sense of the terrain on King's Hill before a mature canopy of trees grew to cover the slope. Most of these homes still stand and are protected under the King's Hill Historic District. The house in the foreground is at the intersection of St. Clair Avenue and Kings Court. (Norm Gholston.)

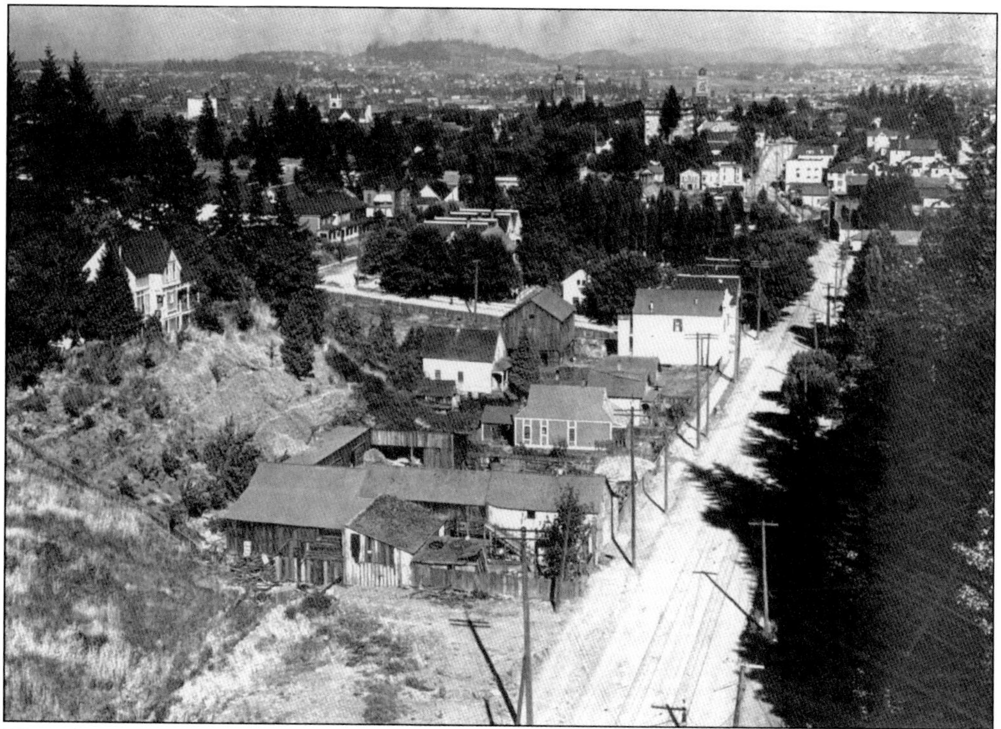

This photograph from around 1905 is of Jefferson Street, below the Ford Street Bridge, looking east. Note the cable car tracks, electrified at this point, for the line that led to the park. (Norm Gholston.)

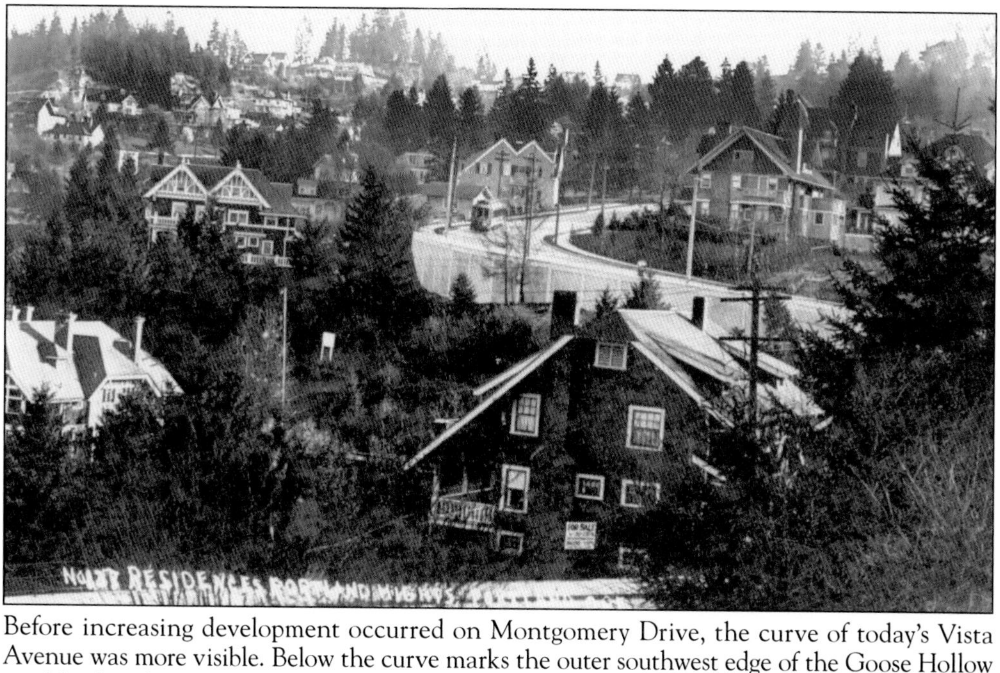

Before increasing development occurred on Montgomery Drive, the curve of today's Vista Avenue was more visible. Below the curve marks the outer southwest edge of the Goose Hollow neighborhood association's boundaries. A streetcar heads down from the heights in this c. 1908 image. (Norm Gholston.)

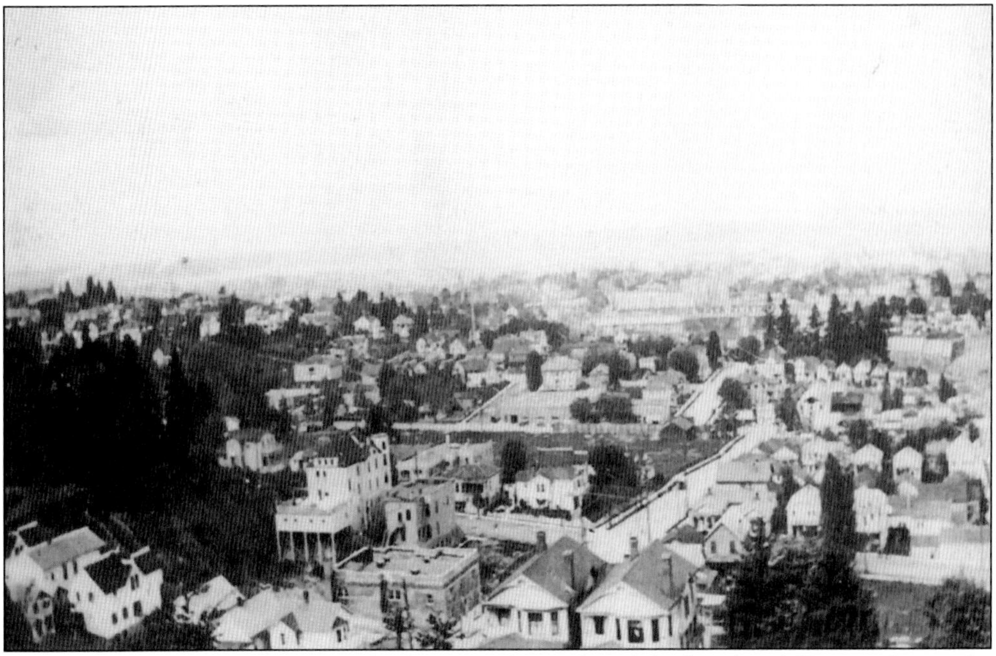

All of the Goose Hollow homes in the foreground were demolished in the 1960s to make way for the Vista Ridge Tunnel. The intersection in the lower center is Southwest Eighteenth Avenue and Market Street Drive. This image is from around 1905. (Norm Gholston.)

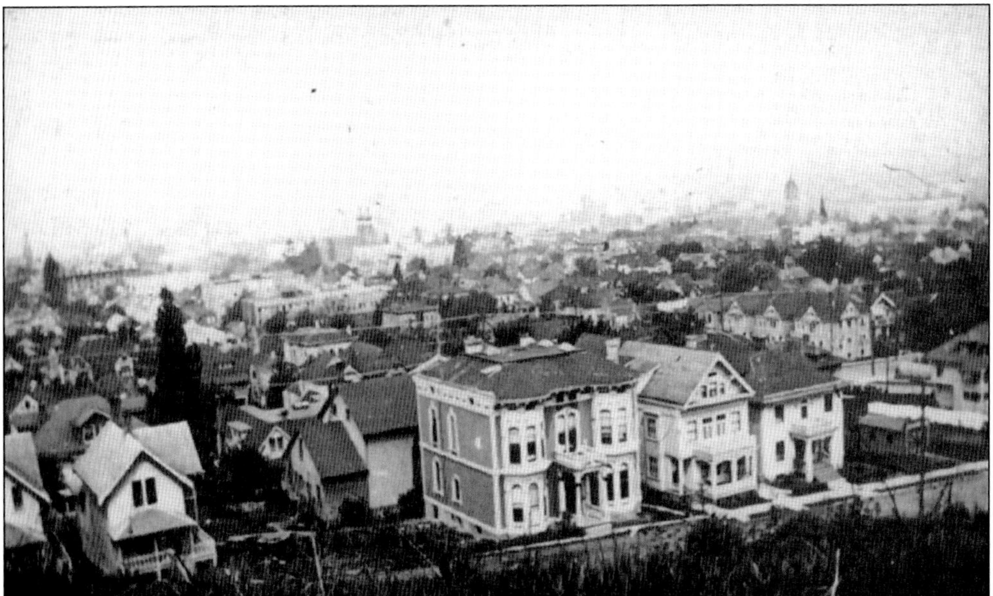

This photograph, looking north, was taken from Gander Ridge around 1905. The houses in the foreground still stand at the 1400 block of Southwest Harrison Street. (Norm Gholston.)

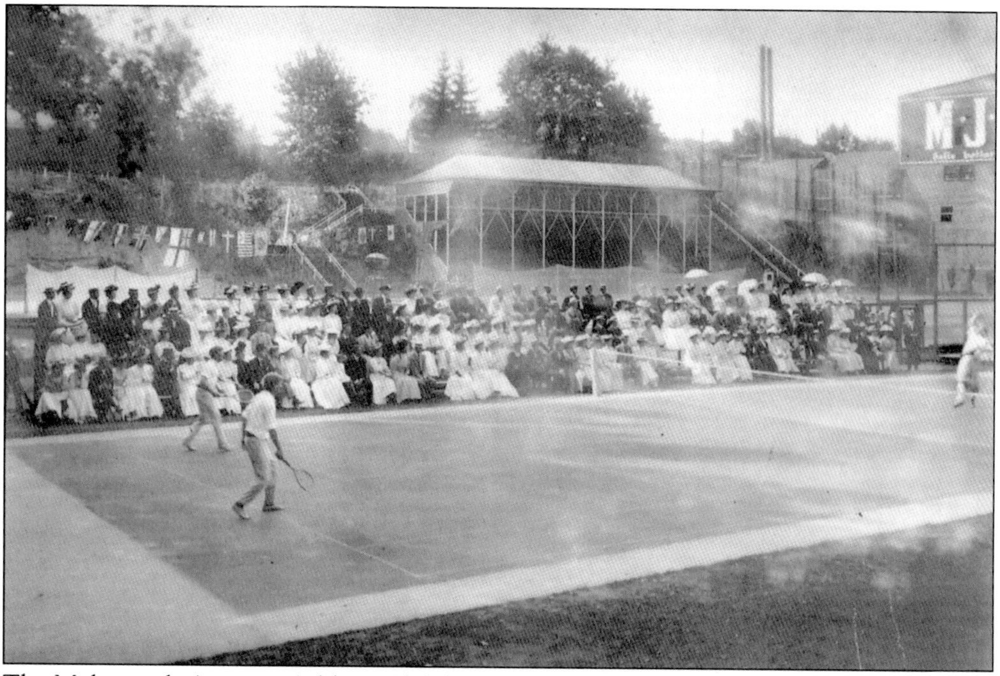

The Multnomah Amateur Athletic Club built this grandstand in 1893, on the northwest end of the field along what is now Twentieth Avenue, behind the Exposition Building. The tennis courts were across the field, next to today's Eighteenth Avenue. Amos King (1822–1901) was a MAC member who liked to attend events on this field and explain that his tannery once stood where the grandstand was. (OrHi-bb007386.)

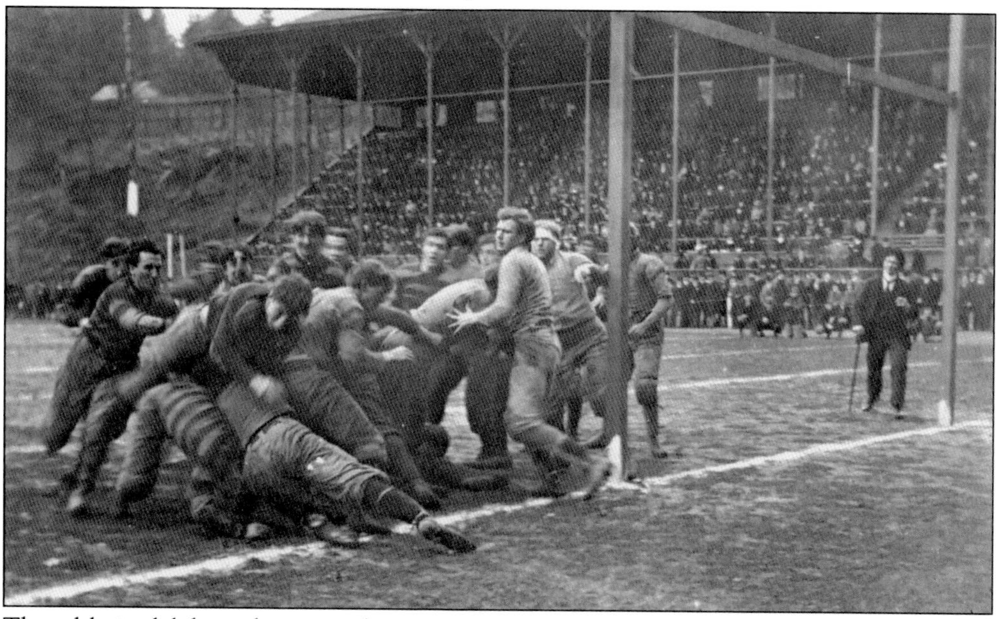

The athletic club hosted many such sporting events. Spectators watch this 1910s football game from what had been the Tanner Creek Gulch only a few years before. Tanner Creek was routed into a culvert and the gulch was graded and filled to accommodate this redevelopment of the terrain. (Norm Gholston.)

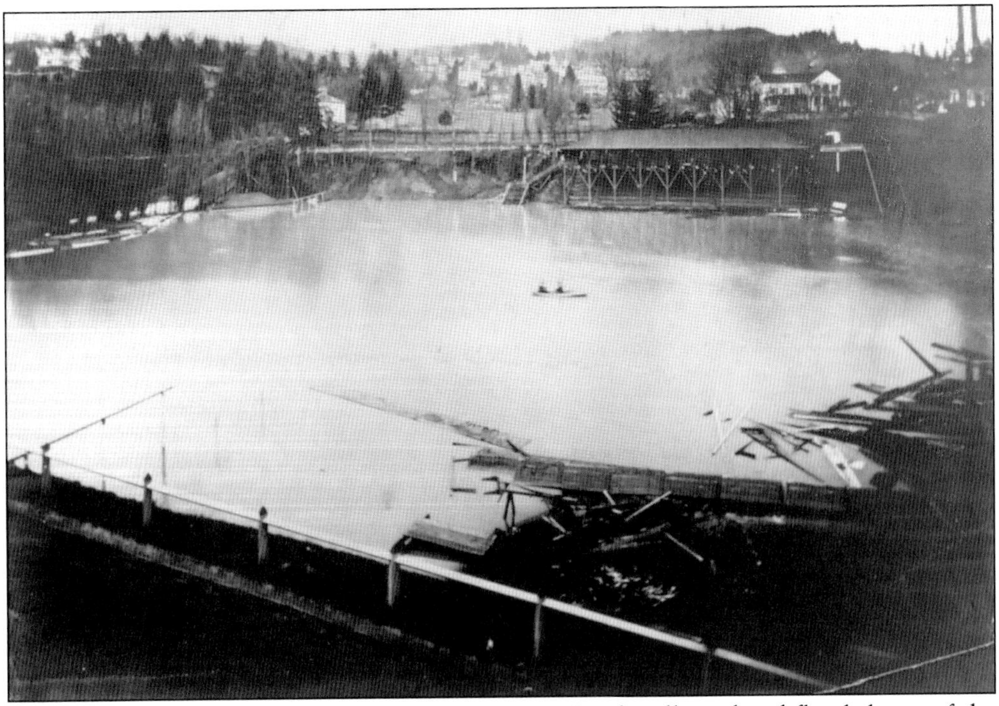

In 1904, the buried bricked culvert carrying Tanner Creek collapsed and flooded part of the Multnomah Athletic Club campus depicted here, looking west. Heavy rains caused the collapse and faulty construction of the culvert was blamed since insufficient mortar had been used in the brickwork. Fire engines pumped 5-feet-deep water off of Multnomah Field, but not before pranksters decided to row across it. (OrHi.)

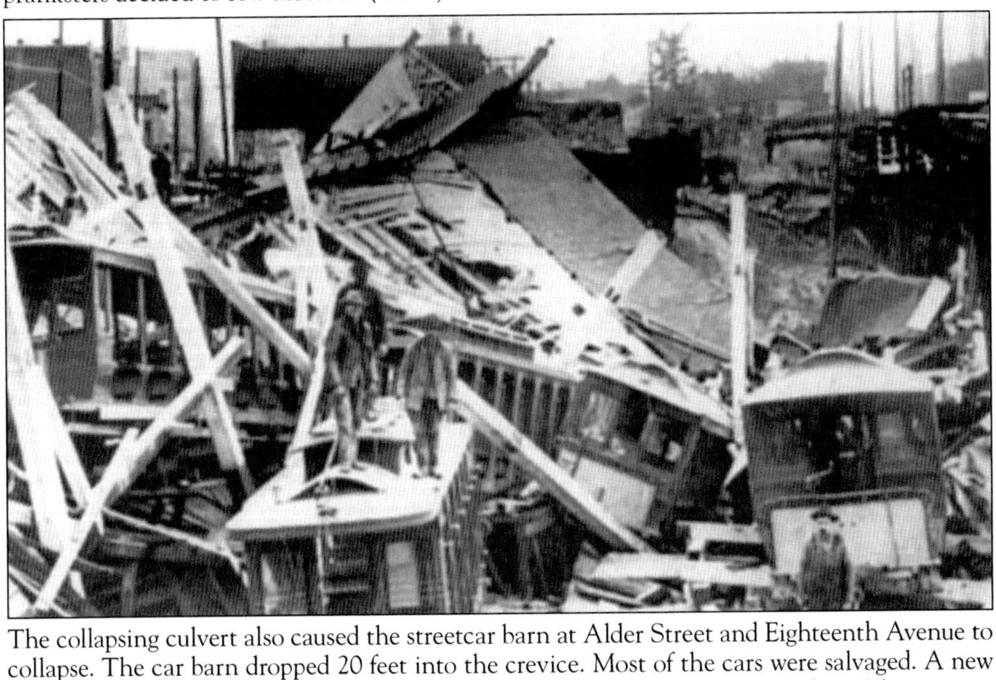

The collapsing culvert also caused the streetcar barn at Alder Street and Eighteenth Avenue to collapse. The car barn dropped 20 feet into the crevice. Most of the cars were salvaged. A new car barn had already been built at today's Vista Avenue and Burnside Street. (CoPA.)

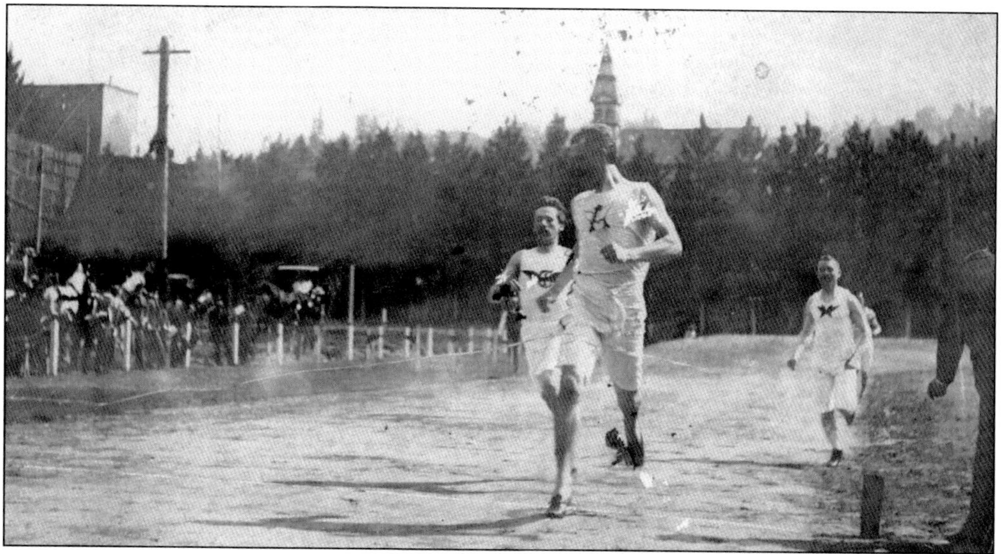

This track meet on Multnomah Field is from around 1909. Though not seen, the corner of Eighteenth Avenue and Salmon Street would be in the upper left where Zion Lutheran's steeple can be seen. Note the size of the poplar trees planted in 1893 to divide the athletic field from the rest of Tanner Creek Gulch. At this time, the Chinese Vegetable Gardens were still in existence on the other side of the trees. (Norm Gholston.)

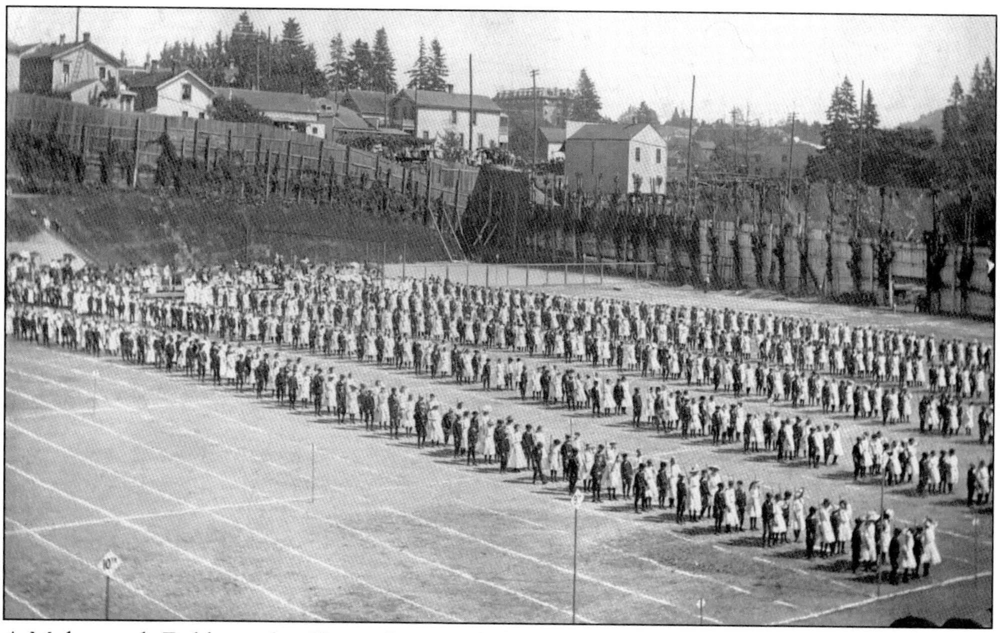

A Multnomah Field parade offers a glimpse of changes in Tanner Creek Gulch. The trees have been dramatically trimmed. They were completely removed in 1910 to expand Multnomah Field, though at this time Chinese gardeners were still farming on the other side of the fence. The house on pilings behind the fence, in the center, fronts Eighteenth Avenue, thus indicating that the infill in that area was not complete. (Norm Gholston.)

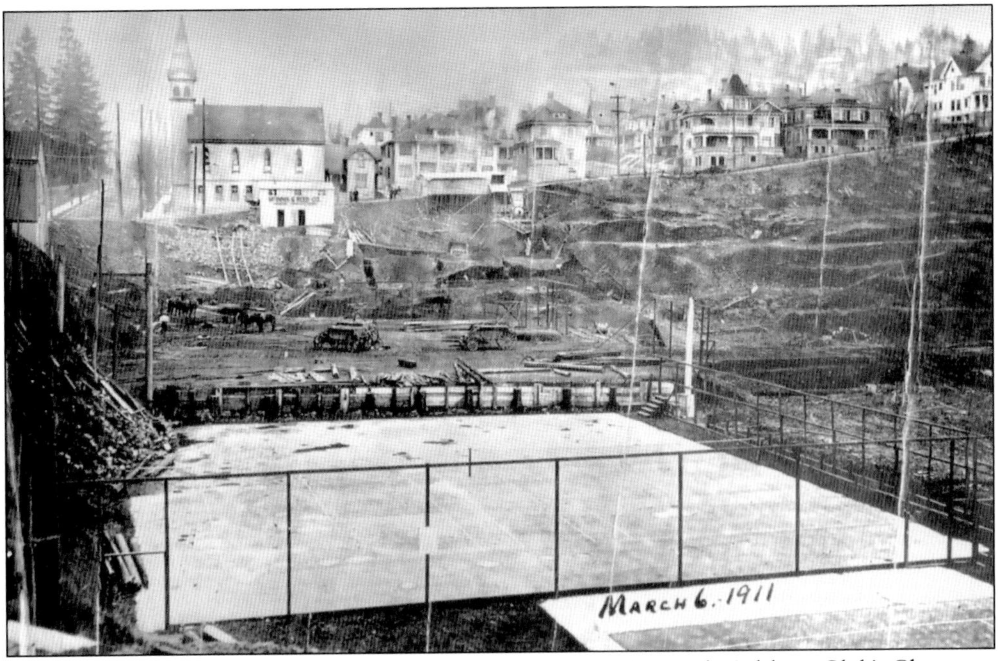

In July 1910, fire destroyed the Exposition Building, the Multnomah Athletic Club's Chapman Street (Eighteenth Avenue) clubhouse, the grandstand, and many nearby buildings. Crews clear the site in this 1911 photograph. Zion Lutheran Church, founded by German immigrants, was spared, as were the lovely homes nearby. Sadly none of these buildings survived the 20th century, replaced by a new church building designed by Pietro Belluschi in 1950, the MAC parking structure, and apartment buildings. (OrHi-bb007448.)

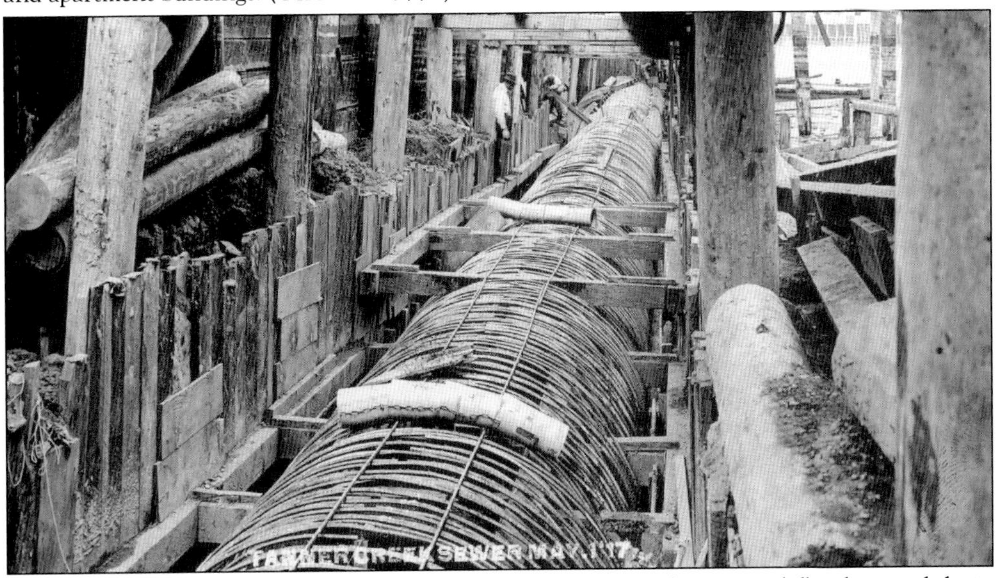

From 1873 to the turn of the century, Tanner Creek was buried to control flooding and drain wetlands. The waterway was sometimes nicknamed Old Barrels Creek because of the tannery vats that apparently remained visible until Multnomah Field was built. Though this image, from 1917, is near Couch Lake, a similar method was used to divert the creek underground in Goose Hollow around Southwest Eighteenth Avenue. (CoPA.)

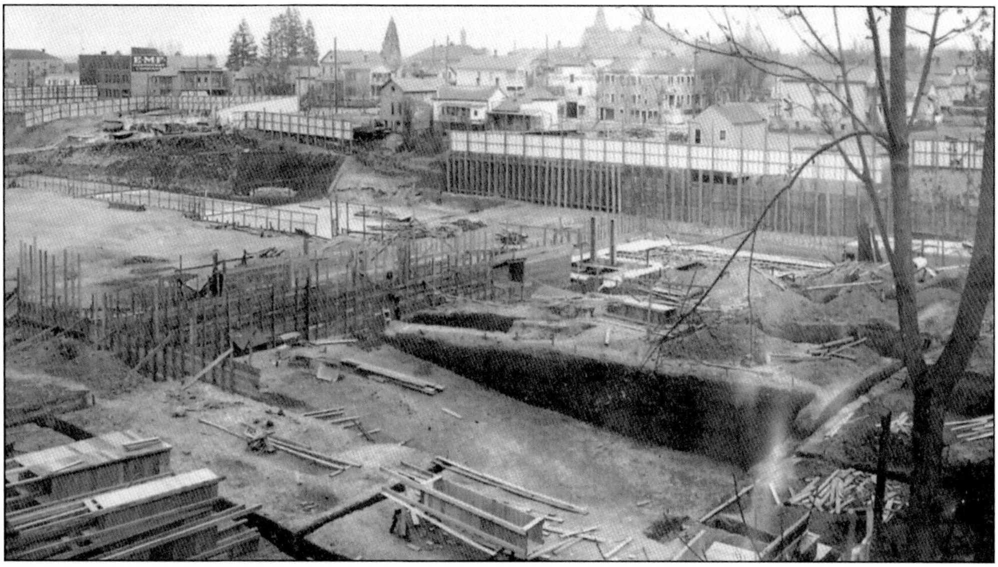

In a 1912 image, excavation is underway for the Multnomah Athletic Club's new building fronting Salmon Street. A lot of earth was moved to reshape the hillside and to finish leveling the gulch that only two years earlier was home to the Chinese Vegetable Gardens. To level and straighten what was once a deep and curving gulch, Eighteenth Avenue was put on pilings that were visible for many years until it was completely infilled. (OrHi-bb007413.)

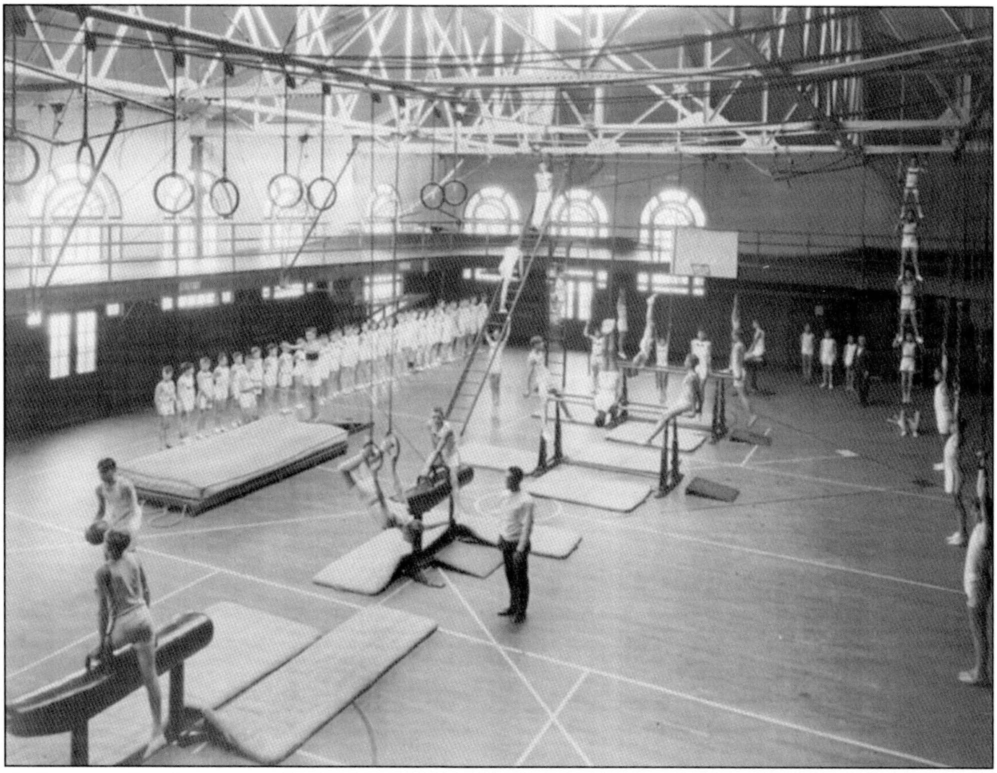

A photograph taken around 1919 inside the Multnomah Athletic Club's Salmon Street clubhouse shows a lively gymnastics class in progress. (University of Oregon.)

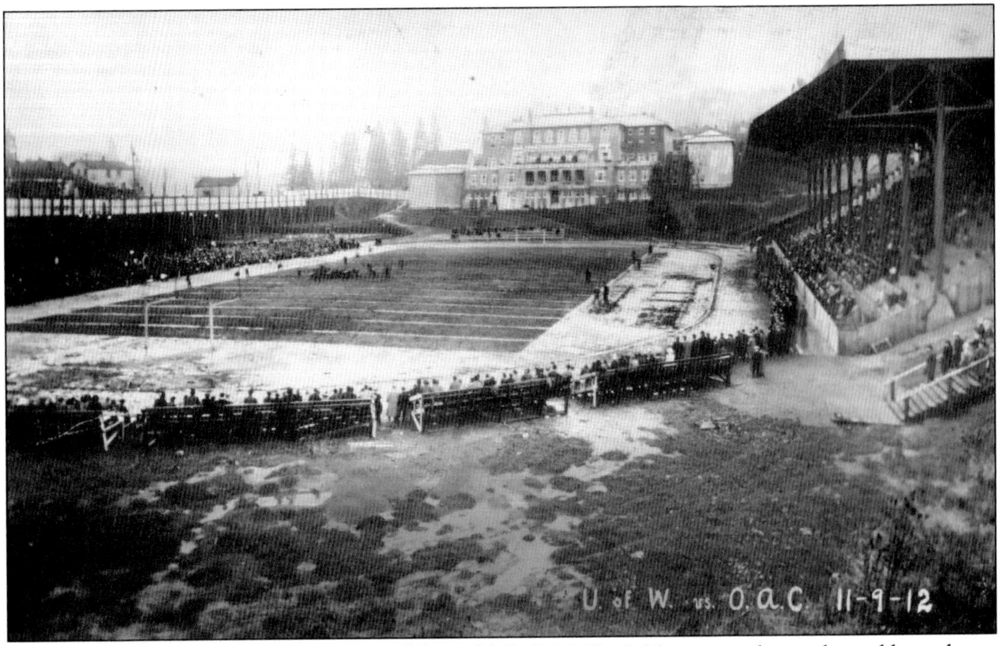

In this 1912 image, the Multnomah Athletic Club (MAC) clubhouse and grandstand have been rebuilt. On the left, Eighteenth Avenue is clearly still on pilings, waiting to receive its fill of infill. (Norm Gholston.)

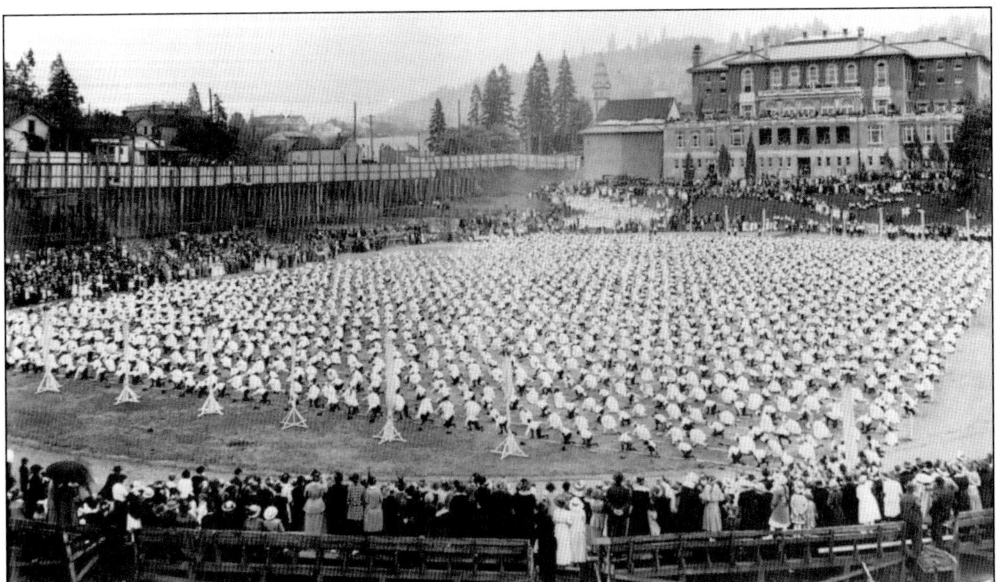

For several generations of Oregonians, Multnomah Field (later the Civic Stadium) was the site of parades, festivals, May Day celebrations, concerts, and presidential visits. Note the Eighteenth Avenue pilings are clearly visible. (OrHi.)

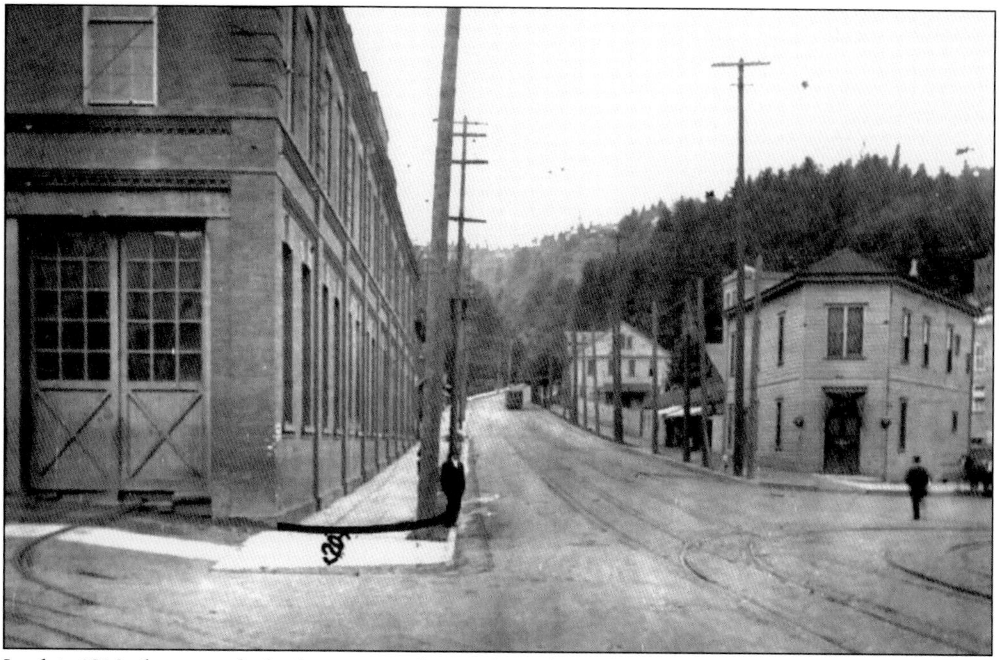

In this 1910 photograph, looking west, the marks indicate how the city planned to cut back the sidewalk on Burnside Street at the Vista Avenue intersection. The corner where the Cedar Hill streetcar barn stands (left) is now a parking lot for the Uptown Shopping Center. (CoPA.)

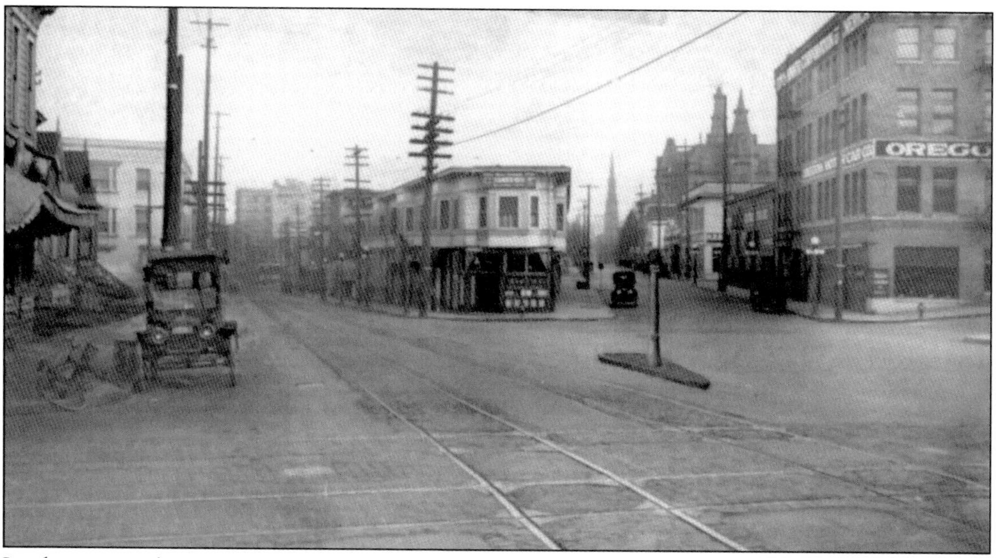

Looking east, this section of Alder Street, at the right, was often referred to at this time as "upper Alder" and was a hub for auto sales, repair, and painting shops. The cross street in the foreground is Burnside Street and Nineteenth Avenue. (CoPA.)

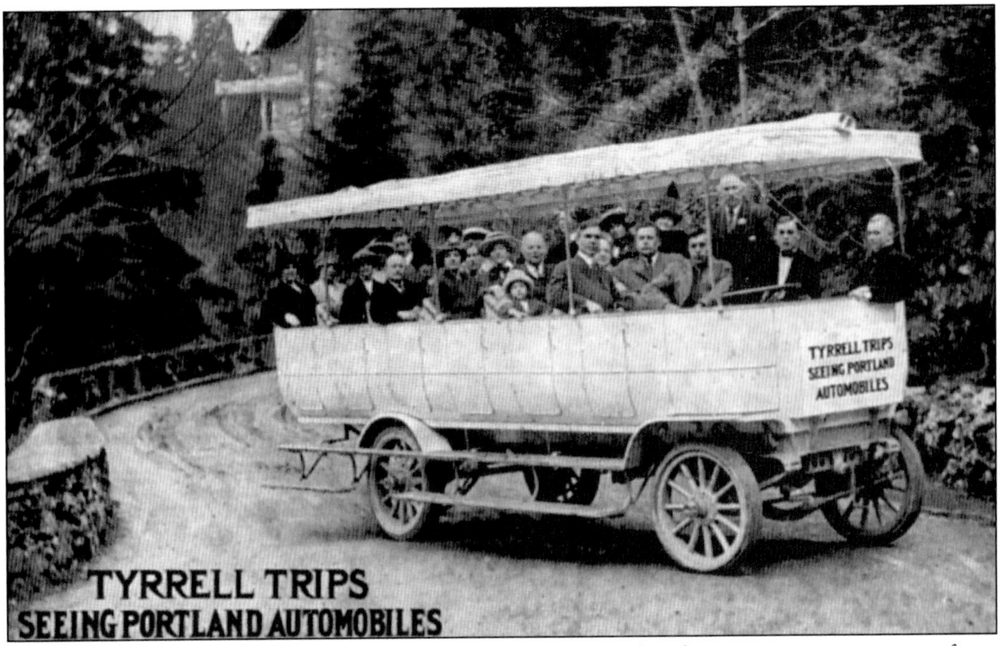

A sightseeing car at the entrance to City/Washington Park takes tourists to see views from the heights in 1913. Sightseeing by electric streetcar was giving way to scenic automobile tours. (Margaret Parypa.)

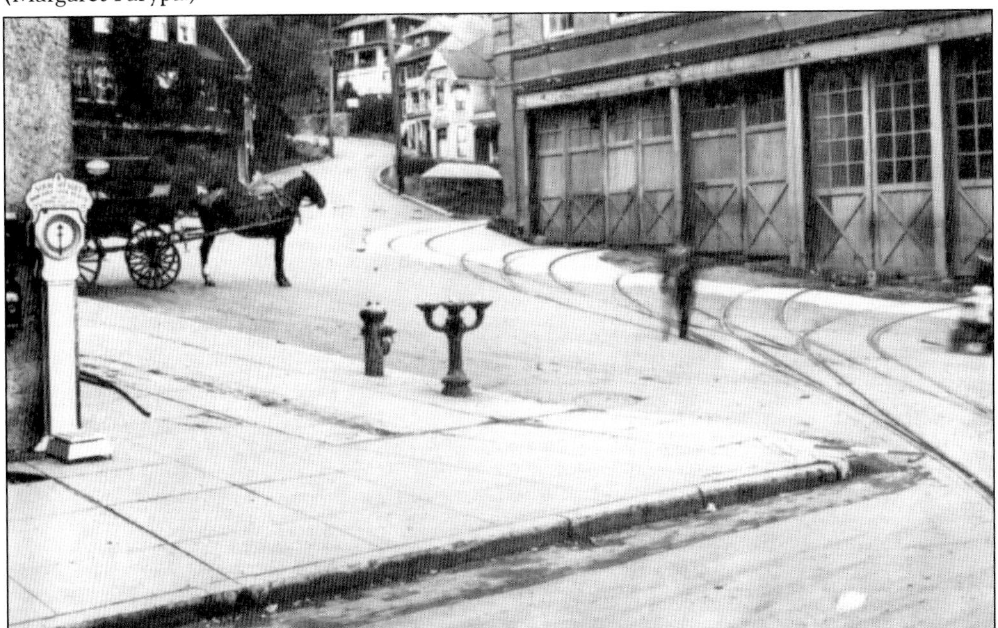

A 1913 photograph of the Cedar Hill streetcar barn at Burnside Street offers a glimpse up Green Avenue, named after Henry Green. This narrow street is home to charming apartment buildings with front doors opening almost into the road. Goose Hollow is lucky to have such quirky, winding streets. The Benson Bubbler is no longer at this spot, though one is on the southeast corner of Morrison Street and Eighteenth Avenue. The streetcar barn was demolished in the 1930s. (CoPA.)

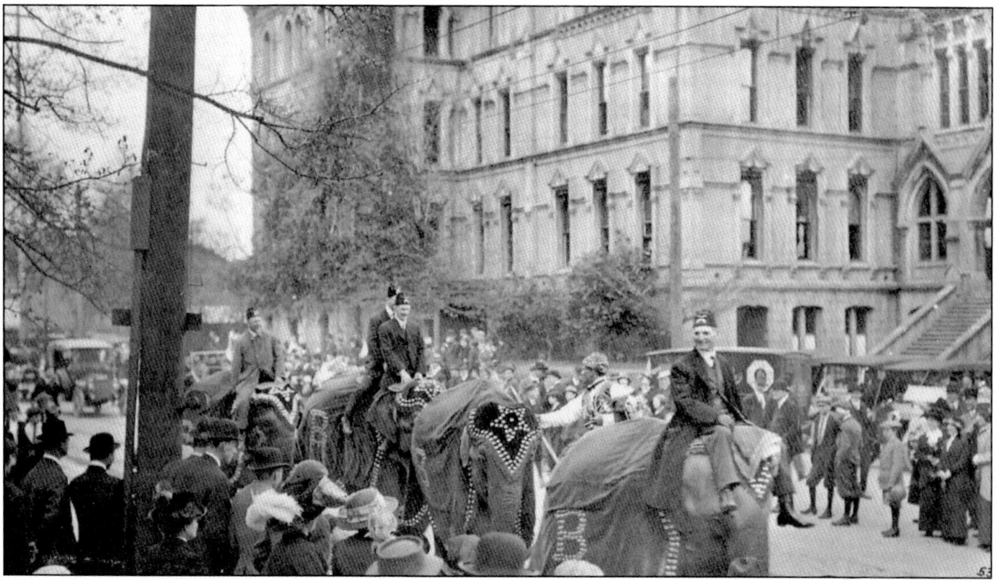

Portlanders dressed in their finest clothes enjoy a day in Goose Hollow as they watch the Shriners pass by Portland High School on elephants as part of the Shrine Circus Parade in 1914. This area was briefly referred to as the Lownsdale District, which was the north end of the lower elevations in Goose Hollow. The name appeared in the *Oregonian* only once, in 1924. (OrHi-bb7431.)

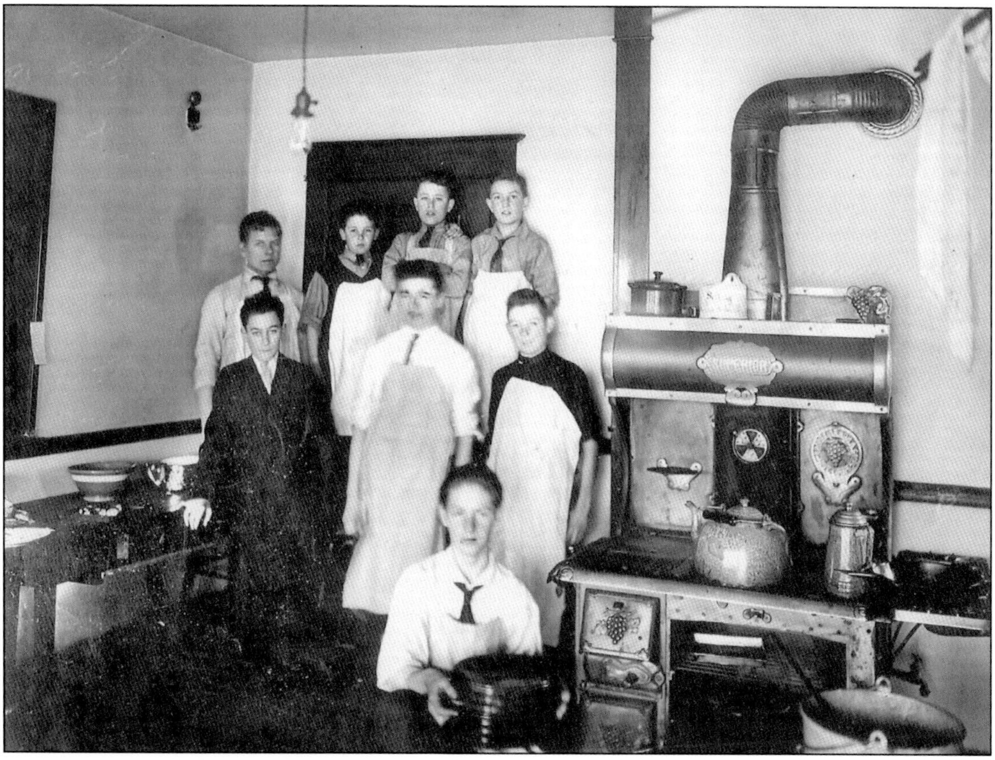

For some reason, Portland High School boys only learned to cook during the war, as seen in this image from 1918, during World War I. Cooking was taught as a sort of survival skill. (OrHi-bb007383.)

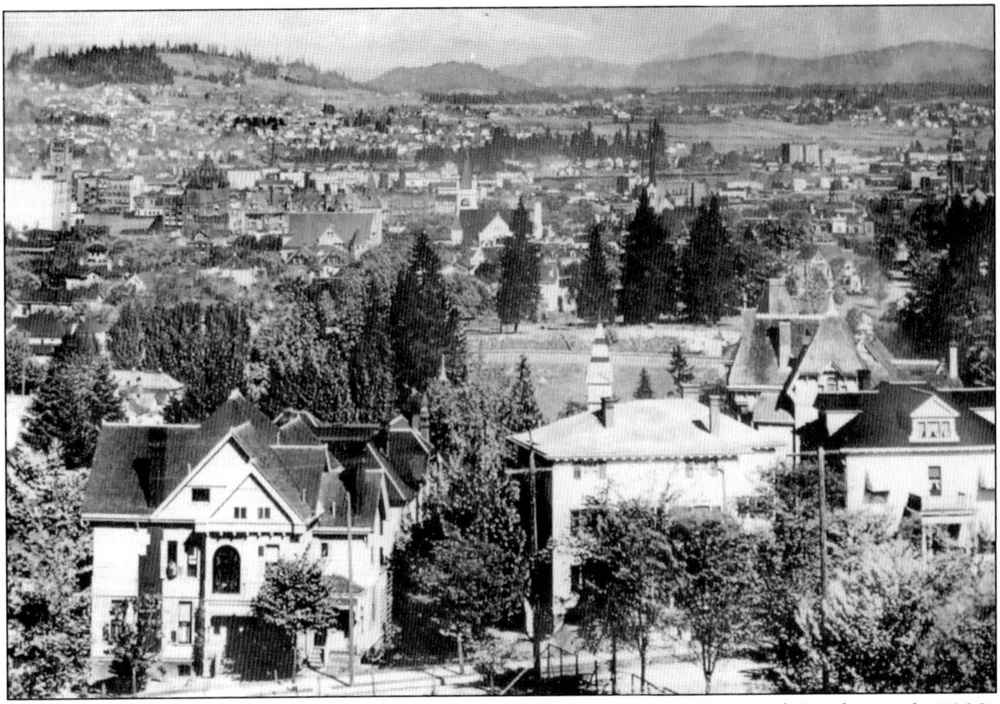

With the ease of access by streetcars, the King's Hill development boomed. In this early 1900s photograph, Mount Hood can be seen in the distance. The homes in the foreground are on King Street: the George Durham house (left), the Judge Wallace McCamant house (center), and the Nahum King house (right). (OrHi-bb007417.)

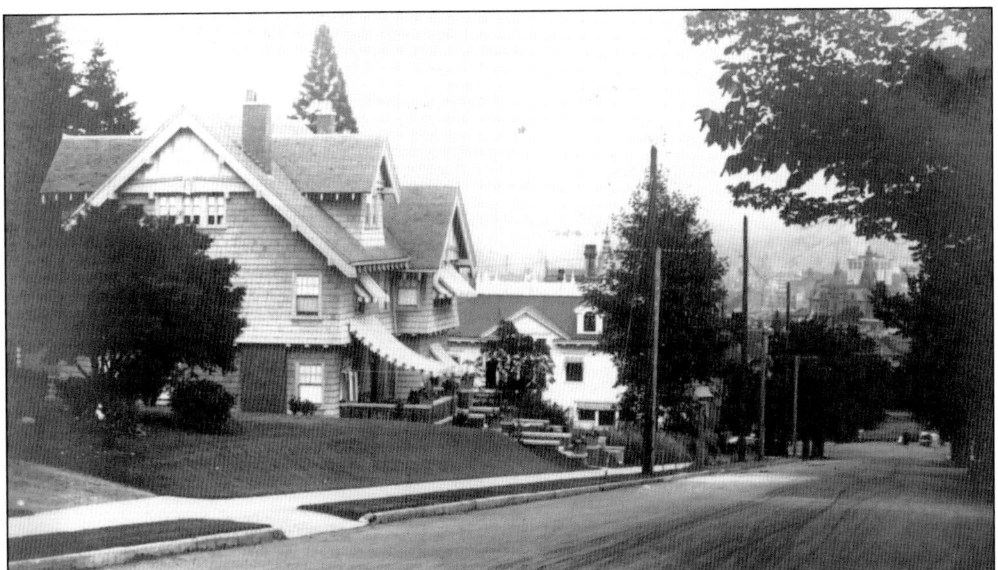

Near the Washington Park entrance on Park Place, looking east at houses on King's Hill, Portland High School can be seen in the distance. (Norm Gholston.)

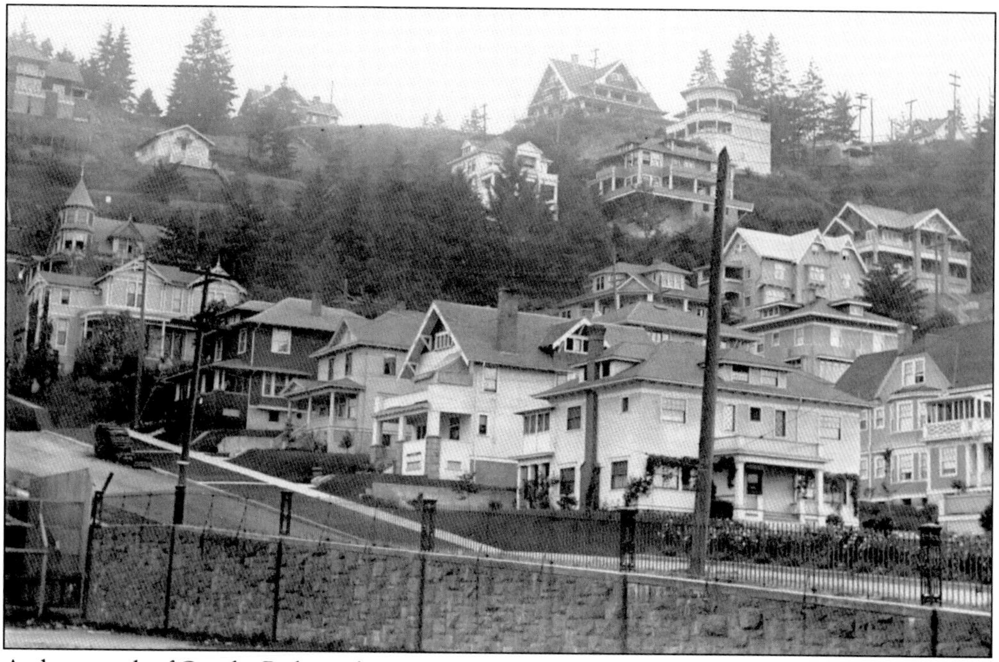

A photograph of Gander Ridge, taken around 1910, gives a sense of what the area was like before it was split from neighboring streets in Goose Hollow by Interstate 405 and the connectors to Highway 26. In the foreground is the intersection of Fourteenth Avenue and Harrison Street. (Don Nelson.)

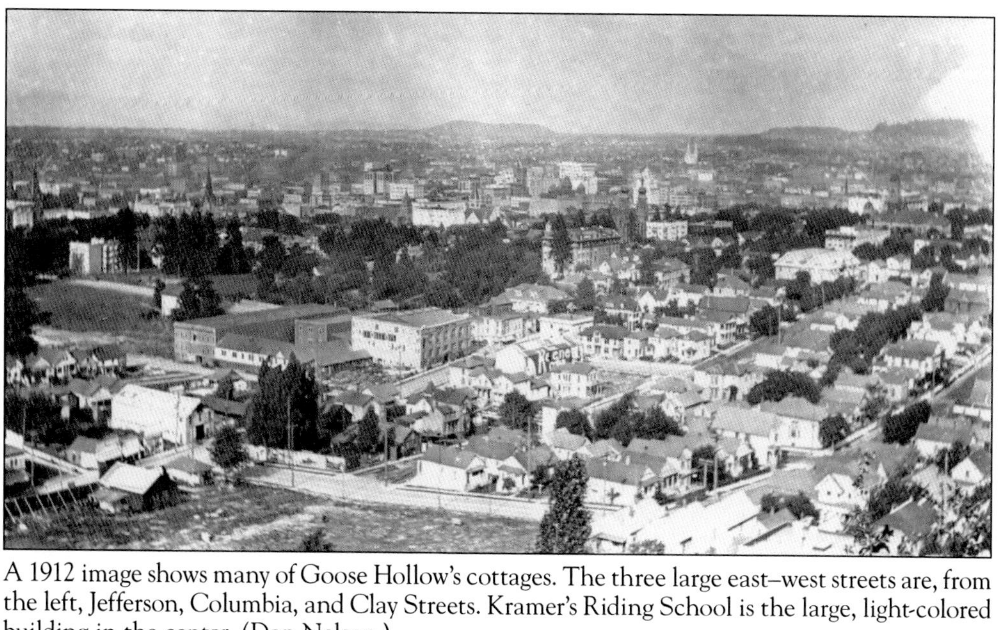

A 1912 image shows many of Goose Hollow's cottages. The three large east–west streets are, from the left, Jefferson, Columbia, and Clay Streets. Kramer's Riding School is the large, light-colored building in the center. (Don Nelson.)

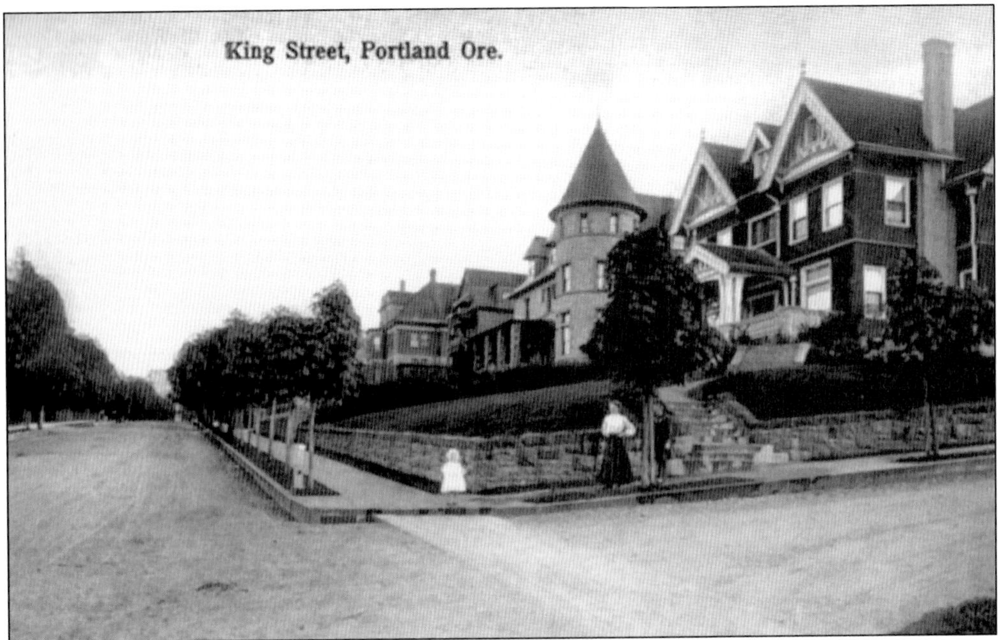

In present-day King's Hill, many homes are more than 100 years old. Styles include Craftsman, Colonial Revival, Mediterranean, Italianate, and Queen Anne designs. From the 1950s to the 1970s, several historic homes were replaced by apartment buildings. Many of the street trees were planted in the original development and have grown to majestically overlook the hillside, including horse chestnut and maple trees along Park Avenue and breath-taking sequoia trees on Vista Avenue. King's Hill is home to several social, civic, and arts organizations, including the Town Club, built in 1930 at 2115 Salmon Street; the Oregon Society of Artists, located at 2185 Park Place; the Portland Garden Club, at 1132 Southwest Vista Avenue; and the Multnomah Athletic Club, located at 1849 Southwest Salmon Street. Above, an adult and two children stand on the corner. Below, on the north end of King Street, a child smells roses with a streetcar to the south on Burnside Street.

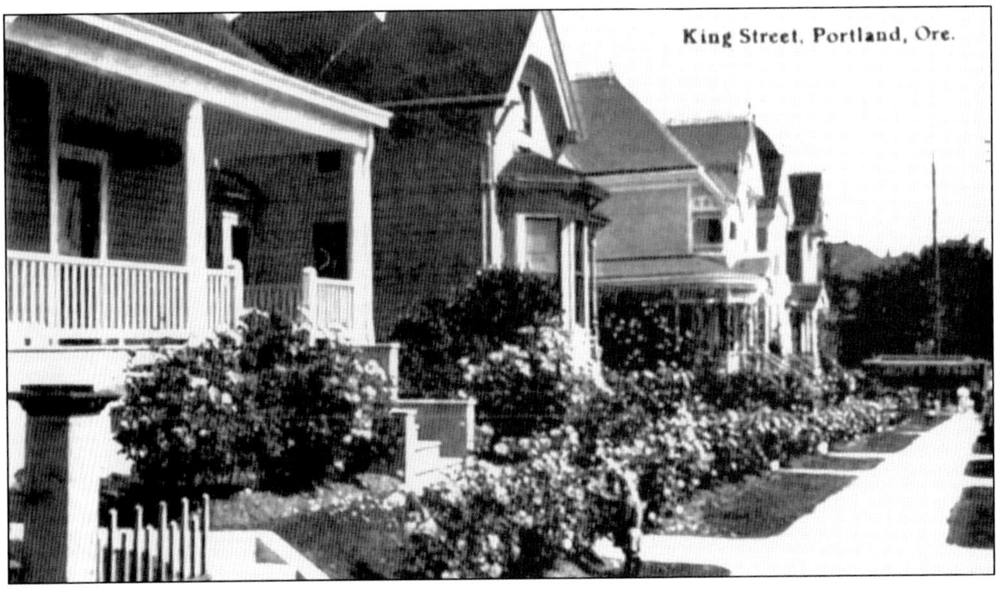

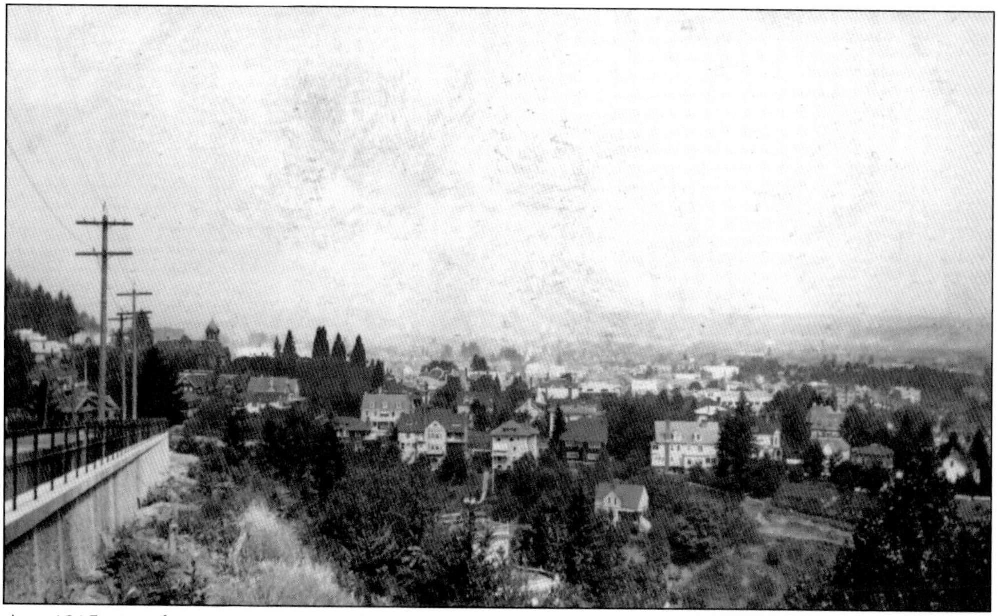

A *c.* 1915 view from Vista Avenue looks across Tanner Creek Canyon north to King's Hill where St. Helen's Hall is visible. (Norm Gholston.)

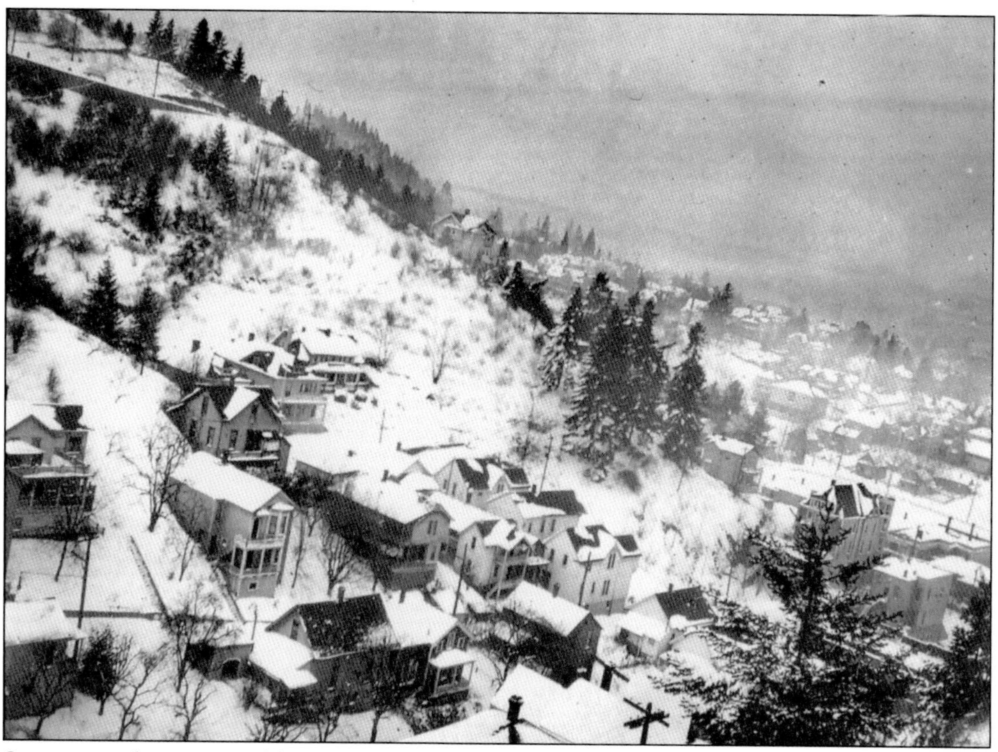

Snow covers houses in Cable Car Canyon around 1920. With Vista Ridge denuded of trees, today's Vista Avenue is visible in the upper left of the image. (OrHi-bb007426.)

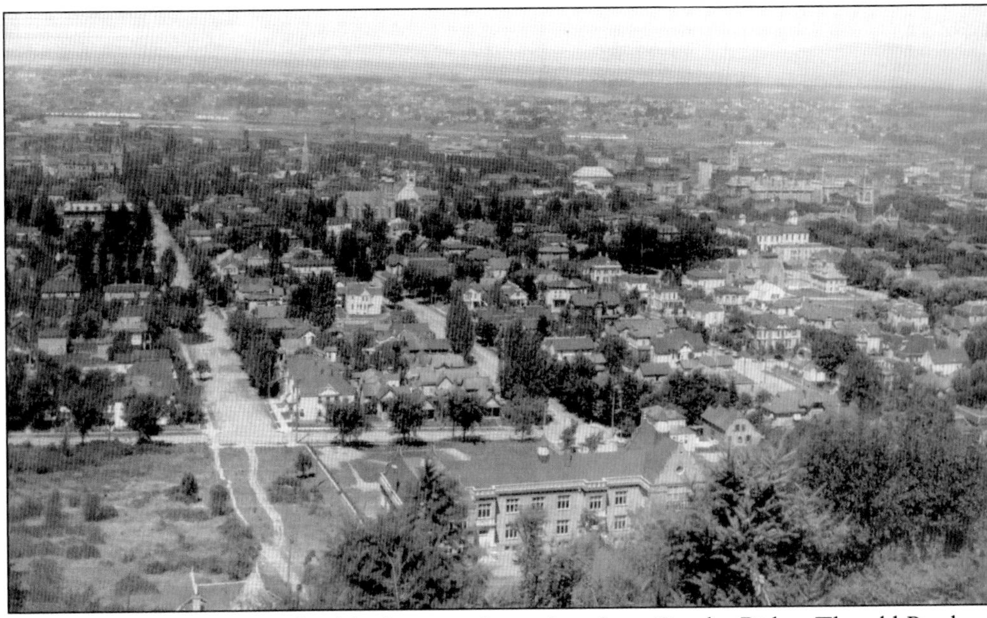

A 1920s photograph of Portland looking north is taken from Gander Ridge. The old Portland Academy, later home to St. Helen's Hall (a precursor to Oregon Episcopal School), is on Montgomery Street in the foreground with Fourteenth Avenue to the left. This area was demolished in the 1960s for urban "renewal." (Norm Gholston.)

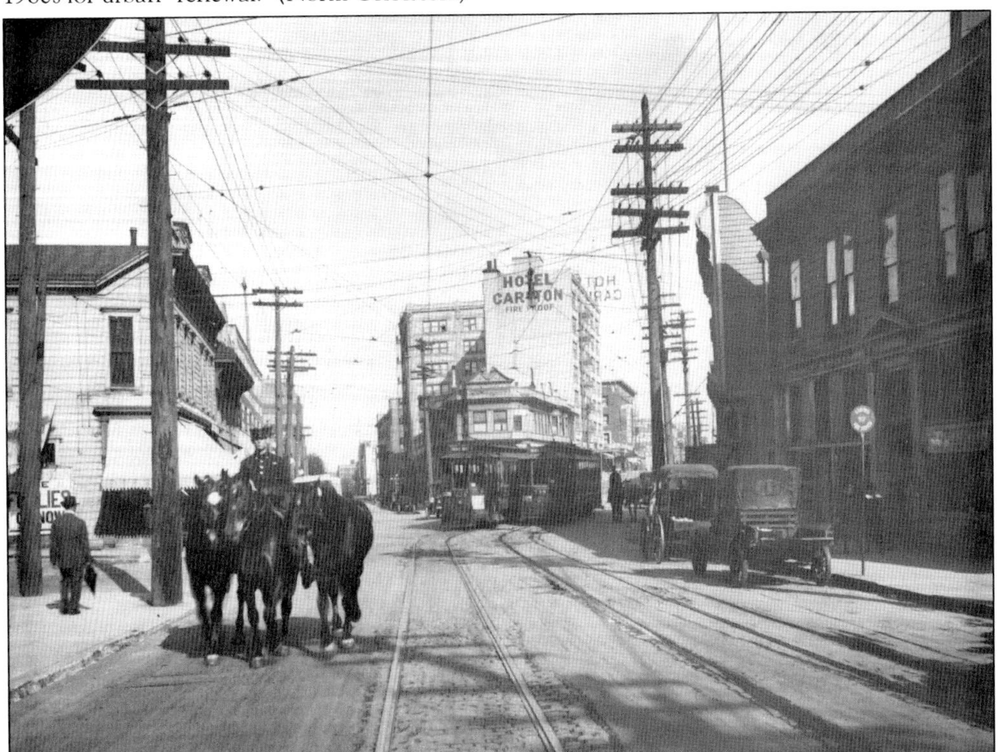

This 1920s image shows Burnside Street as it once connected to Washington Street, before the area around the Hotel Carlton was demolished to accomodate Interstate 405 construction. (CoPA.)

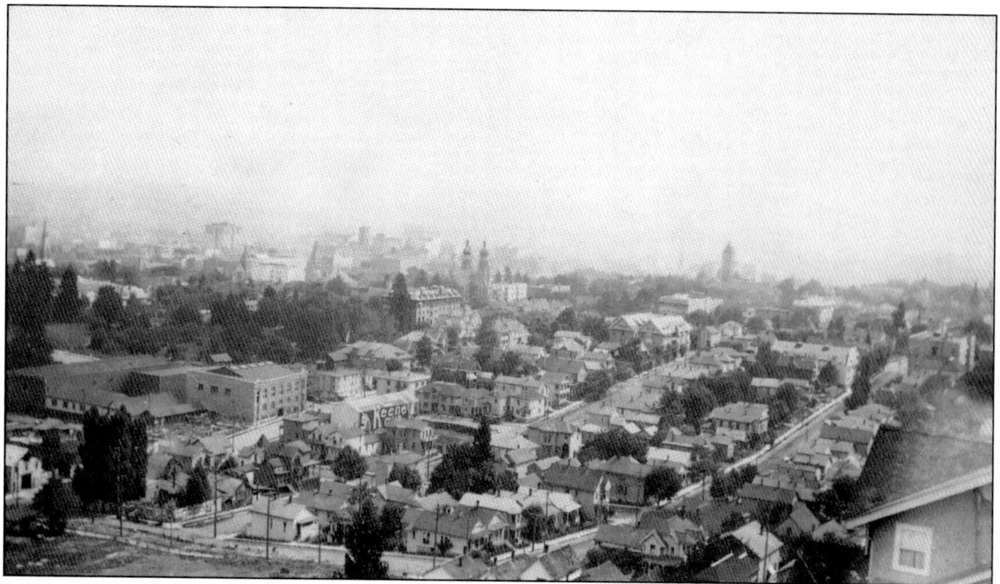

A late 1910s photograph, looking east, shows a section of Columbia Street, near Sixteenth Avenue, up on pilings. (Norm Gholston.)

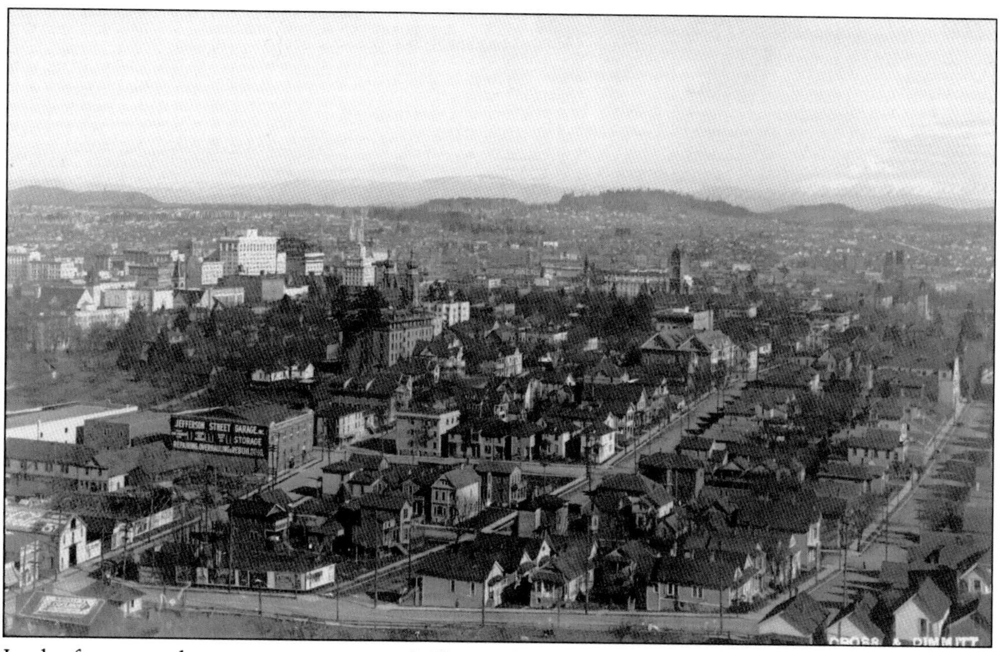

In the foreground, a streetcar passes on Jefferson Street near Eighteenth Avenue in 1920. Mount Hood is in the distance. The twin spires of Temple Beth Israel are near the center of both images, with the Hill Hotel (later called the Maraba West apartments) on Jefferson in front of the temple. (Norm Gholston.)

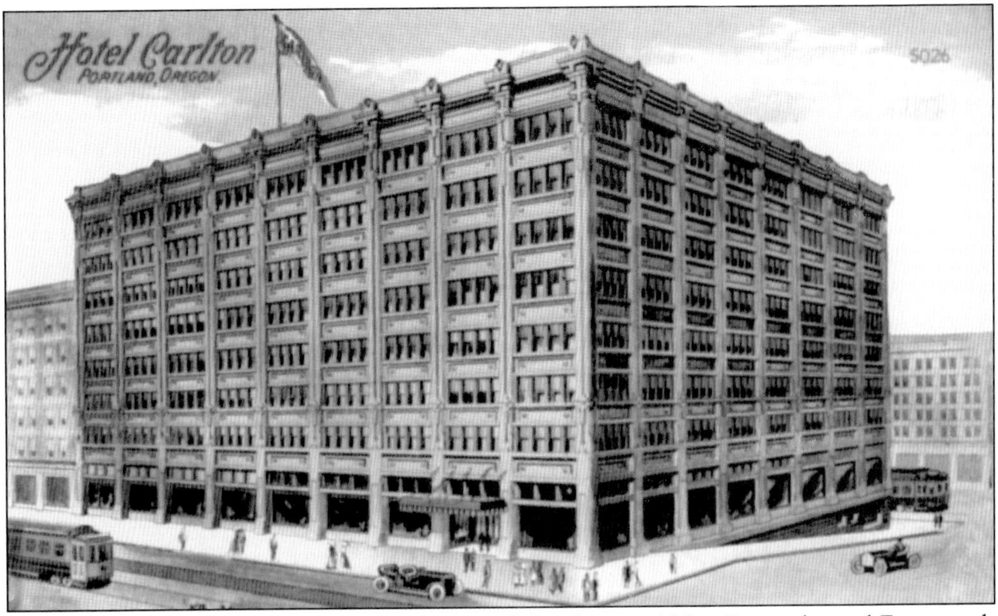

This 1910 postcard shows streetcars and automobiles sharing Alder, Burnside, and Fourteenth Streets around the Hotel Carlton, which was removed for Interstate 405 construction. The old Hellig Theater once stood on this spot. A Portland resident remembered in the June 4, 1921, issue of the *Oregonian* when "the western boundaries of Portland ran about where the Carlton Hotel now stands, and you crossed a bridge over Tanner Creek that took you into the wilds of Oregon." (Norm Gholston.)

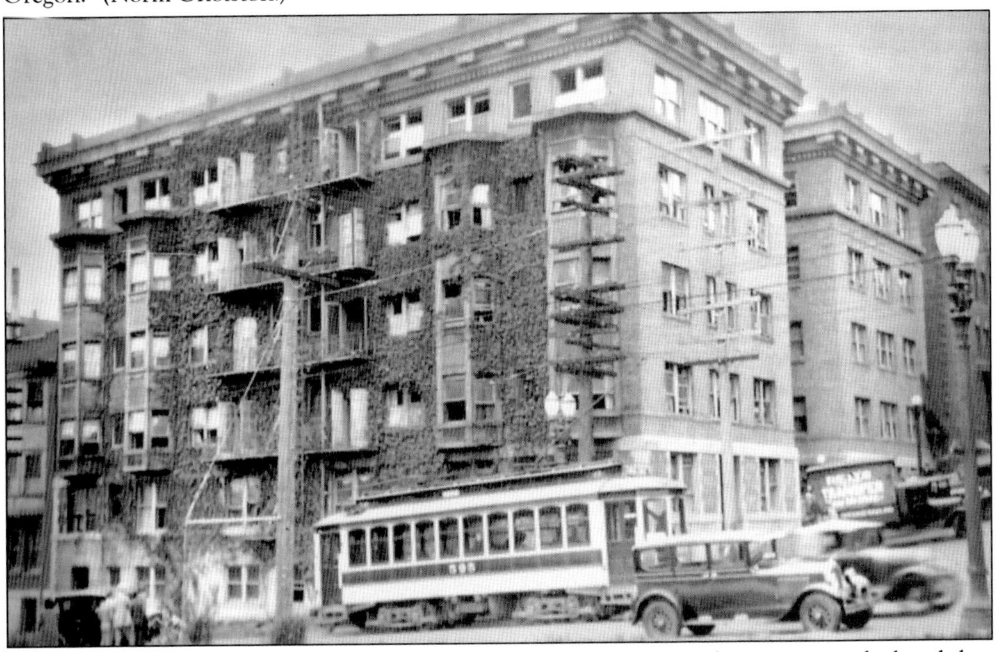

The Stelwyn Apartments had a beautiful roof top garden. Stelwyn advertisements declared that it was "a high class summer home for tourists." Located on the corner of St. Clair Avenue and Burnside Street, it was destroyed by fire in 1974. This photograph was taken in 1930. Even then Burnside Street was bustling. (OrHi-bb007415.)

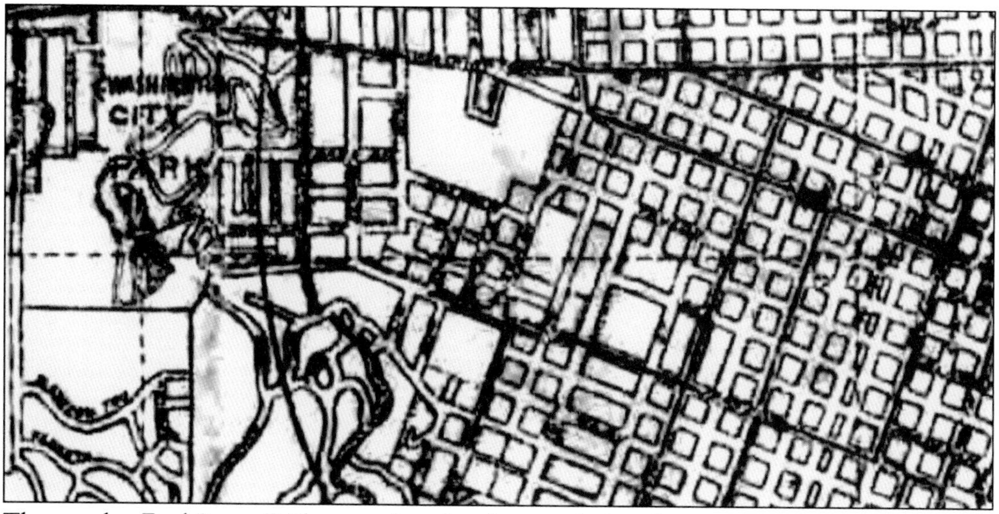

The wooden Ford Street Bridge was thought of as too shaky when streetcars crossed, so a solid, majestic bridge was planned to replace it. Several streets were realigned and renamed at this time. Traffic once flowed up King's Hill and Vista Ridge via Ford Street, which is now an unpaved, dead-end road off Market Street Drive. A new road was cut into the hillside and named Vista Avenue (the section on King's Hill formerly called Ford Street was renamed as Vista) to connect more directly to the heights. In the above image, a 1918 map shows the reconfigurations as seen by the darker north–south line on the left. Curiously, the map shows that a street once connected Prospect Drive to today's Market Street Drive. Remnants of this road can still be seen in a little-used public walkway between Vista Avenue and Prospect Drive. In the below image from 1932, the plans have been implemented. (Both, CoPA.)

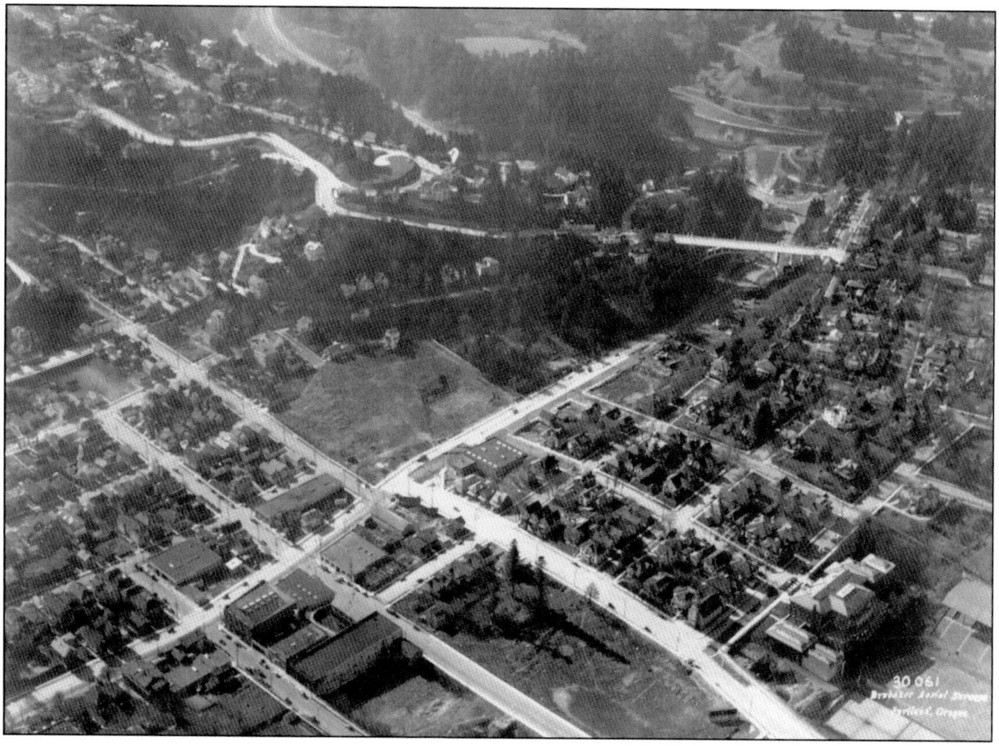

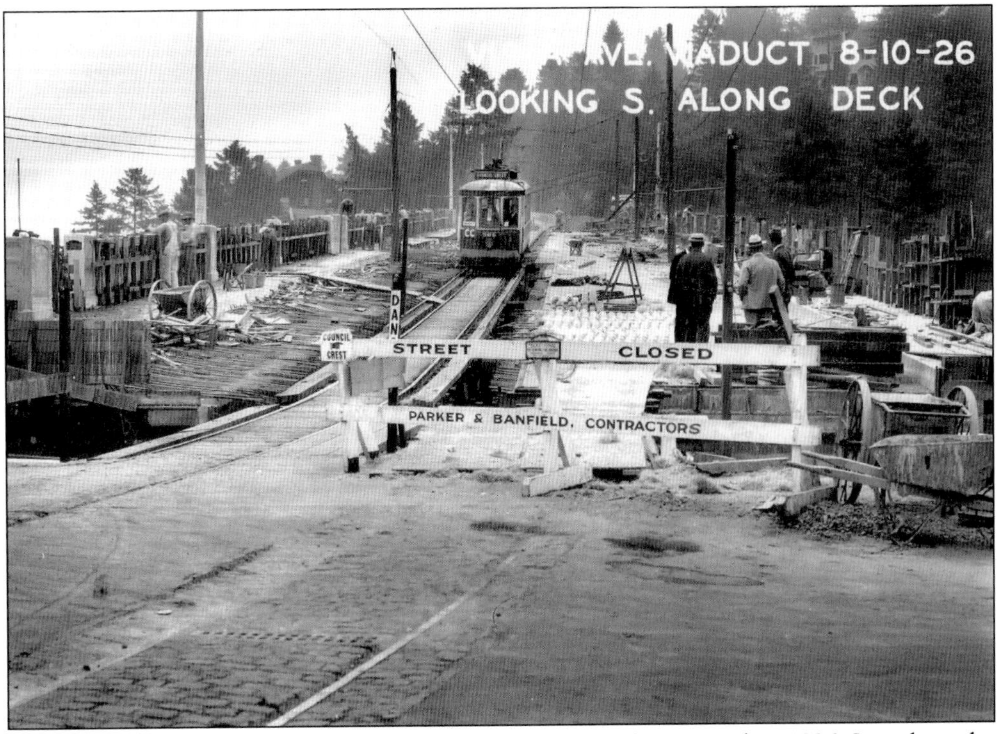

Construction was started on the Vista Bridge in 1925, and it opened in 1926. Listed on the National Register of Historic Places, its official name, Vista Viaduct, is rarely used. In this 1926 photograph, the streetcar operates amidst the construction. A sign directs traffic to reach Council Crest by turning right onto Madison Street, an impossible feat today. The image below shows construction from the base of the bridge seven months earlier. (Above, OrHi-cop02195, No. 1656.; below, OrHi.)

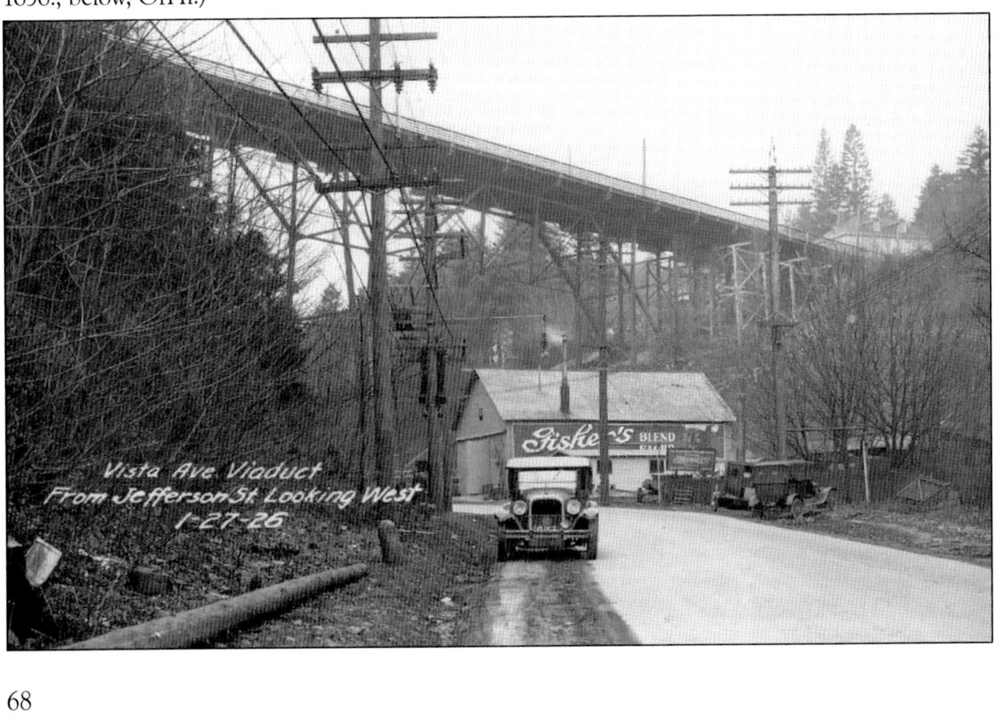

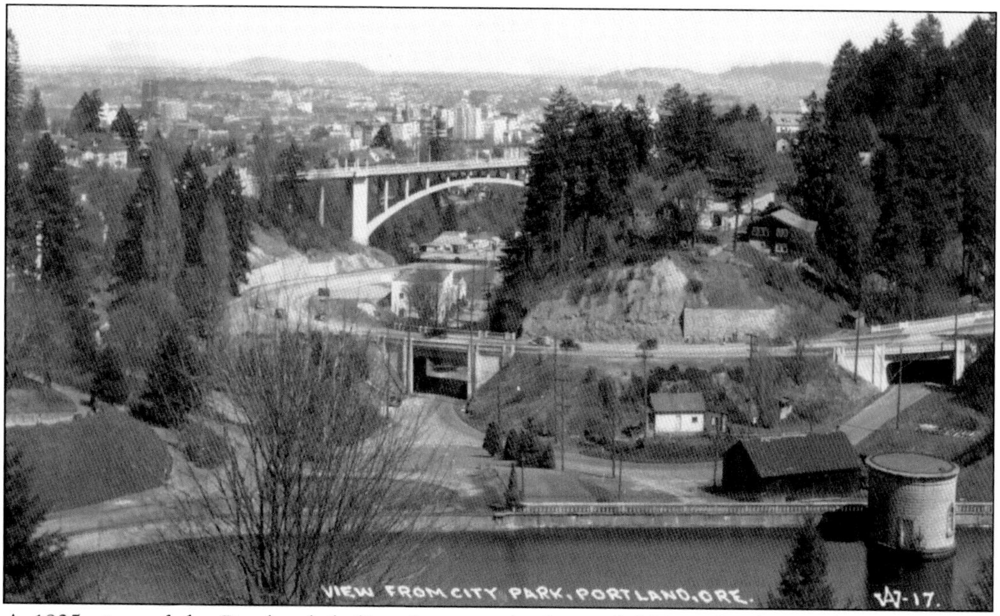

A 1935 view of the Portland skyline features the beautiful Vista Bridge in the center. The Washington Park reservoirs are in the foreground. (CoPA.)

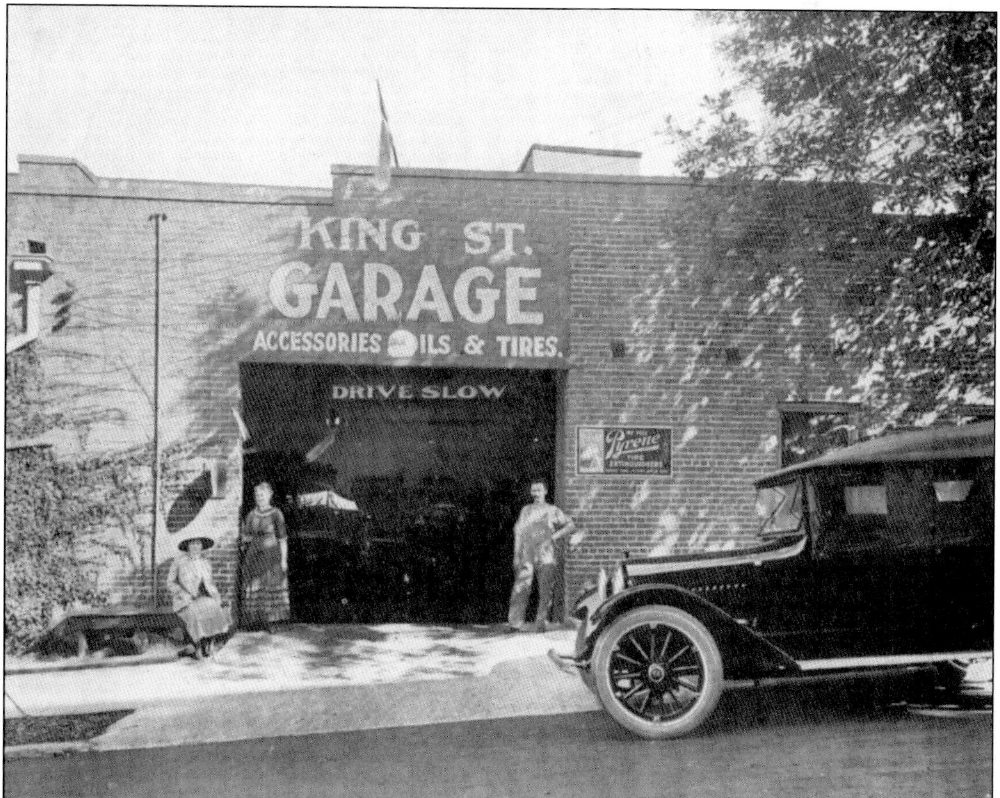

The King Street Garage, pictured around 1918, was on Southwest King near Burnside Street. (Don Nelson.)

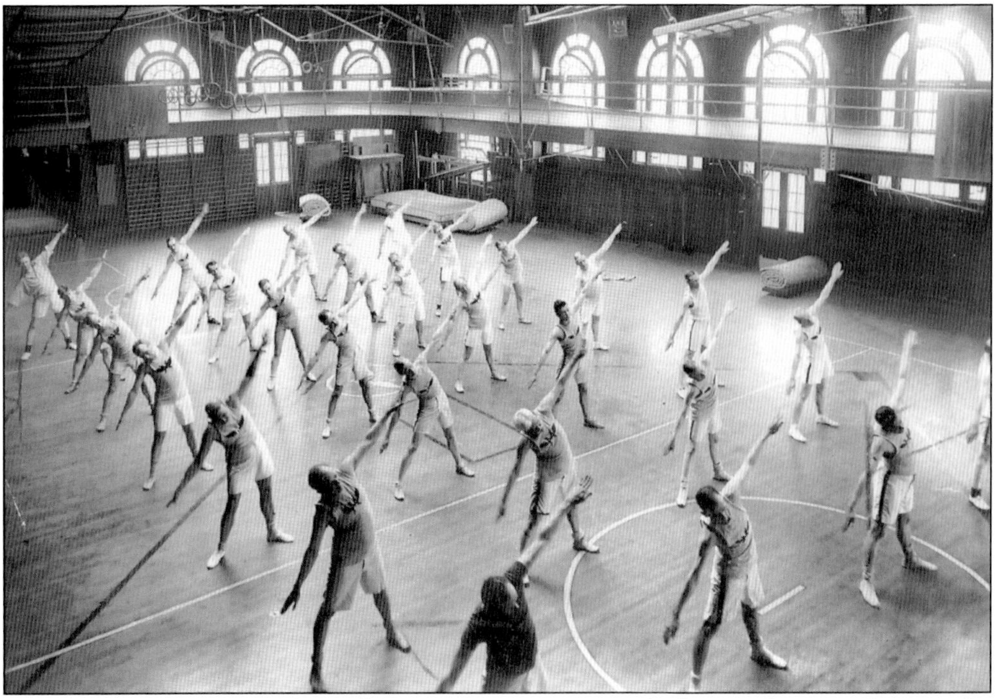

Inside the Multnomah Athletic Club gymnasium, a men's calisthenics class is underway. The elevated track runs alongside enormous arched windows. (OrHi-bb007436.)

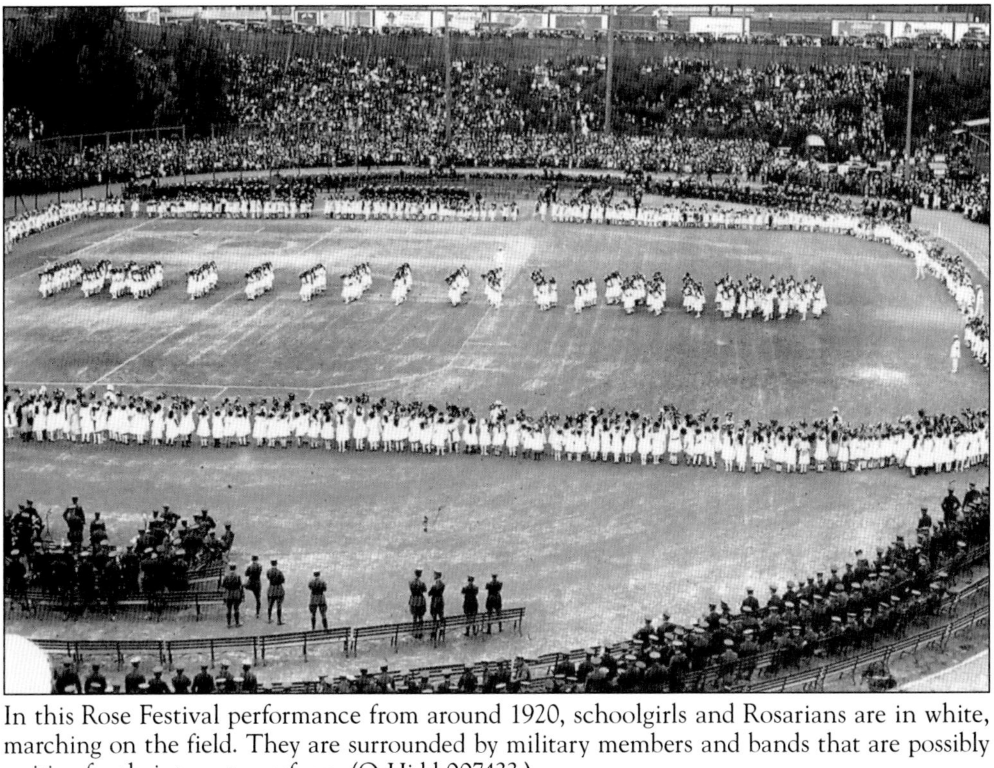

In this Rose Festival performance from around 1920, schoolgirls and Rosarians are in white, marching on the field. They are surrounded by military members and bands that are possibly waiting for their turn to perform. (OrHi-bb007433.)

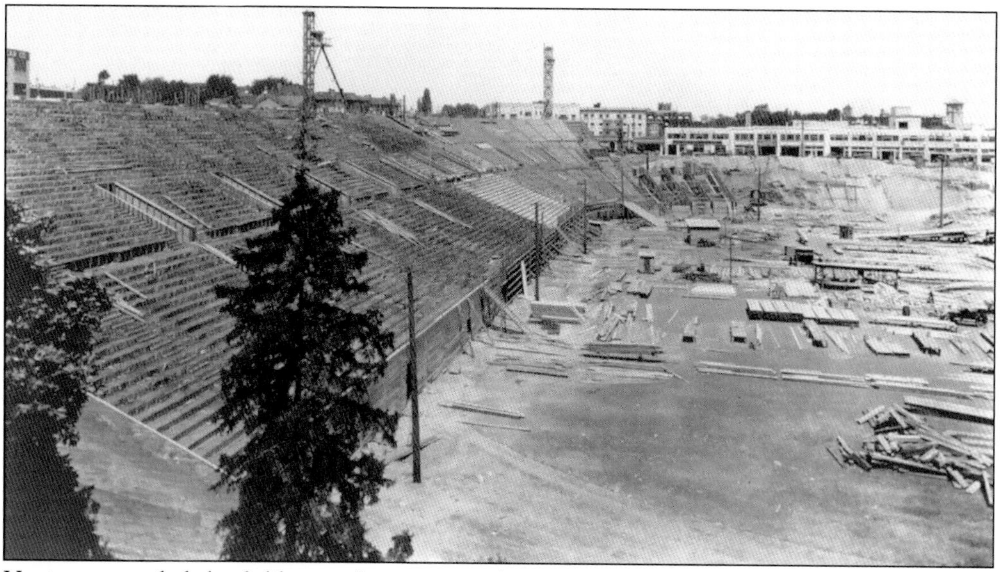

Having expanded the field several times over the years, the Multnomah Athletic Club built a 28,000-seat stadium in 1926. Architect A. E. Doyle designed a complete horseshoe shape for the stadium. Thankfully the club did not own all of the land along Eighteenth Avenue so it could not build the entire horseshoe. Today the neighborhood treasures the open side of the stadium where glimpses of games can be seen as pedestrians and trains pass by. (OrHi.)

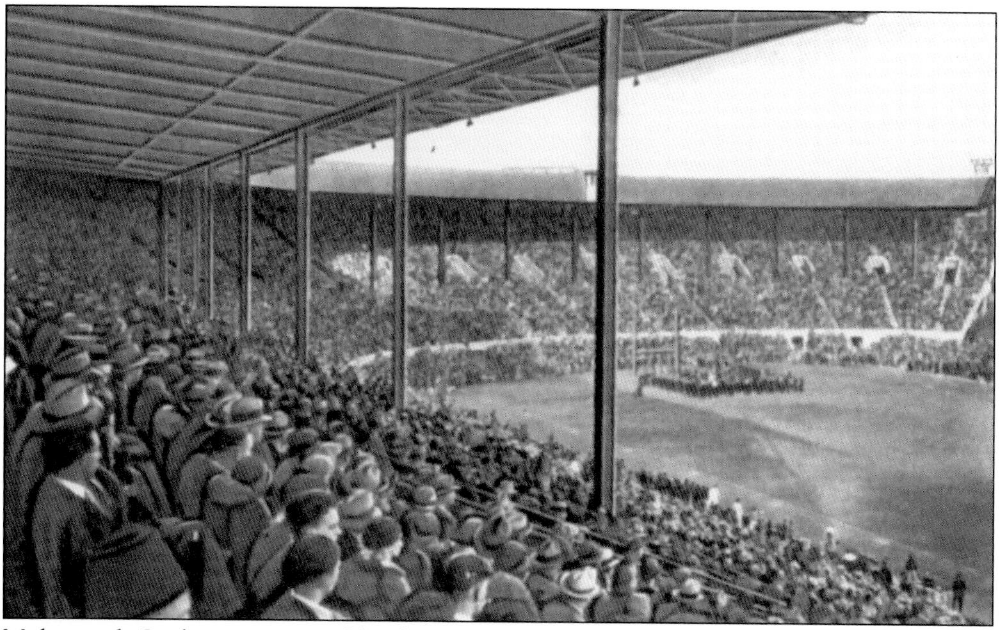

Multnomah Stadium was owned by the Multnomah Athletic Club until 1966 when the city purchased it for $2.1 million and renamed it Civic Stadium. In 2001, the naming rights were sold and it became PGE Park. At the beginning of the 20th century, Portland summer traditions included attending Starlight Symphonies at Multnomah Stadium, performed by the Portland Symphony. (Margaret Parypa.)

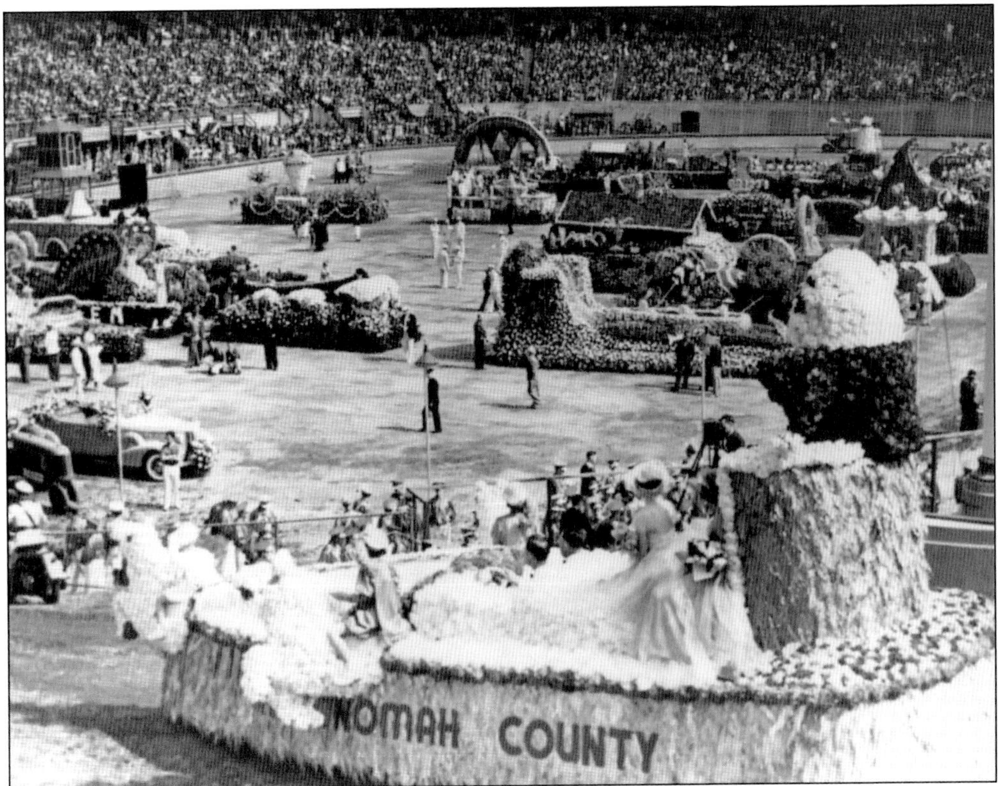

The stadium hosted this 1930s exhibition of Rose Festival floats. Dog races, boxing, presidential speeches, and concerts were also part of the stadium's history. (Mike Ryerson.)

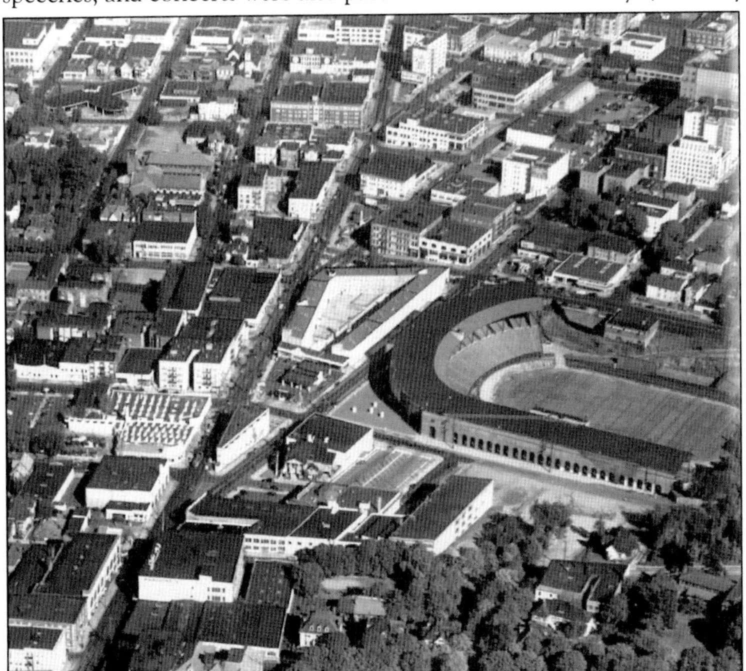

A 1947 aerial view shows the open side of the stadium with other landowners still occupying buildings along Eighteenth Avenue. (CoPA.)

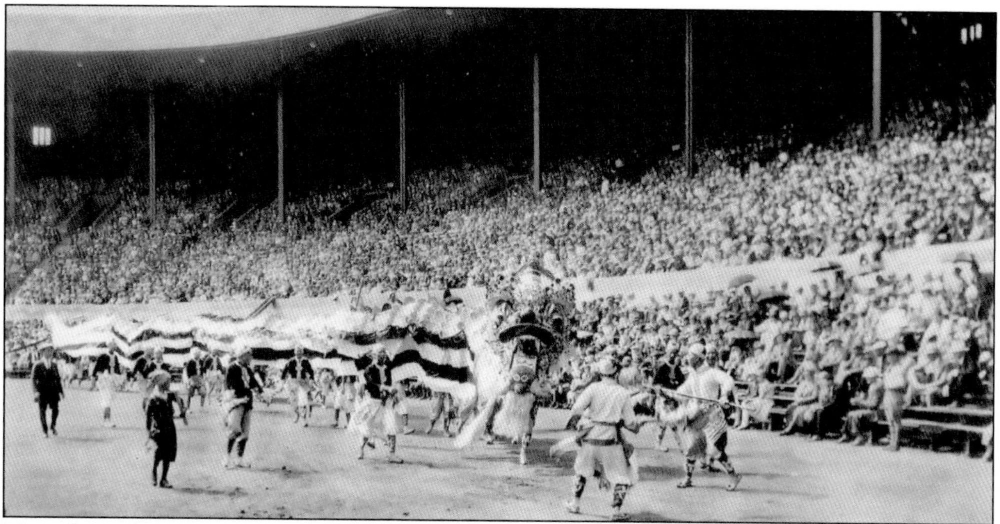

Though Portland's Chinese community and Goose Hollow had several decades of shared history, the connection was lost once Tanner Creek Gulch was infilled and the land developed, thus displacing the Chinese Vegetable Gardens. In this image, a Chinese dragon dance is being performed in Multnomah Stadium in the 1930s or 1940s, probably for the Rose Festival. (OrHi-bb007421.)

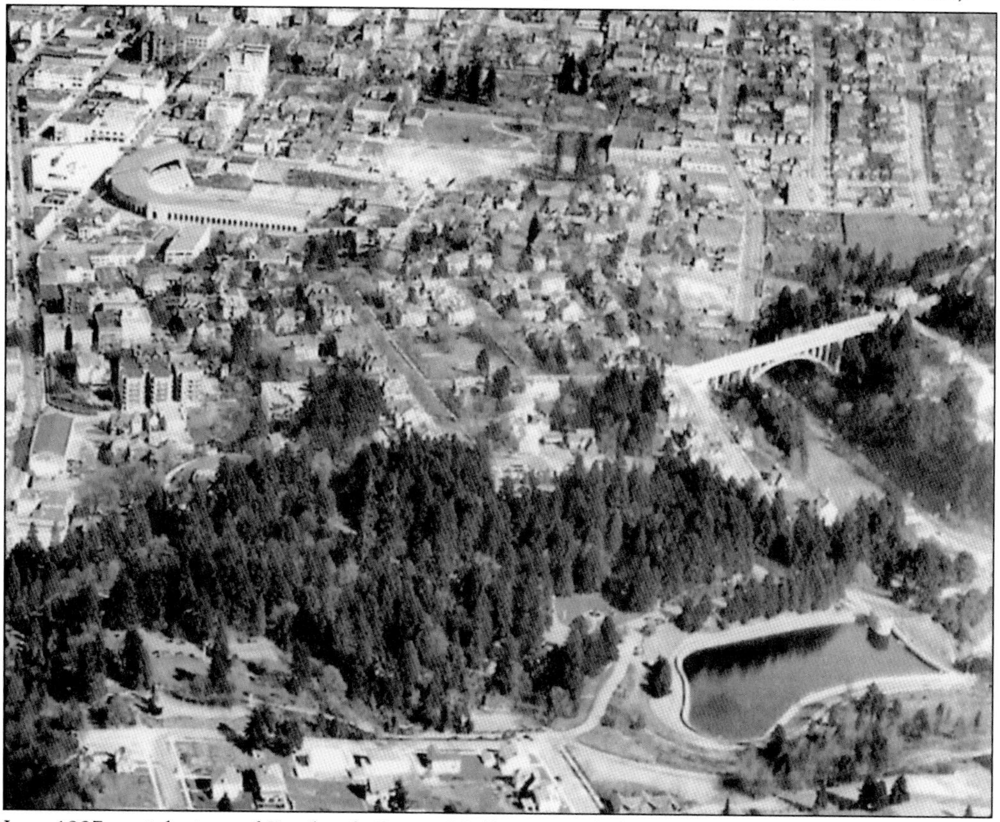

In a 1927 aerial view of Portland, Goose Hollow's newly built Vista Bridge and Multnomah Stadium can be seen, with a Washington Park reservoir and Arlington Heights in the foreground. (OrHi-bb007450.)

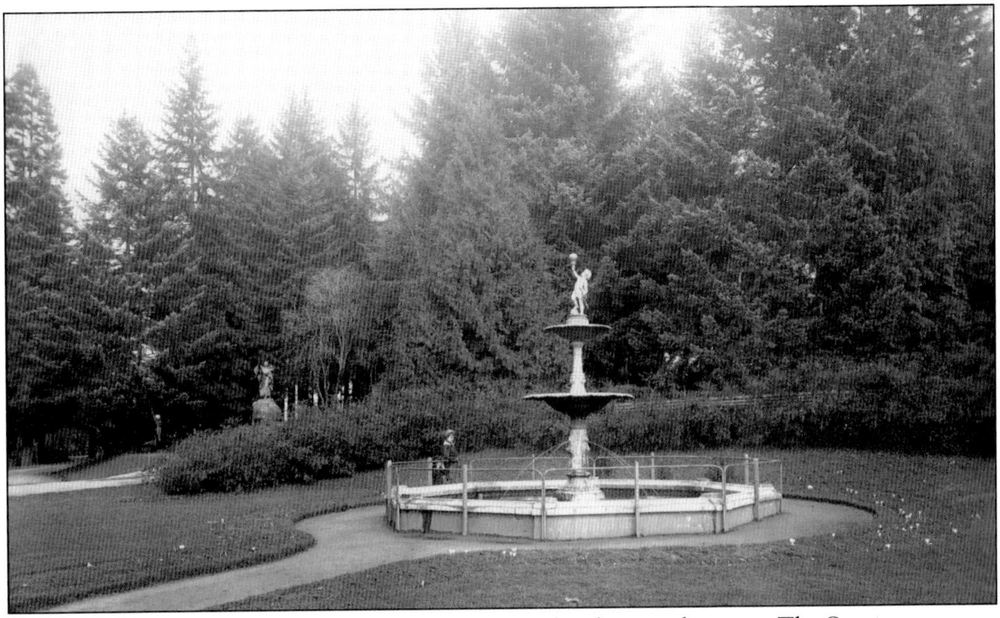

In the 1930s, a woman and boy enjoy Washington Park's chiming fountain. The Sacajawea statue at left was first displayed at the Lewis and Clark Centennial, then moved to the park in 1906. Nearby the *Coming of the White Man* sculpture depicts two Native Americans facing east, toward the Oregon Trail. The Oregon Holocaust Memorial north of the fountain is a moving experience with small poignant sculptures. (Norm Gholston.)

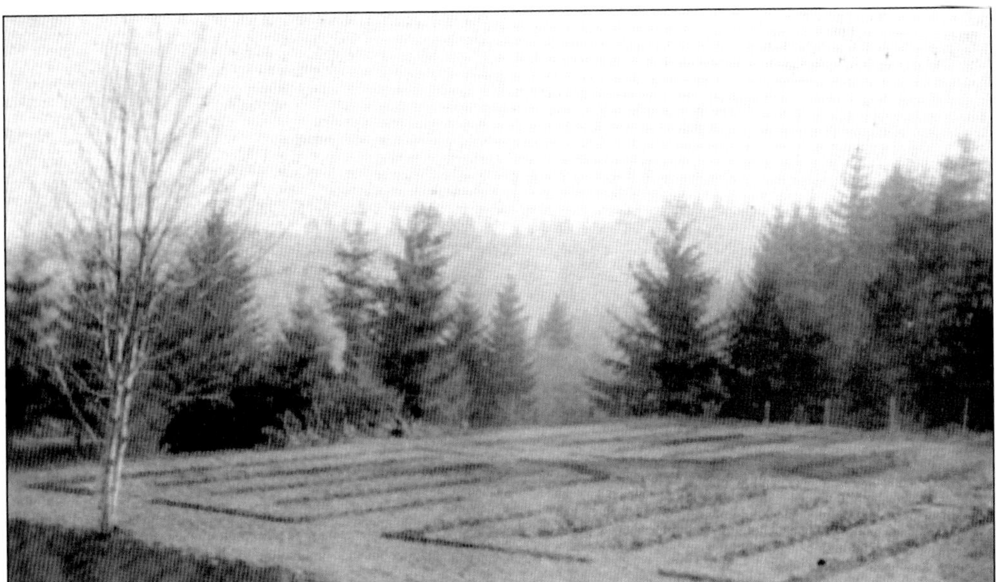

This 1918 image is of an early plot of what later developed into the International Rose Test Garden. Rose boosters like Jesse Curry convinced Portland to start this garden. During the 1905 Lewis and Clark Centennial, visitors to Portland were awed by the more than 200 miles of rose-lined streets, which led to Portland becoming known as "the City of Roses."

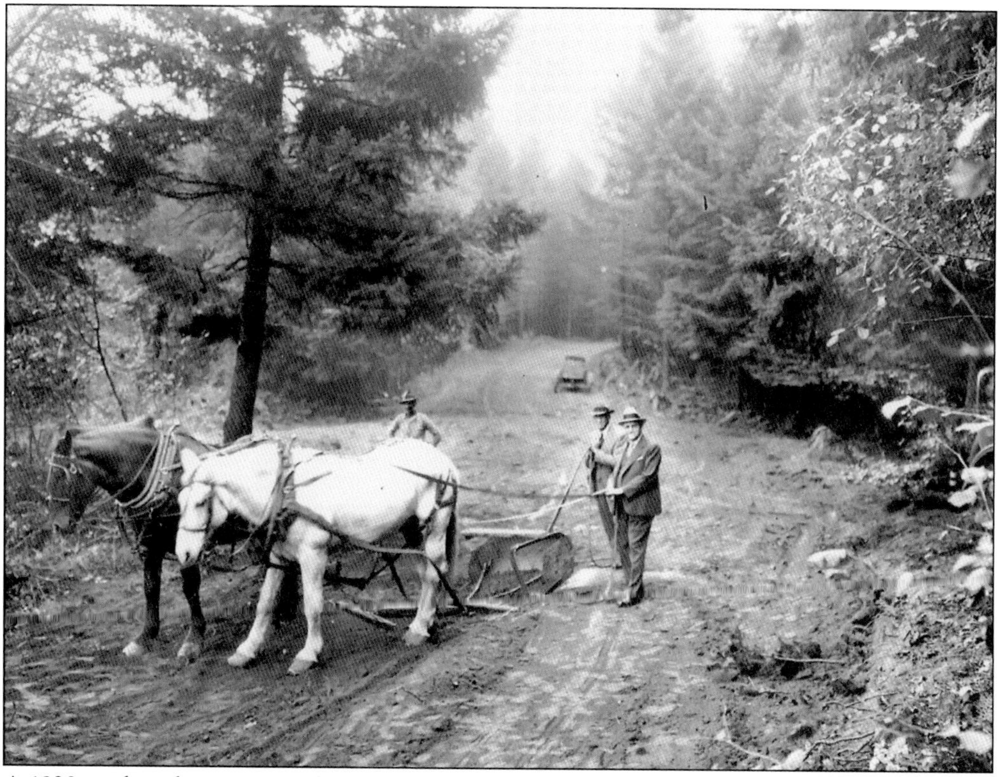

A 1930 road grading team works on cutting a road through the forest to create Hoyt Arboretum. The first trees were planted there in 1931. Part of the land that later became the arboretum was in the Amos King land claim. (OrHi-bb005772.)

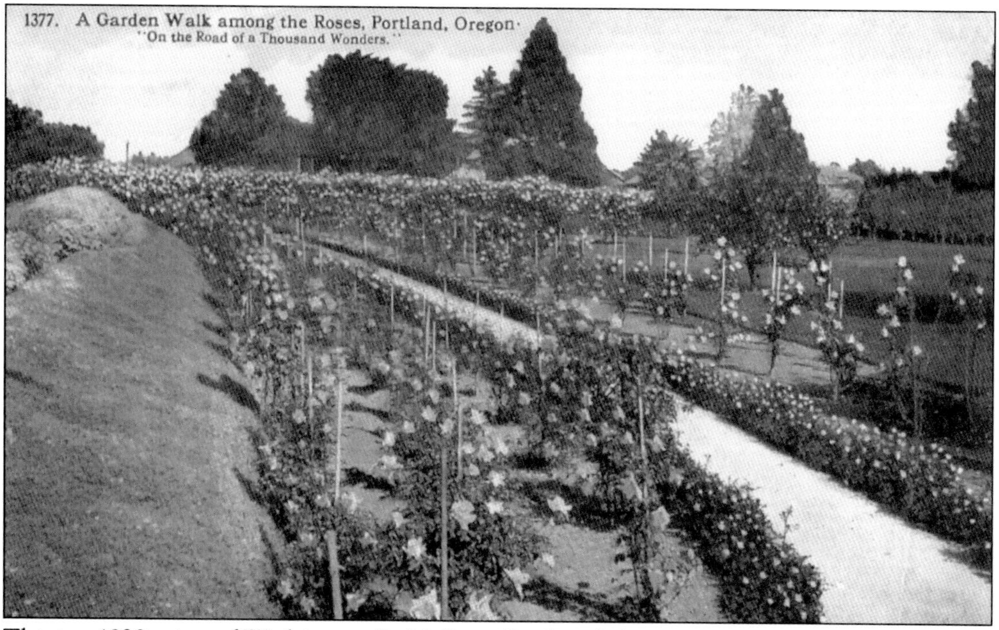

This is a 1930s view of Washington Park's Rose Garden. A favorite pastime of Portlanders, then and now, was to stroll through the paths in the Rose Garden.

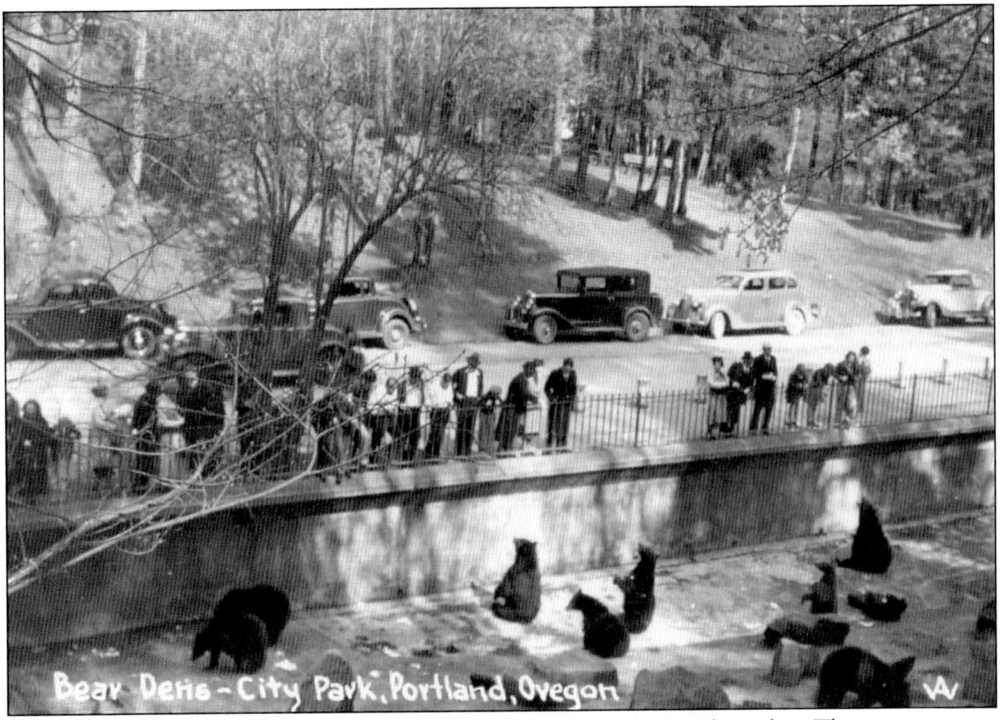

These 1935 and 1947 photographs show the Washington Park Zoo's bear den. The zoo was once located near today's Rose and Japanese Gardens. In a nearby playground well-used by Goose Hollow children, families still picnic in what was once the old elephant house. The zoo started with pharmacist Richard Knight, who kept exotic animals near his drugstore. In 1887, he donated his animal collection to the city. At first, the animal enclosures were spread throughout the park; eventually they moved near today's Japanese Garden. The zoo moved to its current location in 1959. (Above, CoPA; below, OrHi-bb007380.)

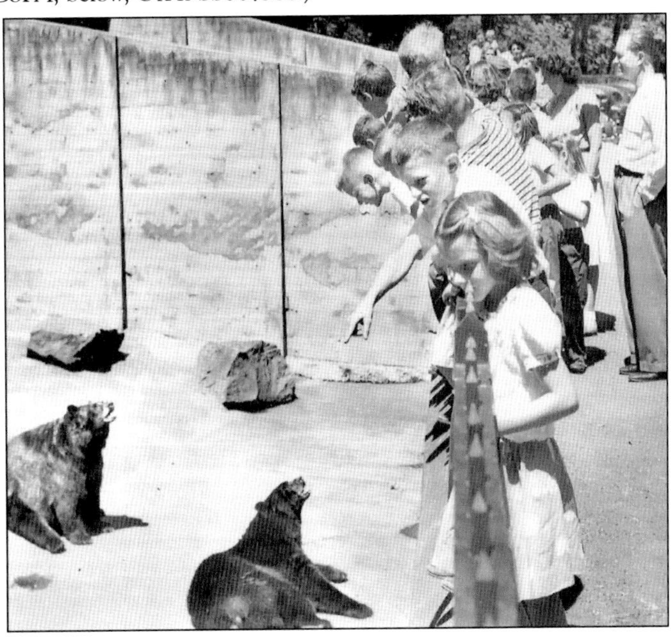

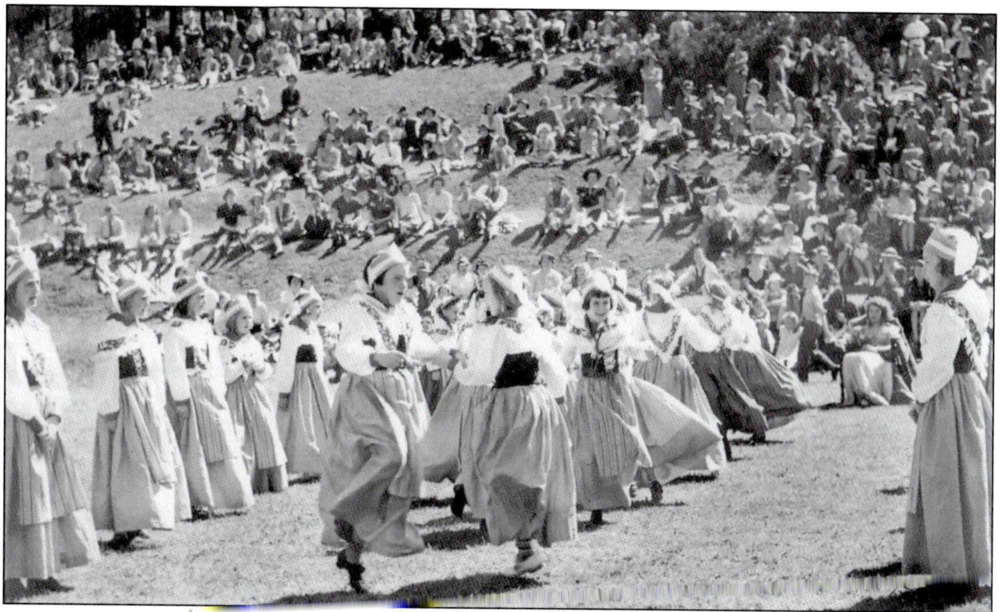

Blue Birds, once the name for junior Camp Fire Girls, perform a folk dance in the Washington Park amphitheater in 1938. Performances at the amphitheater have always been a popular outing for Goose Hollow residents, who can be seen walking to summer concerts and plays. (OrHi-bb007419.)

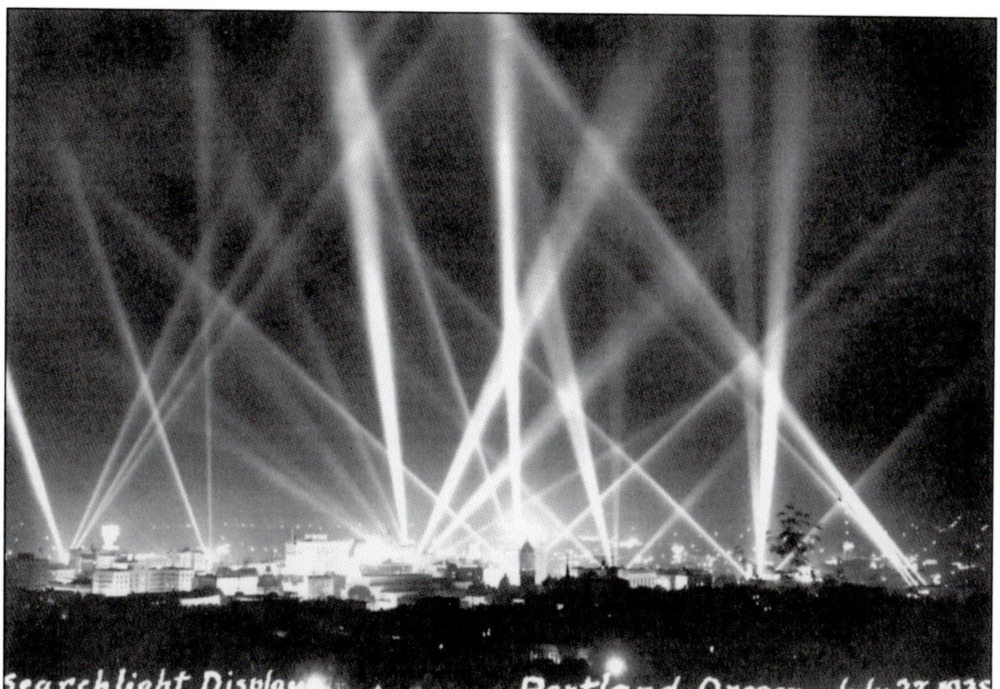

A 1938 searchlight display from U.S. Navy boats was demonstrated while the vessels were in town for Fleet Week. This spectacular nighttime view was taken from Goose Hollow, with cottages in the lower elevations visible in the foreground. (OrHi-bb007387.)

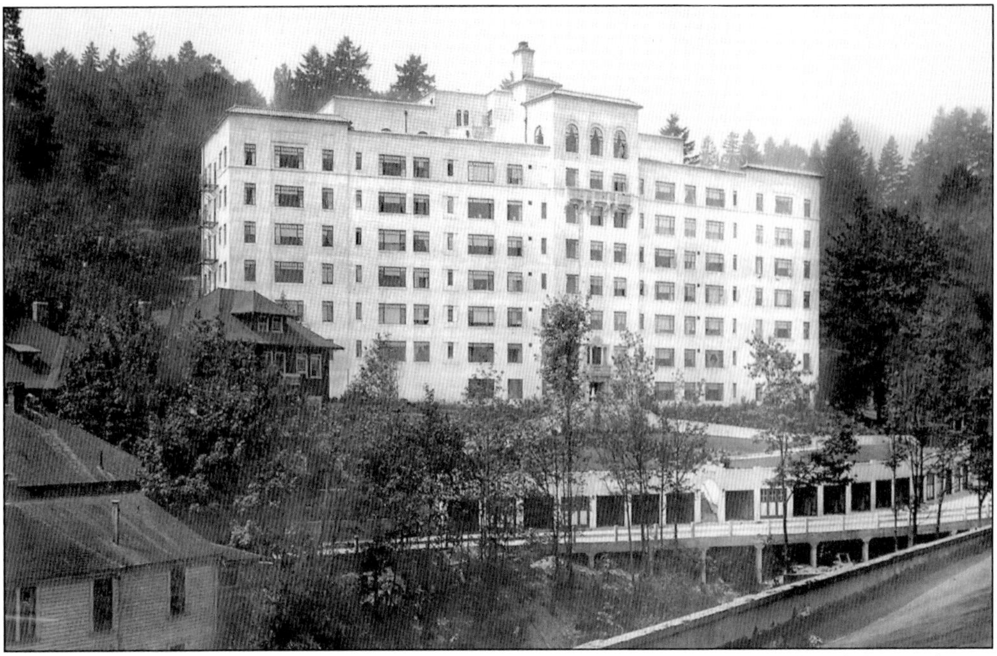

The Envoy Apartments, which are now condos, have been a delightful landmark located near the Burnside Street entrance to Washington Park since 1929. Note the elevated Osage Street in front of the Envoy's covered parking. The roof of the Cedar Hill streetcar barn is visible in the foreground. (OrHi-bb007418.)

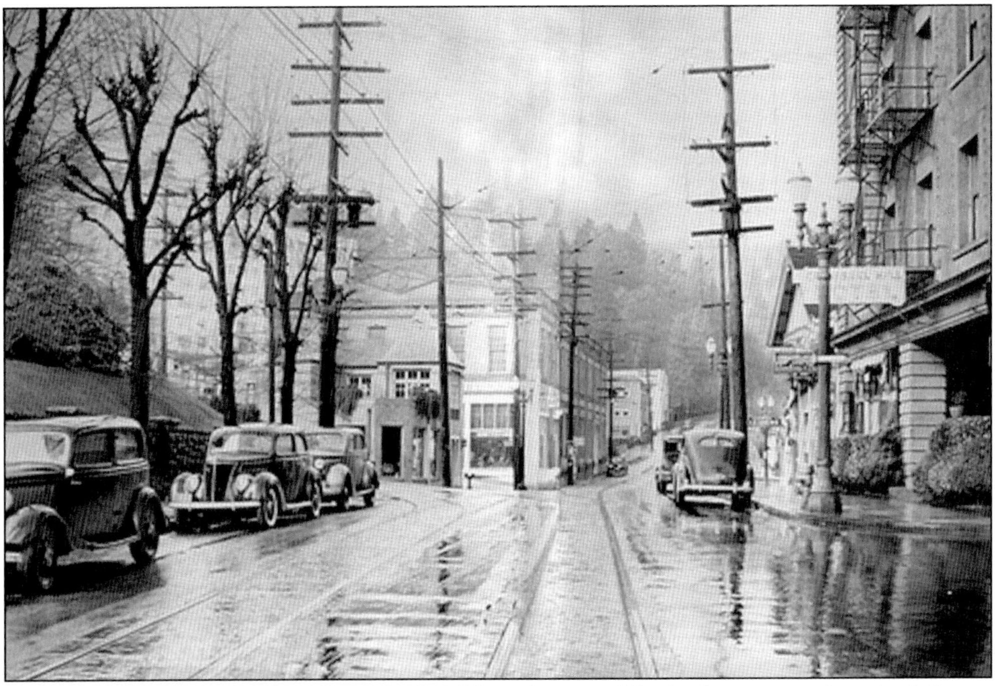

Burnside Street is pictured as it approaches Vista Avenue. The high green yard to the left was part of the Solomon Hirsch estate, built in 1907. The Hirsch mansion was demolished in 1938 and the hillside leveled to make way for a gas station. (CoPA.)

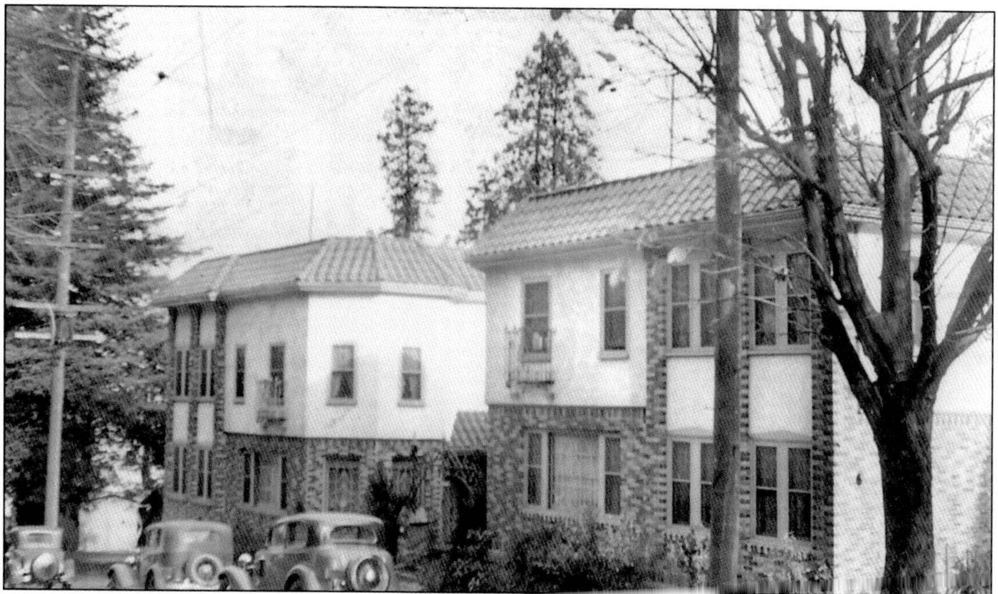

The Gleneagles Apartments, pictured here in 1936, still exist at 912 Southwest Vista Avenue, though they are now called the Vista Townhouses. (OrHi-bb007401.)

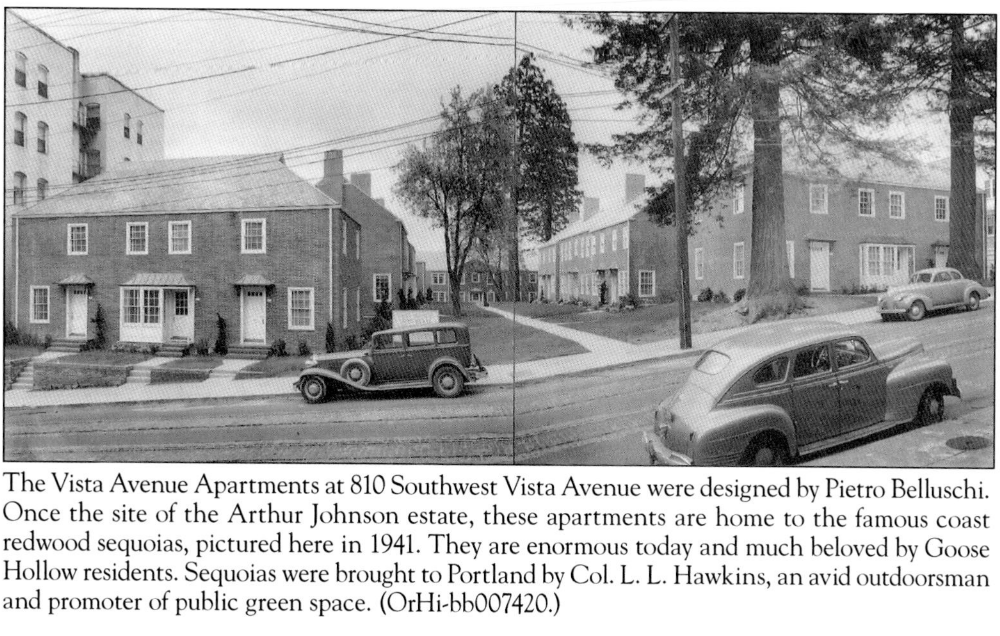

The Vista Avenue Apartments at 810 Southwest Vista Avenue were designed by Pietro Belluschi. Once the site of the Arthur Johnson estate, these apartments are home to the famous coast redwood sequoias, pictured here in 1941. They are enormous today and much beloved by Goose Hollow residents. Sequoias were brought to Portland by Col. L. L. Hawkins, an avid outdoorsman and promoter of public green space. (OrHi-bb007420.)

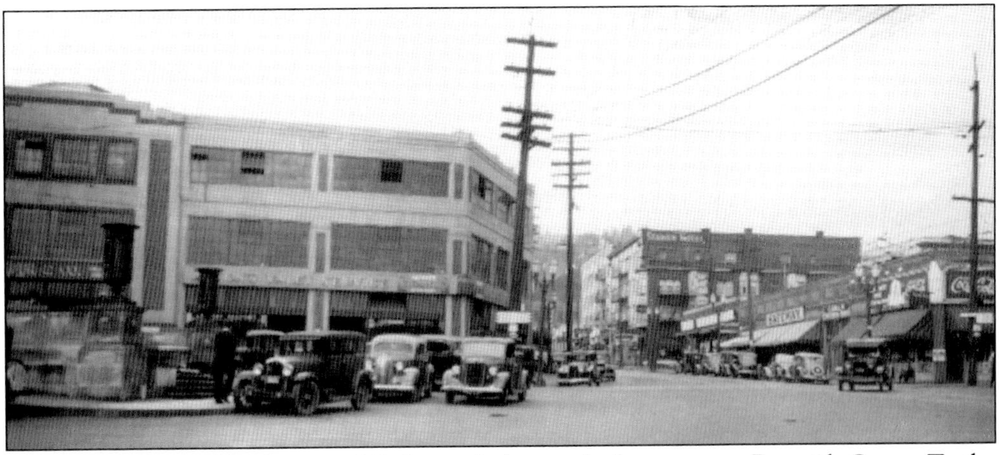

A 1935 view from Alder Street and Eighteenth Avenue looks west onto Burnside Street. To the left is a memorial to fire chief David Campbell, who died in 1911 in the line of duty. Firefighters hold a memorial service here each June 26. (CoPA.)

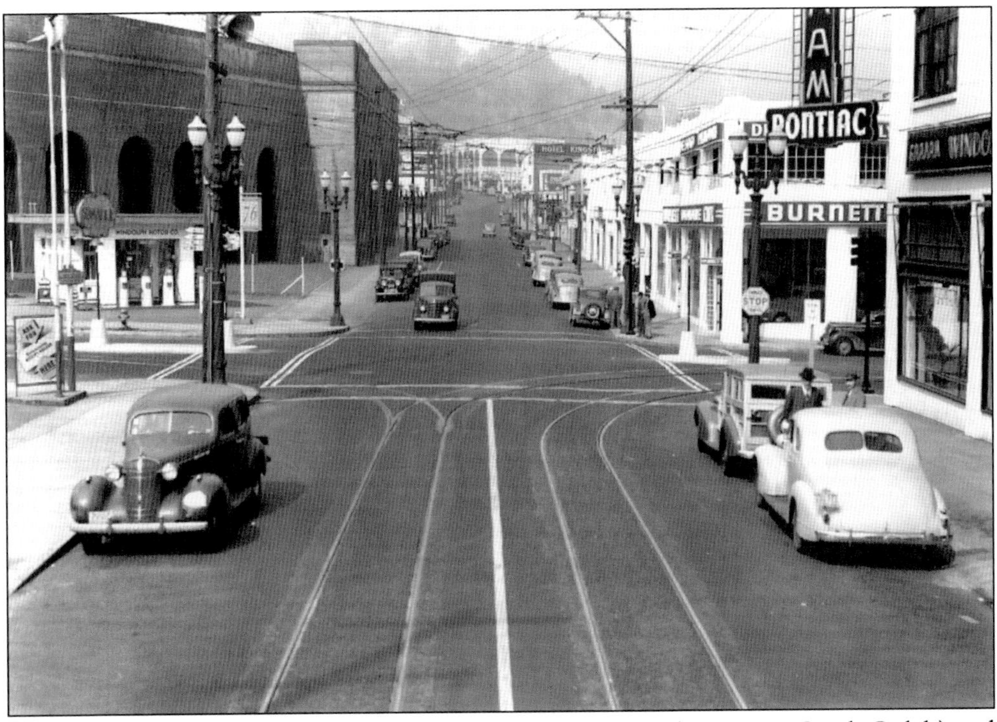

This 1939 street scene depicts Morrison Street (once part of the Tanner Creek Gulch) and Eighteenth Avenue looking west, with Multnomah Stadium, a gas station, and car dealers. Like many parts of Goose Hollow, crossing the flat terrain around this area means crossing 50 feet of infill with Tanner Creek still flowing underground. (CoPA.)

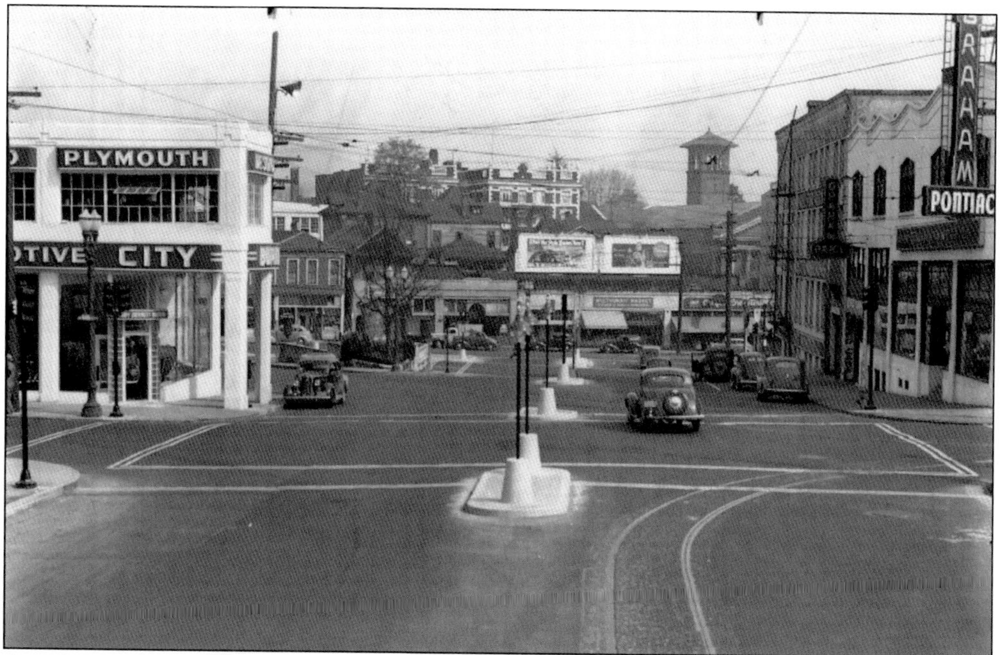

Another 1939 image of the Morrison Street and Eighteenth Avenue intersection looks north toward the Campbell Memorial. Trestle bridges once crossed here, connecting to Burnside Street. (CoPA.)

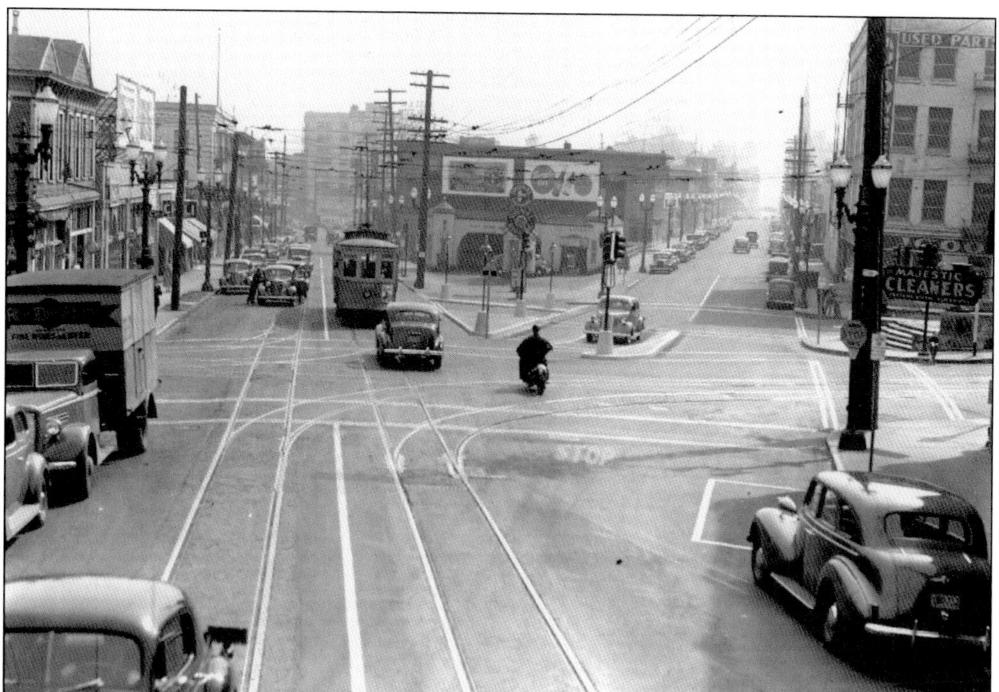

From Burnside Street, looking east, a 1939 photograph shows busy streets with streetcars and automobiles sharing the road. Alder Street, to the right, was once a several-block-long gulch with buildings built on pilings hanging over the chasm. (CoPA.)

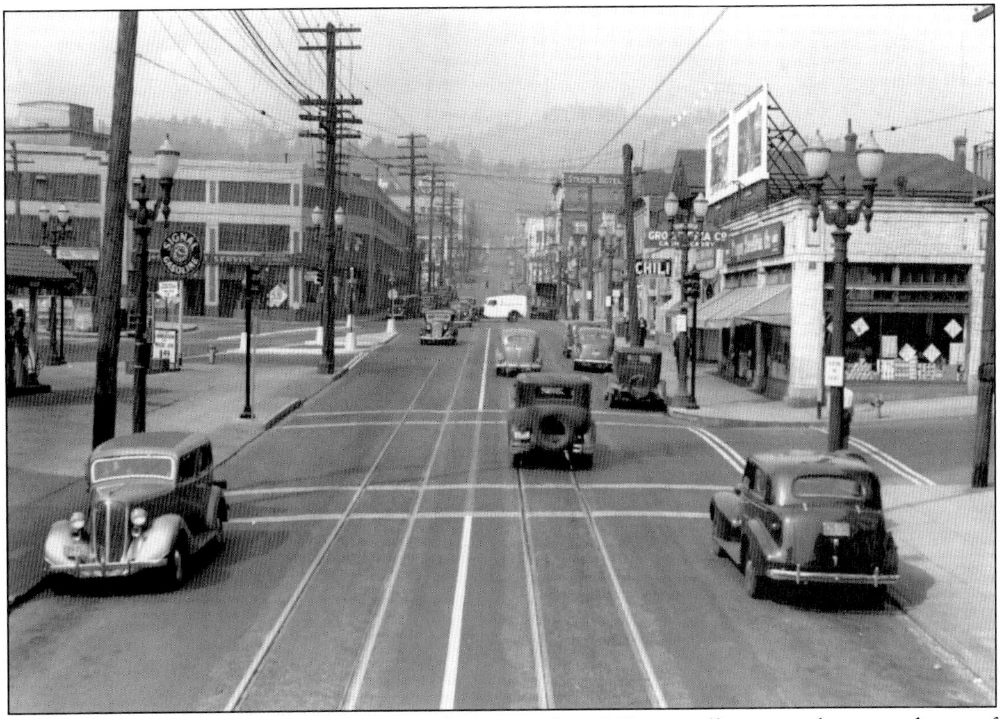

Looking toward the West Hills on Burnside Street, this 1939 view illustrates the ascendancy of the automobile, though streetcar tracks are still visible. (CoPA.)

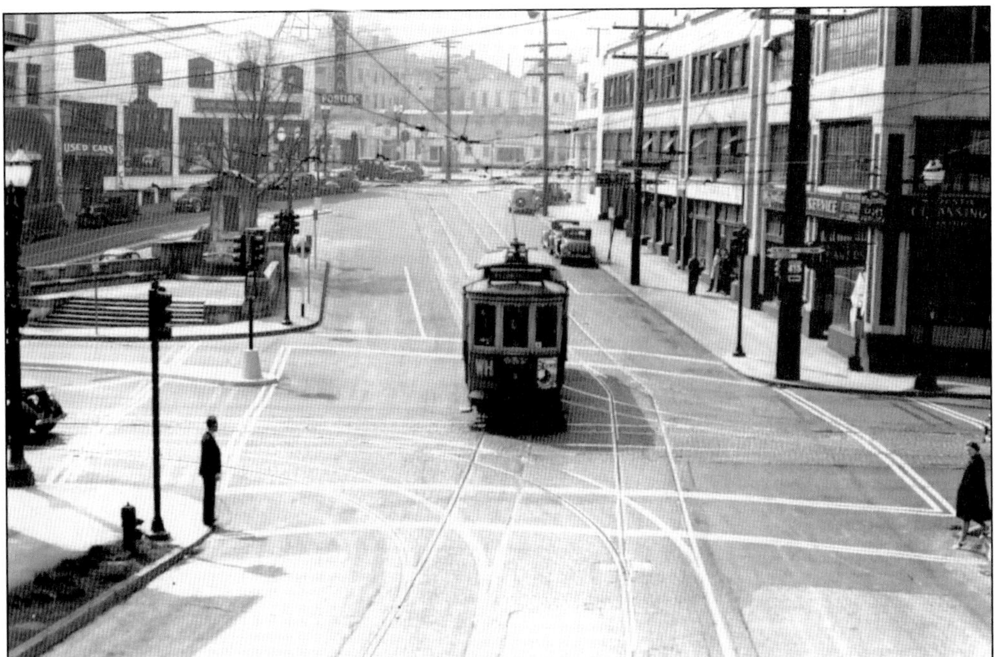

A 1939 view south at the same intersection is where The Civic condominiums now stand on the right. (CoPA.)

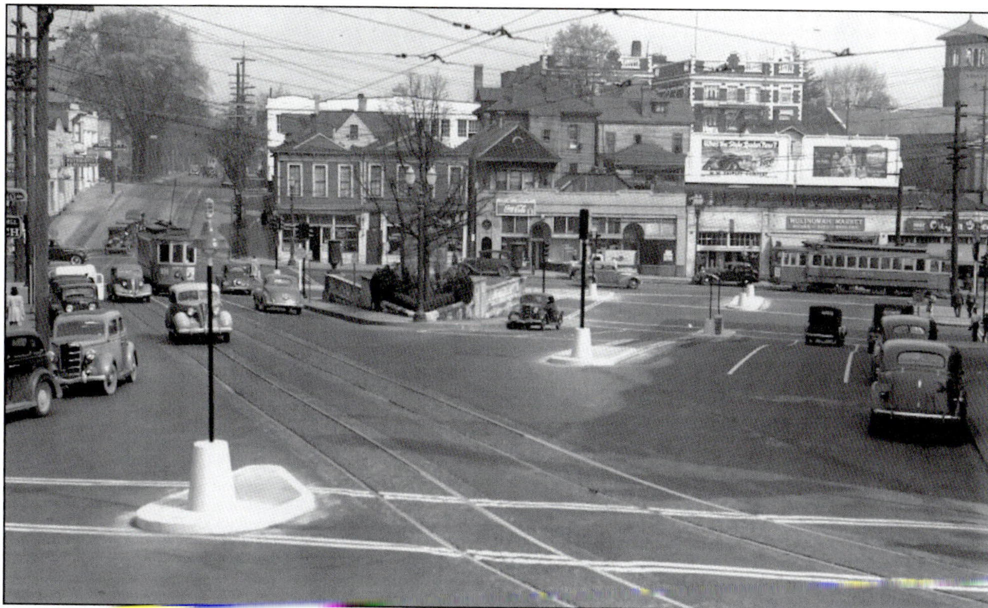

Looking north as streetcars cross Burnside Street and Nineteenth Avenue, the row of buildings across from the Campbell Memorial no longer exists. A fast food restaurant now covers that block. (CoPA.)

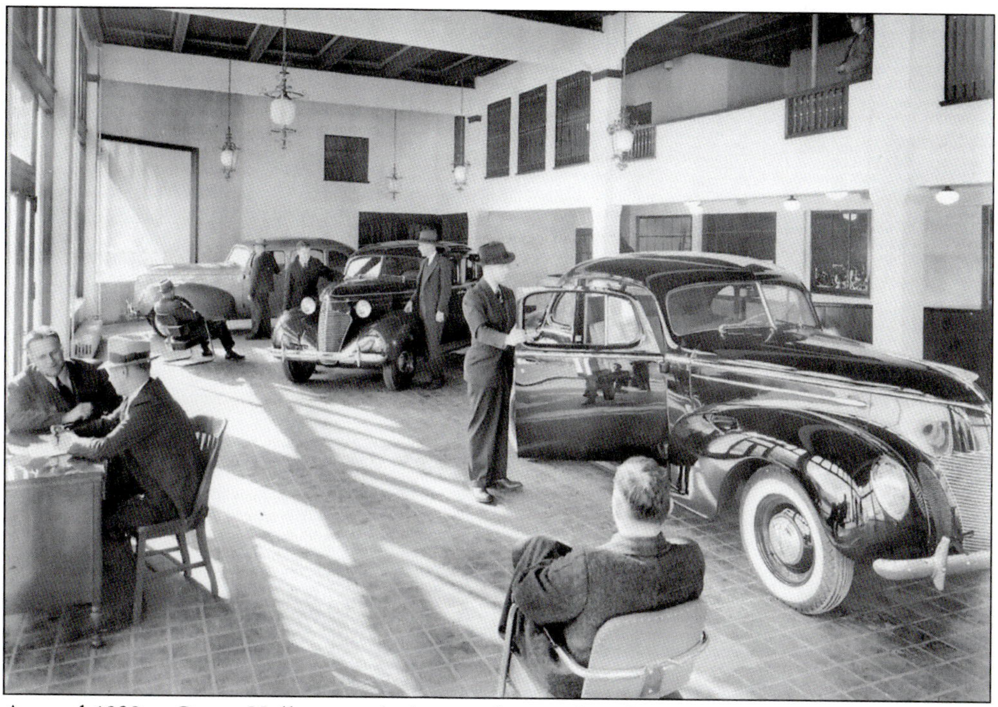

Around 1939, a Goose Hollow car dealer was famous for advertising himself as "the Mayor of Goose Hollow." Apparently this was a strategy to differentiate himself from the other automobile dealers in Goose Hollow, perhaps implying that he could give customers the best deals. The interior of Portland Motors is shown at 2054 West Burnside Street. It was the Hudson headquarters for Oregon. (OrHi-bb007412.)

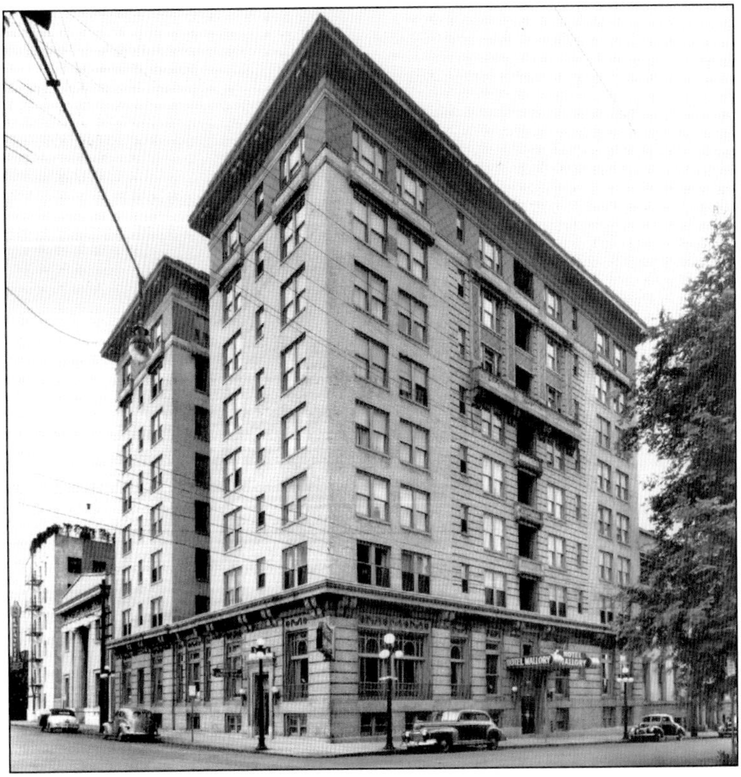

Pictured here in the 1930s, the Mallory Hotel—renamed Hotel deLuxe in 2005—was built in 1912 by Judge Rufus Mallory at Yamhill and Lownsdale Streets, now Southwest Fifteenth Avenue. Mallory lost the hotel in the Great Depression. The Gentner family bought it in 1943. The original Driftwood Room, a lounge with a film noir effect designed by Jim Coppedge in the 1950s, still survives and is a cherished Portland landmark. (Albert Gentner.)

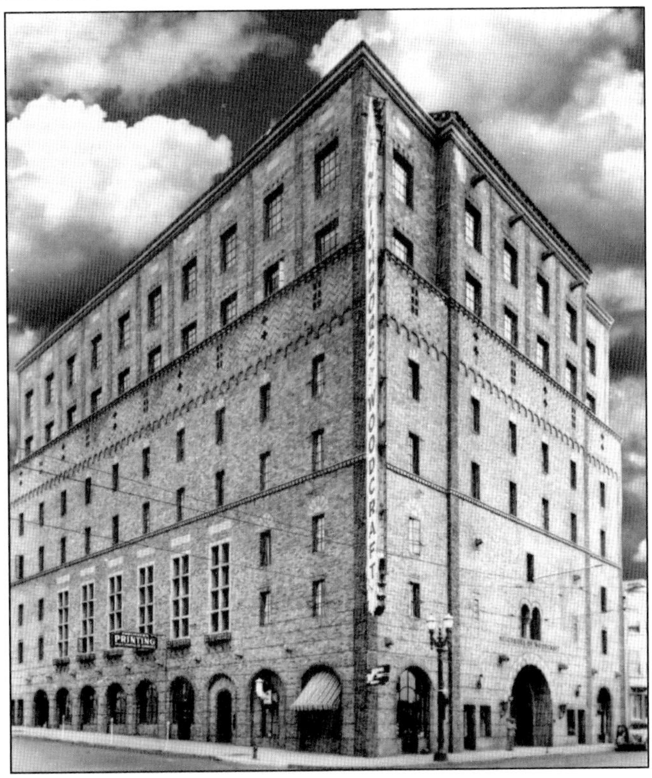

Formed in 1897, the Women of Woodcraft was a fraternal society providing a social outlet and safety net for women whose husbands worked in the timber industry. In 1917, the name was changed to Neighbors of Woodcraft since the organization was accepting men and women into its membership. Pictured here in 1949 is the headquarters building for the organization at 1410 Southwest Morrison Street. Now the Tiffany Center, this Moorish Revival building was erected in 1928. (Norm Gholston.)

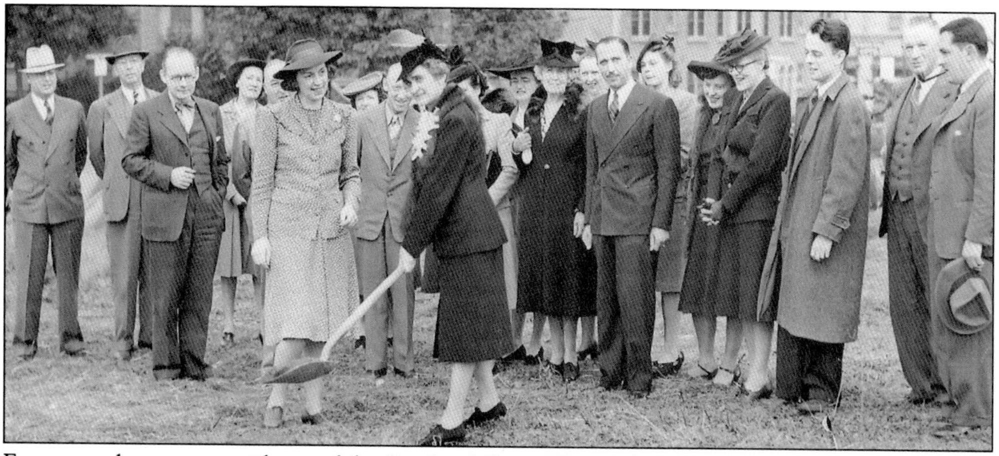

Former and current presidents of the Portland Civic Theater break ground for a new building on Sixteenth Avenue and Yamhill Street in 1941. Mallory Hotel owner Albert Gentner remembered the Civic Theater as a thriving cultural center for Portland with very fine actors. Sadly the theater closed in 1990 and the building was demolished and replaced by a U.S. Social Security office. (OrHi-bb007408.)

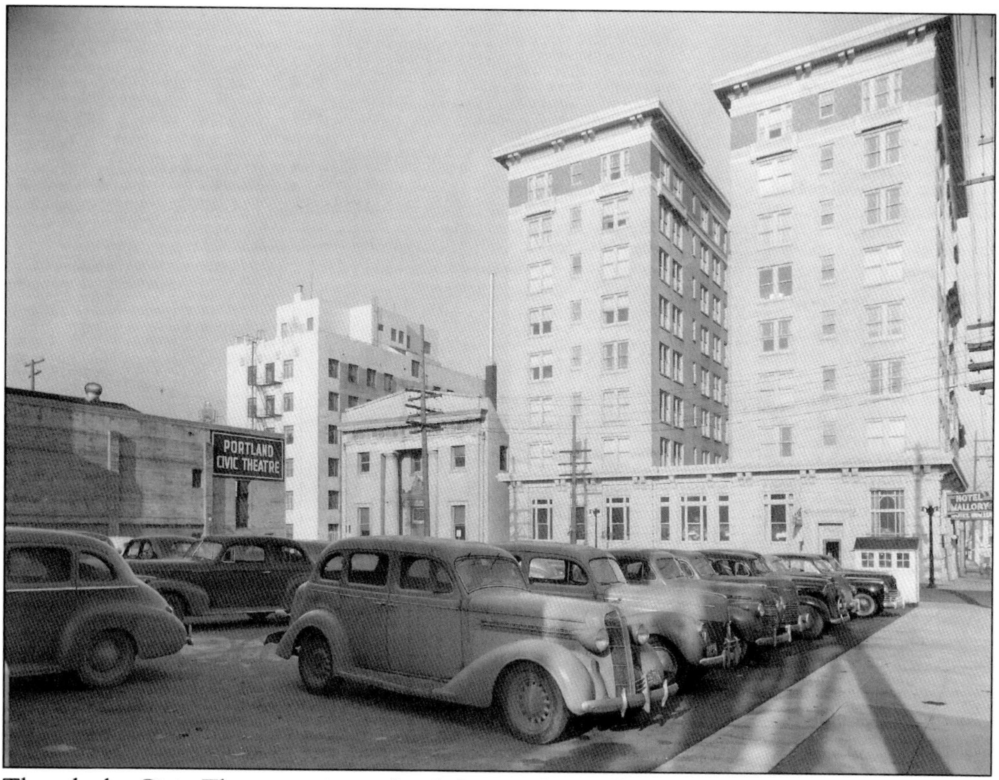

Though the Civic Theater—pictured at left near the Mallory Hotel in the 1940s—no longer exists, theatrical performance art remains strong in Goose Hollow. The Artists Repertory Theatre located at 1515 Southwest Morrison Street is Portland's oldest professional theater. And the Portland Actors Conservatory, housed in a lovely old firehouse on 1436 Southwest Montgomery Street, offers performances and professional actor training. (Albert Gentner.)

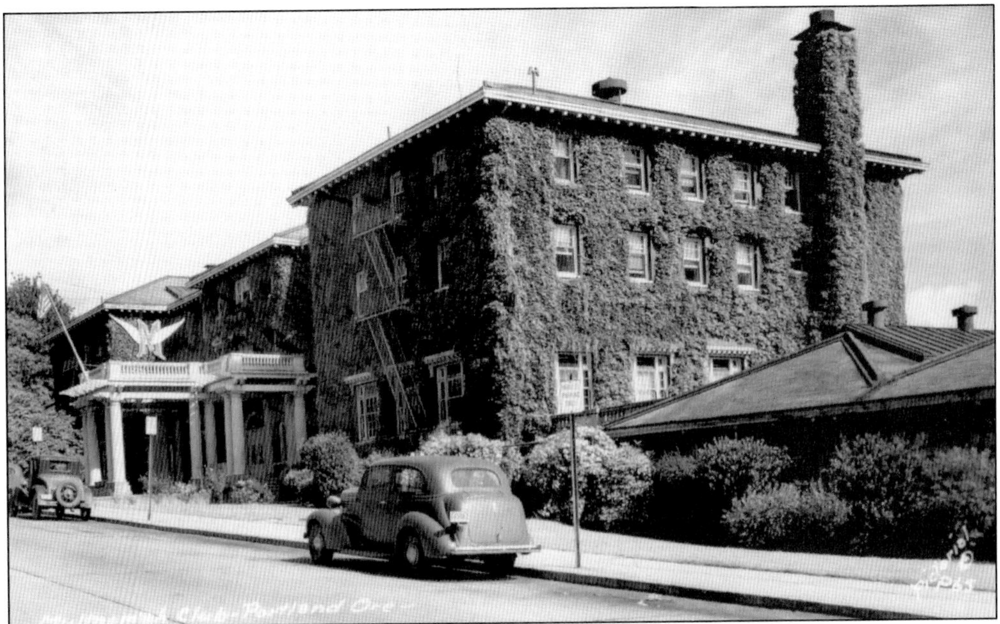

This 1940s photograph shows the regal, old, vine-covered building that was once the Multnomah Athletic Club's home on Salmon Street. Its signature winged M logo is displayed over the entrance. (Norm Gholston.)

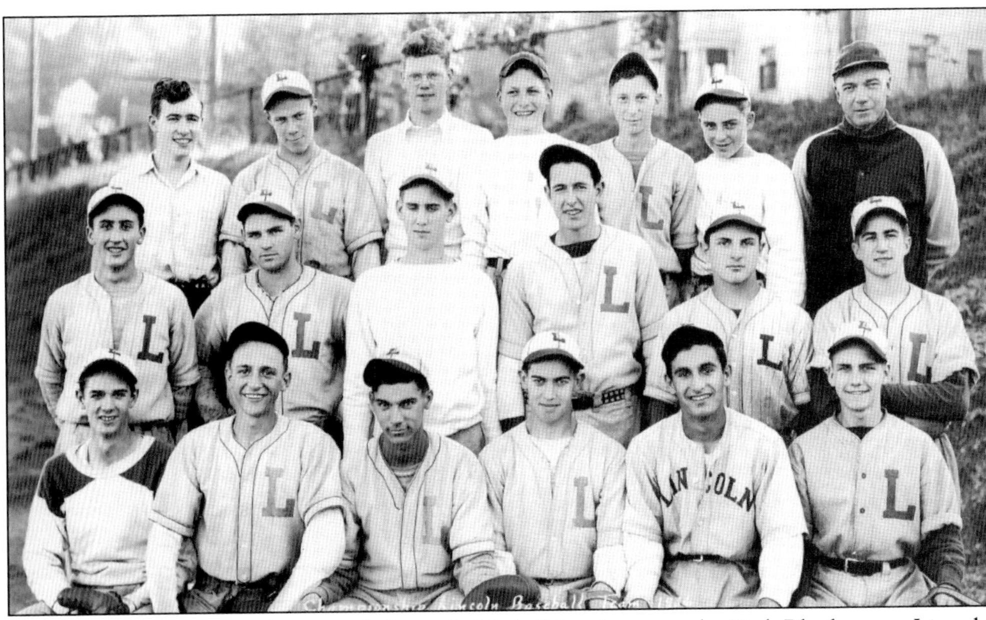

At the time of this 1936 photograph, Lincoln High School was on the Park Blocks, now Lincoln Hall at Portland State University. Since Lincoln students used Kamm field for sports activities, they often held events in Goose Hollow, sometimes at the MAC clubhouse or field. (Mike Ryerson.)

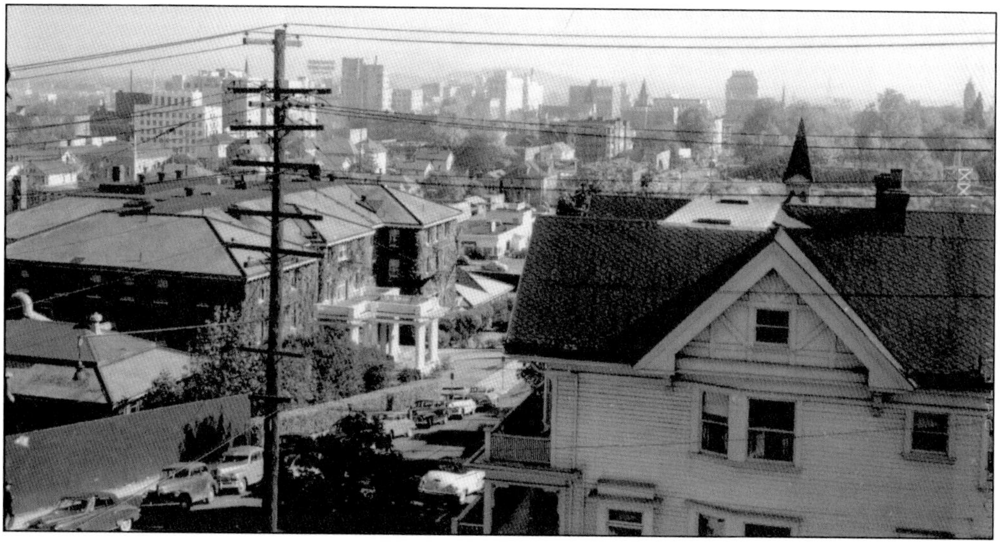

These two images help demonstrate how Goose Hollow has suffered from the blight of automobile infrastructure. In the photograph above from the late 1940s, houses line the hillside across from the Multnomah Athletic Club on Salmon Street. In the photograph below, an aerial view from the 1980s shows the newly constructed MAC building with a rounded roof. The hillside across from the MAC has been stripped of the homes that once lined the street to make room for a parking structure that now covers an entire block. (Above, Norm Gholston; below, Mike Ryerson.)

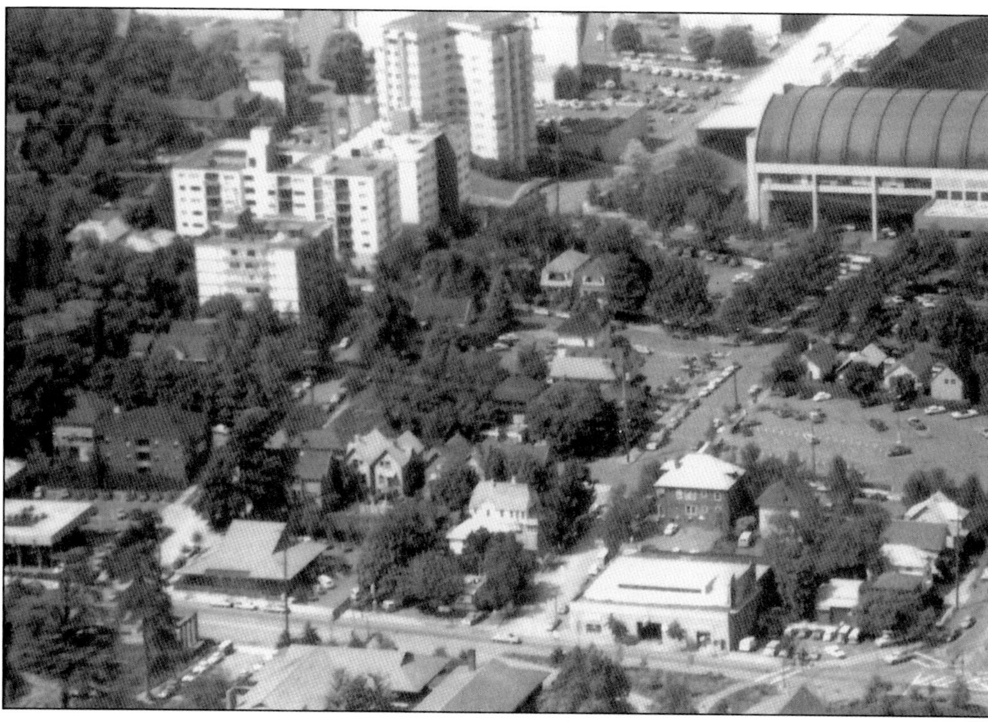

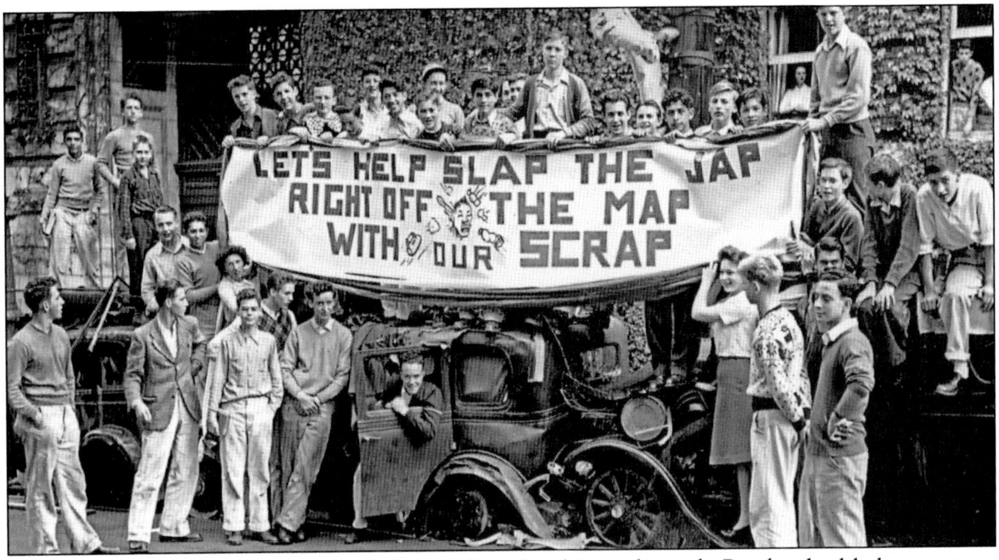

During World War II, Oregonians believed that the shipyards made Portland a likely target, so they had genuine fear of a Japanese attack. The government treated the Pacific Coast as a combat zone, and blackout drills prepared residents for possible air attacks. In fact, a Japanese hot air balloon bomb landed in Bly, Oregon, killing 6 people. Above, Lincoln High School students filled jalopies with scrap metal, enthusiastically participating in the war drive in 1942. Standing outside the Multnomah Athletic Club, their sign induces cringes today but was an effort to show patriotism at the time. In the bottom photograph, Lincoln students celebrate the war's end in 1945. The Bluejackets sing in Multnomah Stadium for a Victory Day show. Note the Eighteenth Avenue garage advertising "Machine Work" in the upper left, the same building on the cover of this book. (Above, OrHi-bb002576; below, OrHi-bb007400.)

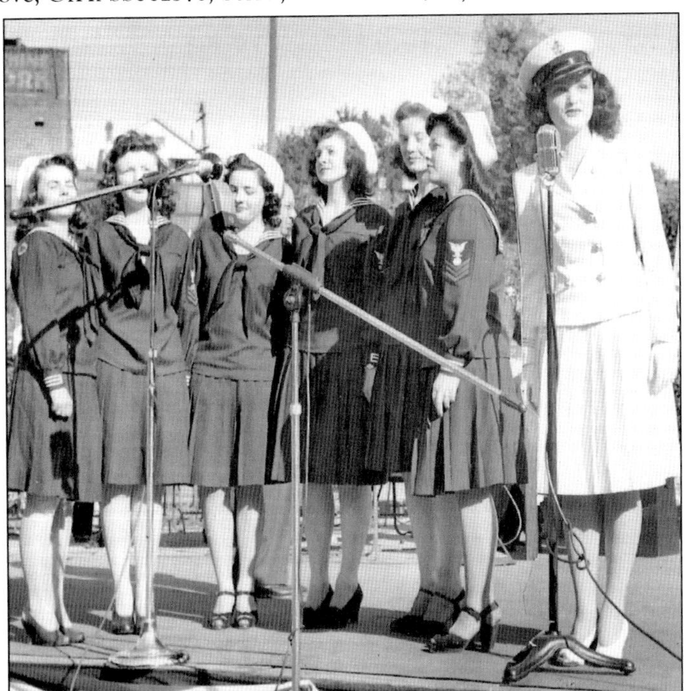

Four

URBAN "RENEWAL" AND RECLAIMING NEIGHBORHOOD IDENTITY 1950–1985

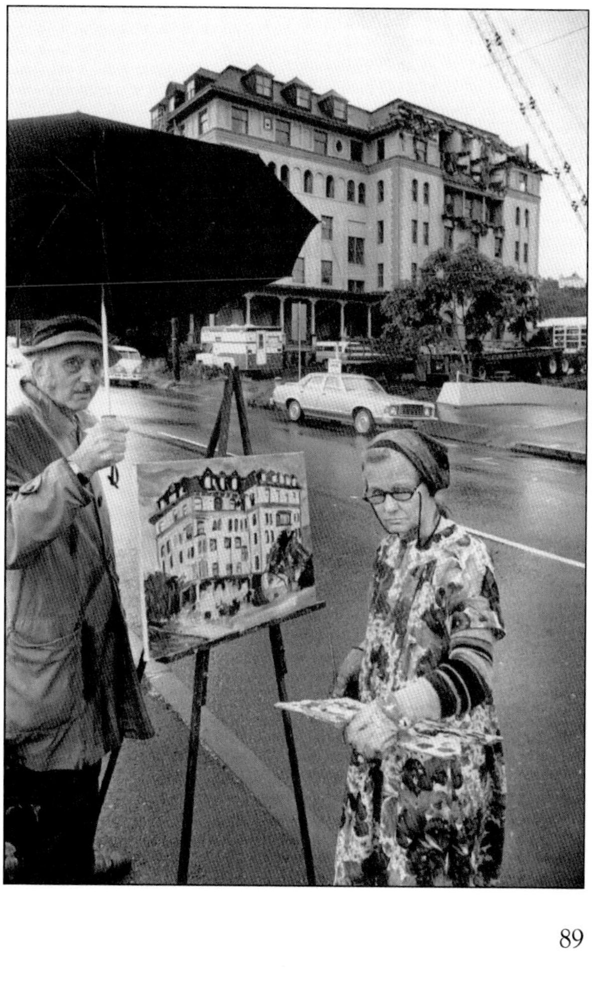

In 1977, this woman's priceless look expresses the stress felt as so-called urban "renewal" ripped through Goose Hollow during the 1960s and 1970s. This hotel/residence hall stood at 1215 Southwest Fourteenth Avenue near Jefferson Street from 1891 until 1977, when it was demolished, making way for KGW's parking lot. Through the years, it was known as the Hobart-Curtis Hotel, The Hill, Jeanne d'Arc (a Sisters of Mercy residence for women), and Maraba West. John Reed's family once lived here. (Norm Gholston.)

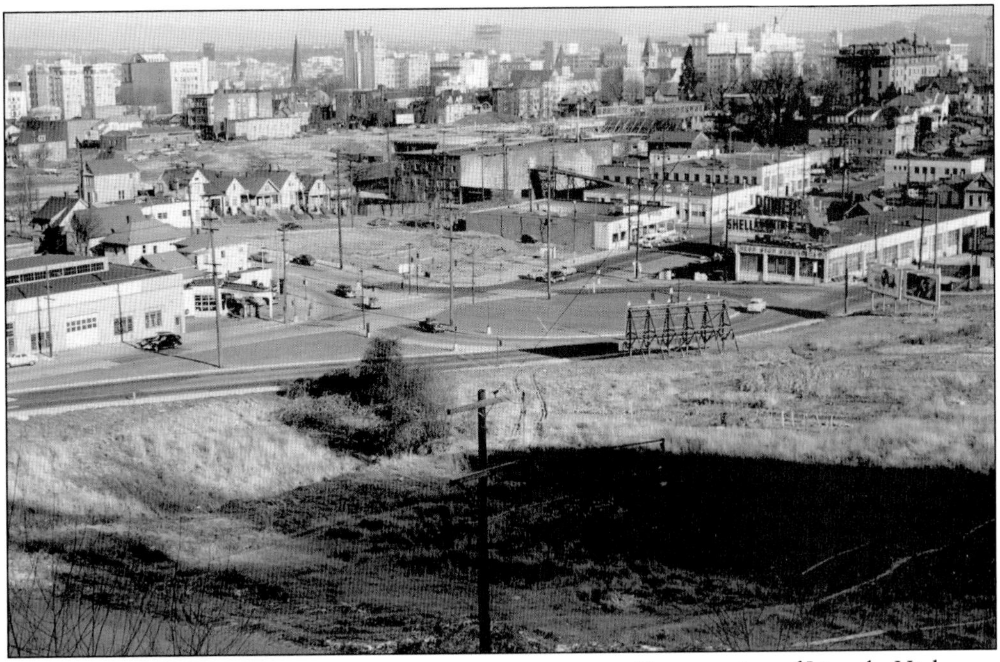

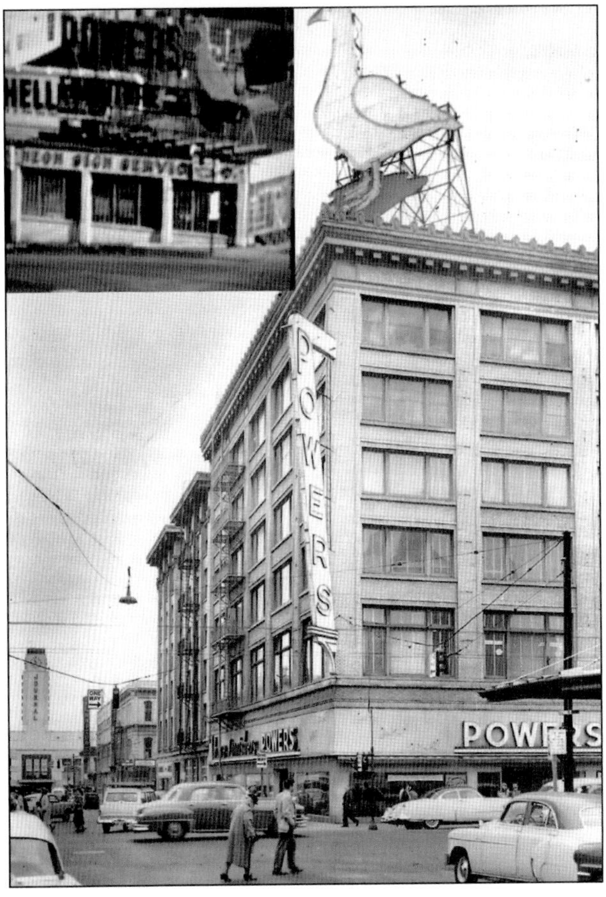

Construction of Lincoln High School is seen above in 1951. Collins Circle, at Eighteenth Avenue and Jefferson Street, is dominated by a Powers Furniture sign with a giant goose (inset left). The current site of the First United Methodist Church is an empty lot (foreground), once the site of Thomas Carter's home and Chinese Vegetable Gardens. The service station (above, left) was once the site of Canyon Gardens. A huge neon goose looming over such a prominent spot in Goose Hollow was merely coincidence. From the 1930s to the 1960s, many 36-foot high neon geese graced the rooftops of Powers Furniture stores, such as at the one seen on the left at Third and Yamhill Streets. The store's first location was on First Street, and the goose marketing concept was developed around the turn of the century, long before a store was opened in Goose Hollow. (Above, CoPA; left, OrHi-bb007407.)

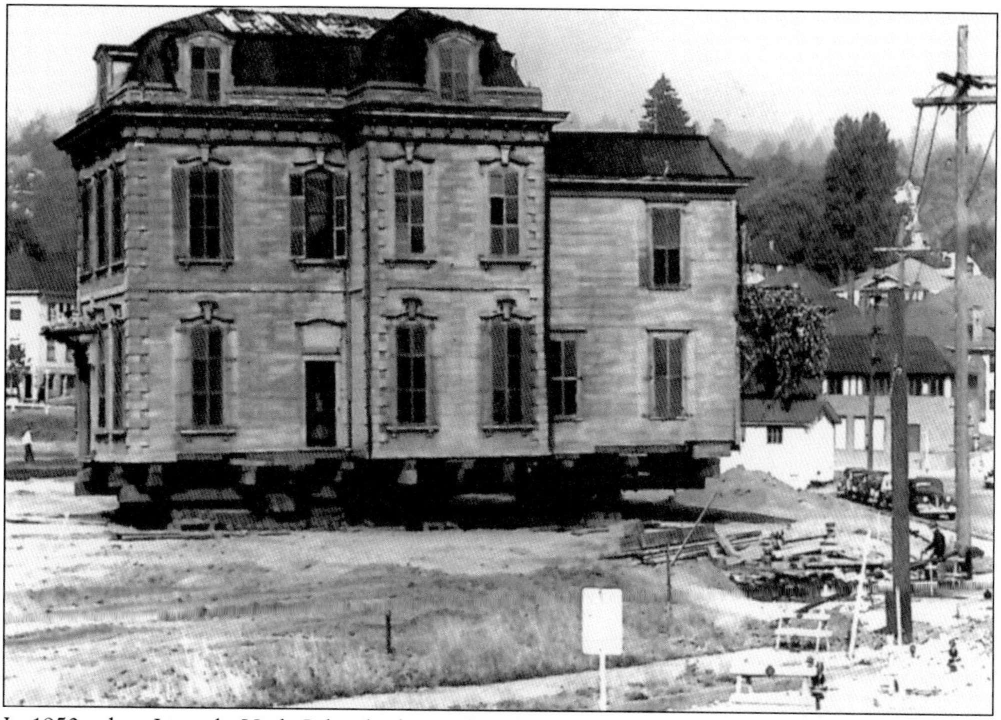

In 1950, when Lincoln High School relocated to the old Jacob Kamm estate, Eric Ladd saved the house from demolition and moved it to 1425 Southwest Twentieth Avenue to join his colony of rescued historic buildings. The Colony also included a chapel from St. Mary's Academy and a replica of President Lincoln's house built for the Lewis and Clark Centennial. After years of neglect, both buildings were demolished, though the foundation of the Lincoln house is still visible next to the Kamm house. Embracing the Portland reuse/preserve ethic well before most, Ladd spruced up the Kamm house with salvaged architectural details and briefly opened the Kamm House Restaurant. The Kamm house survives today as a Goose Hollow gem. (William Hawkins.)

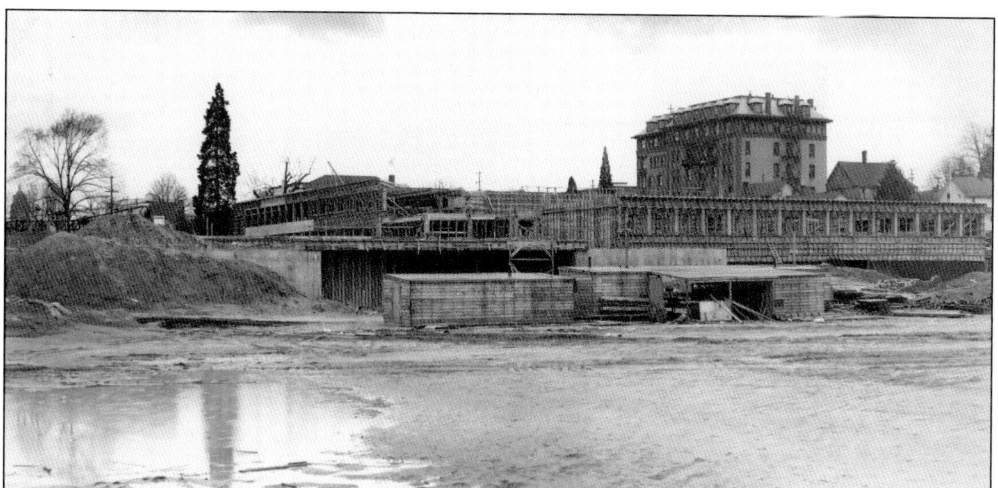

A 1951 photograph shows construction well underway for Lincoln High School. Since the original terrain at this site was a hill leading down into a gulch, a lot of earth was rearranged to bring what is now the football field up to grade. (Norm Gholston.)

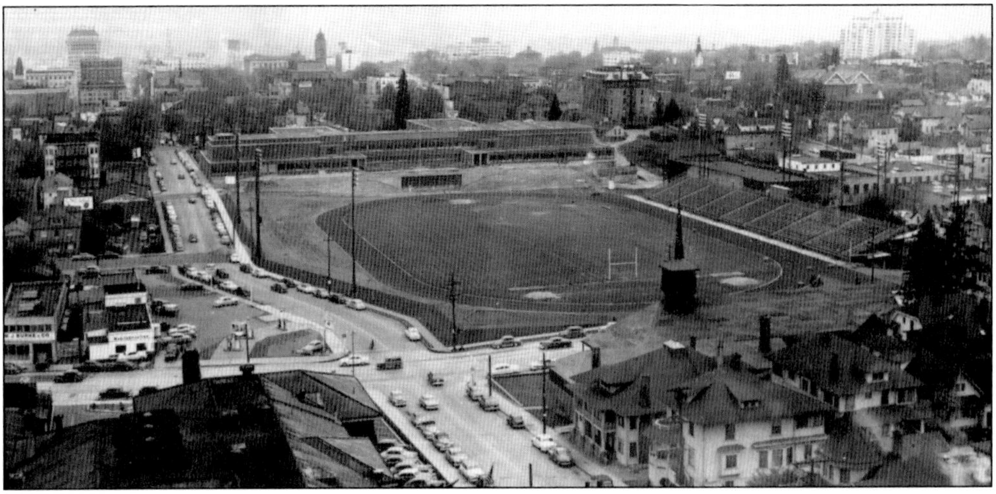

The final touches are being put on Lincoln High School in this 1952 photograph, looking east. Butler's Service Station is on the left. Matt Groening, creator of *The Simpsons*, is a famous Lincoln High School graduate. He sketched Bart Simpson in the wet cement of the sidewalk along the west end of the field.

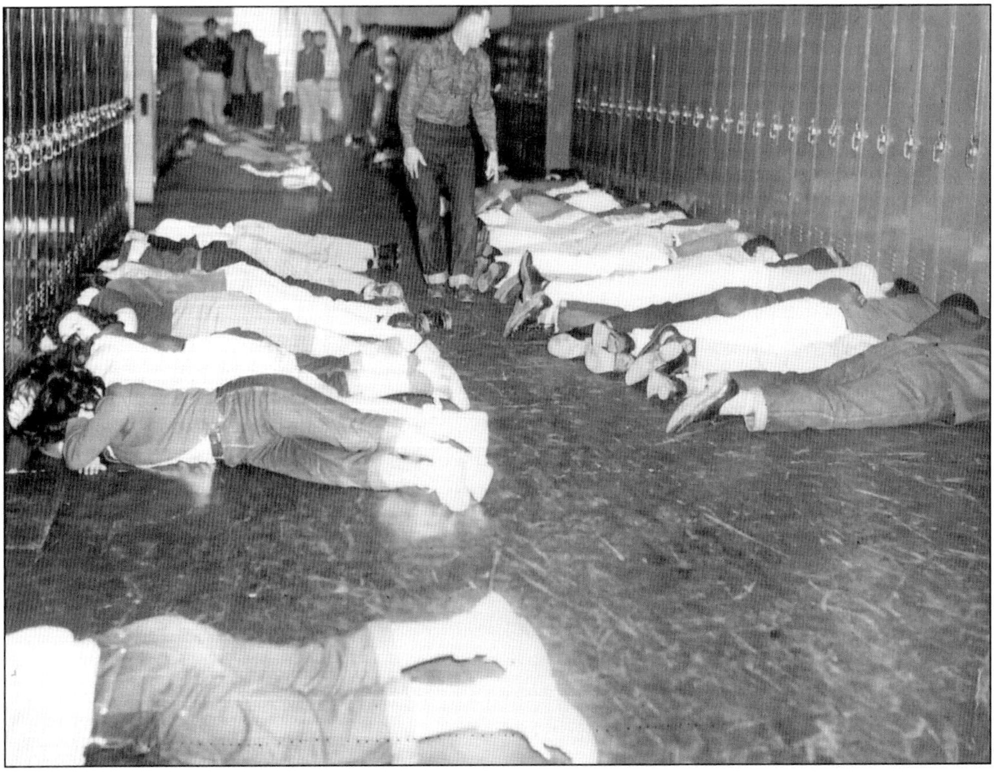

During the Cold War, with worry about possible nuclear attacks by Russia a palpable part of American life, air raid drills became a routine addition to school life. The Federal Civil Defense Administration taught Cold War survival skills through such films as *Duck and Cover*. This 1950s image is of Lincoln High School students conducting an air raid drill. (OrHi-ba025119.)

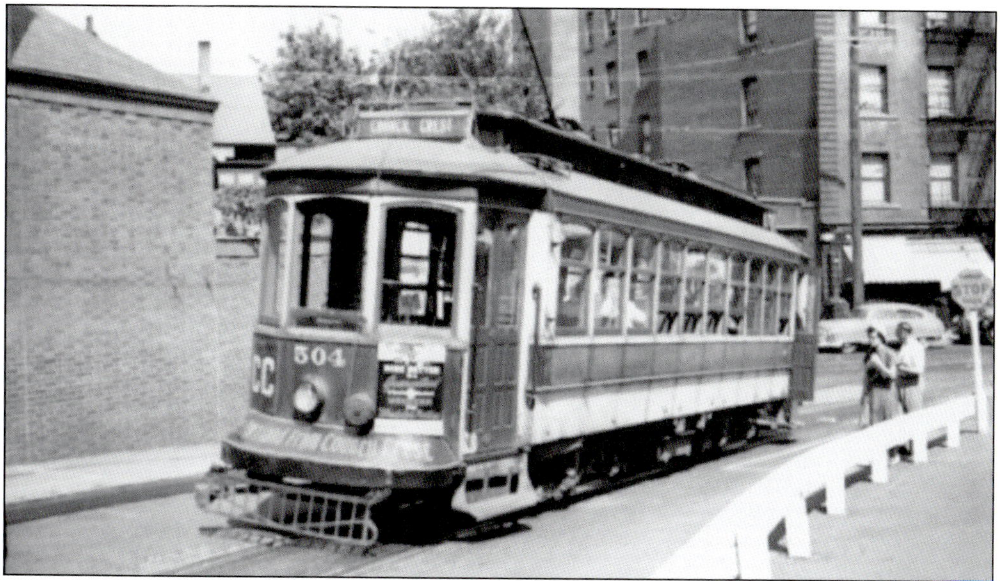

In February 1950, service on Portland's last three streetcar lines—the Council Crest, Willamette Heights, and Twenty-third Avenue lines—ended. A photograph from that year shows passengers waiting as the streetcar passes behind the triangular building on Burnside Street and Vista Avenue in Goose Hollow. (CoPA.)

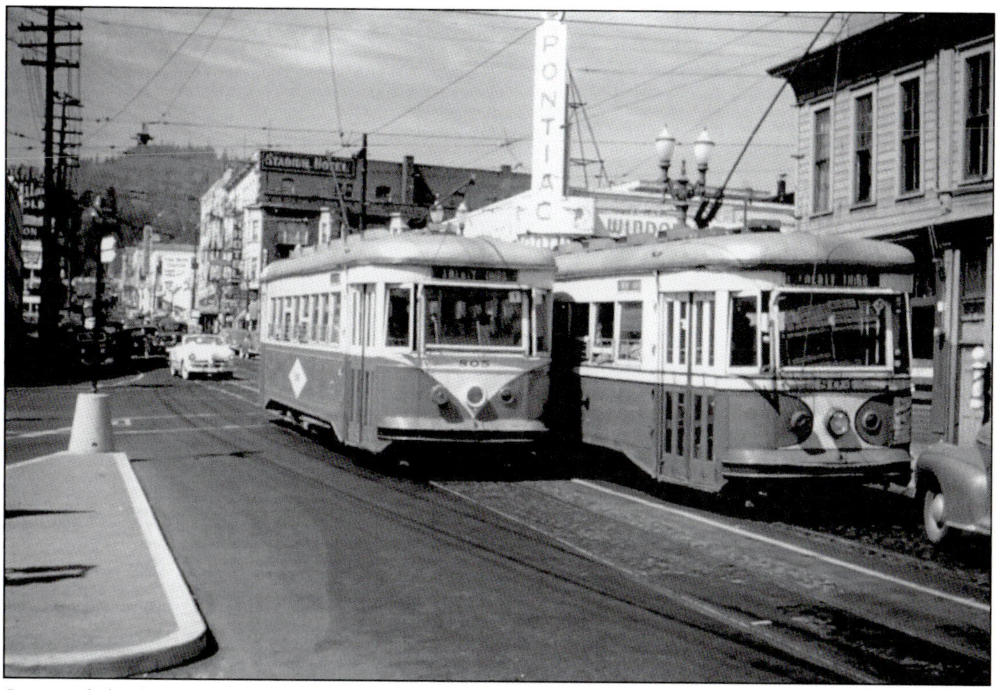

Some of the last streetcars running in Portland, these were on the Twenty-third Avenue line, shown here on Burnside Street, heading downtown. (CoPA.)

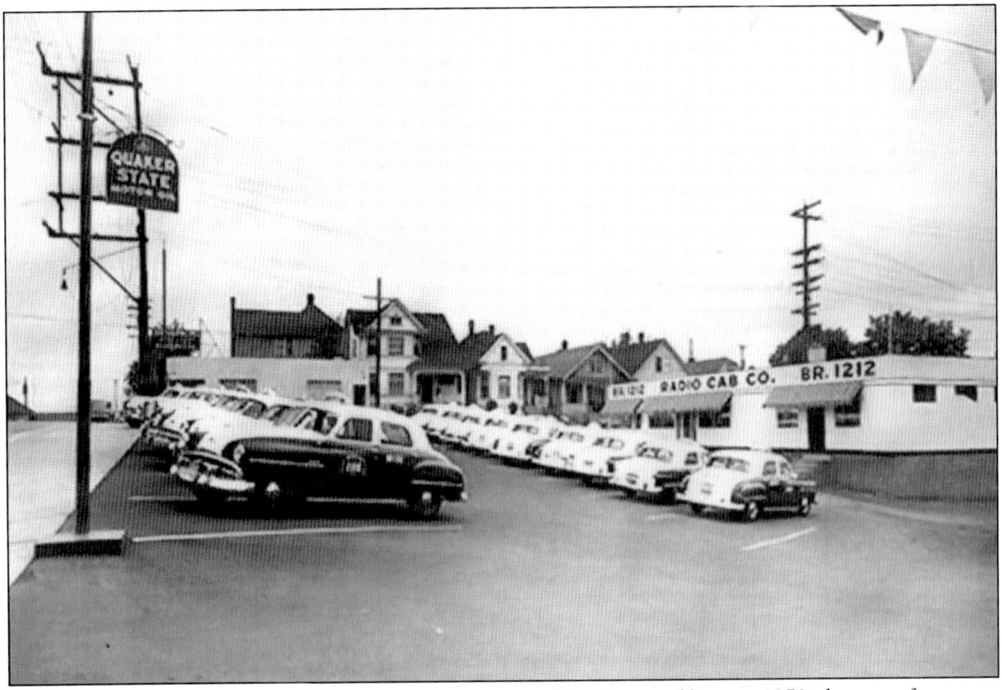

The Radio Cab Company was once located in Goose Hollow. Pictured here in 1950, the row of cottages behind the lot, on Madison Street near Eighteenth Avenue, survives today. (Mike Ryerson.)

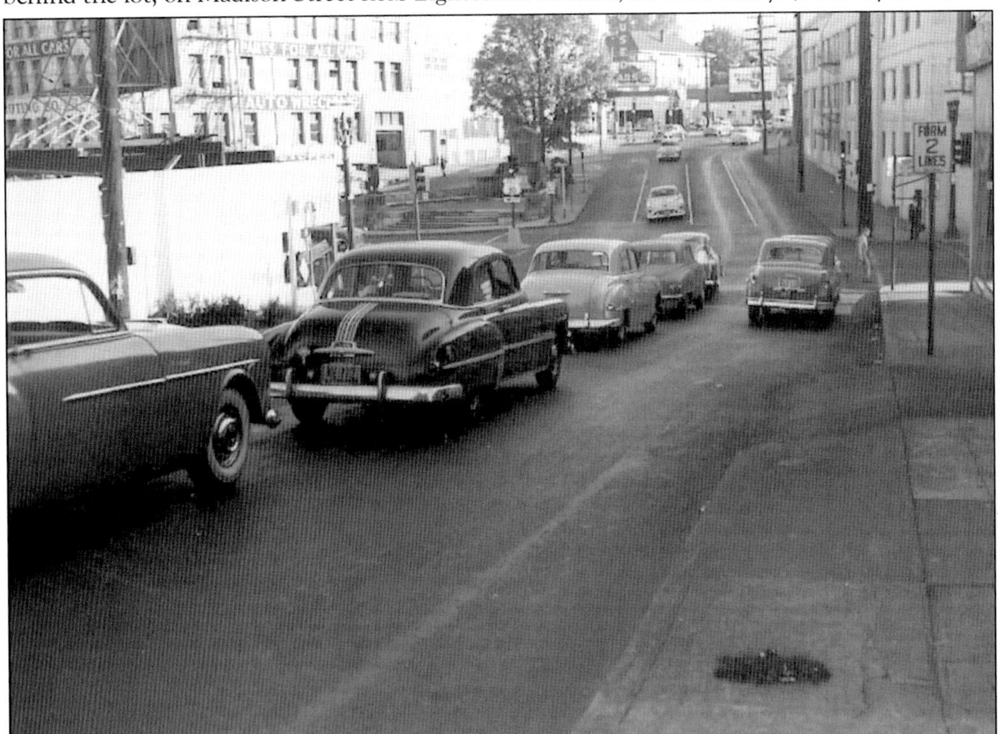

A 1952 photograph looks south toward the intersection of Nineteenth Avenue and Burnside Street as the automobiles head into Goose Hollow. (CoPA.)

A 1953 image looks west on Burnside Street as it crosses Twenty-first Avenue. This was the "before" shot in a street-widening proposal. (CoPA.)

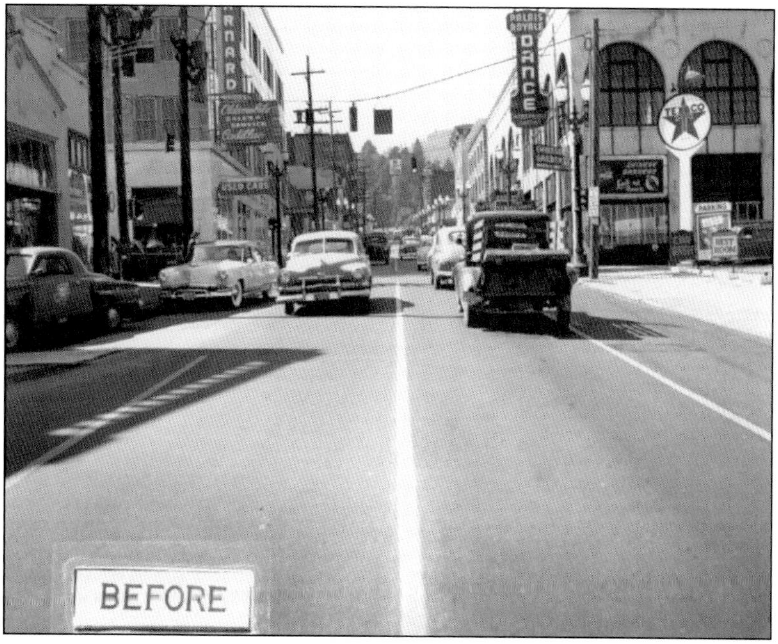

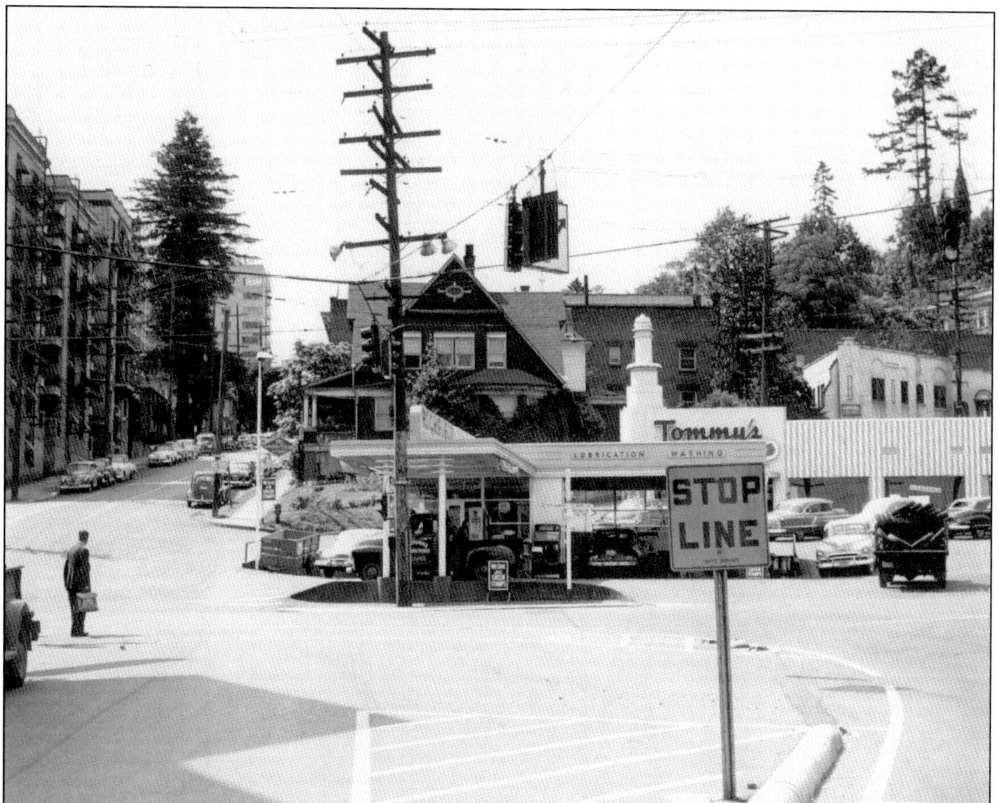

On Burnside Street, looking south onto Vista Avenue in 1953, a service station is now on the site of the old Cedar Hill streetcar barn. (CoPA.)

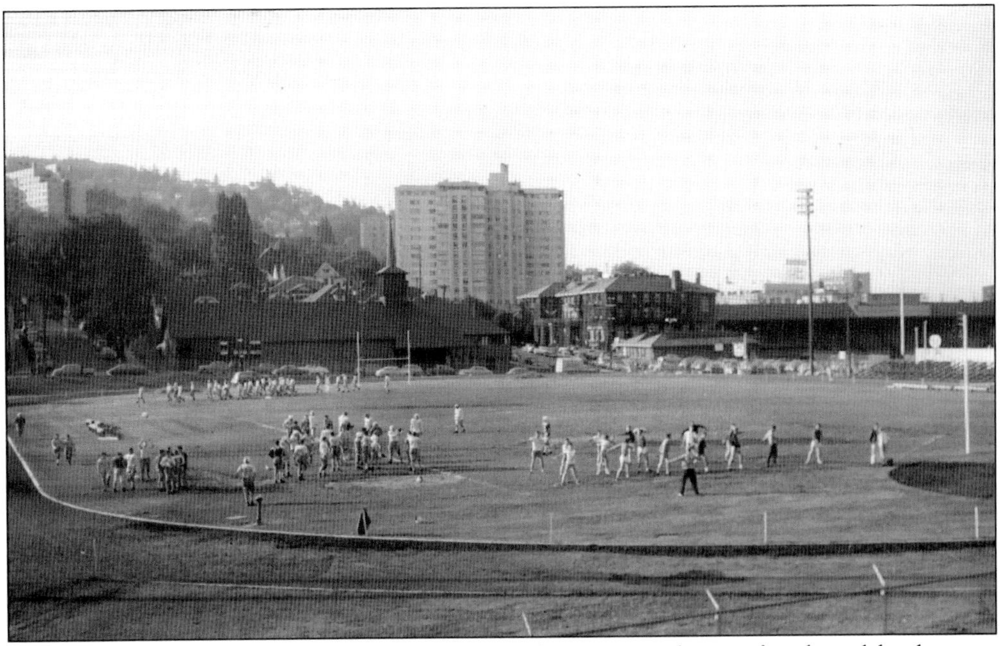

In this late 1950s view from Lincoln Field looking west, the increasing density of residential development in Goose Hollow is clear, with high-rise apartments dotting the hillside. (Norm Gholston.)

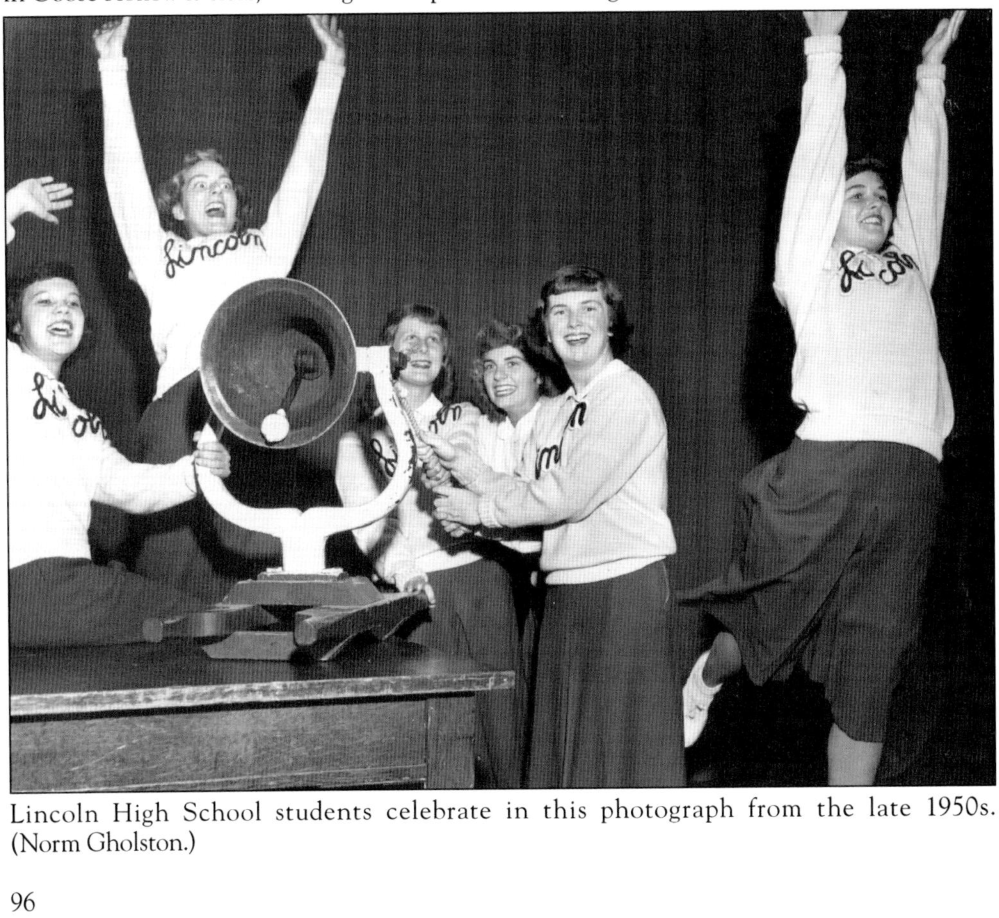

Lincoln High School students celebrate in this photograph from the late 1950s. (Norm Gholston.)

In 1957, Elvis Presley performed at Multnomah Stadium and Portland lost its mind! He was interviewed by the local press at the Multnomah Athletic Club, then performed before an estimated audience of 14,000 people who packed Multnomah Stadium. (*Oregonian*.)

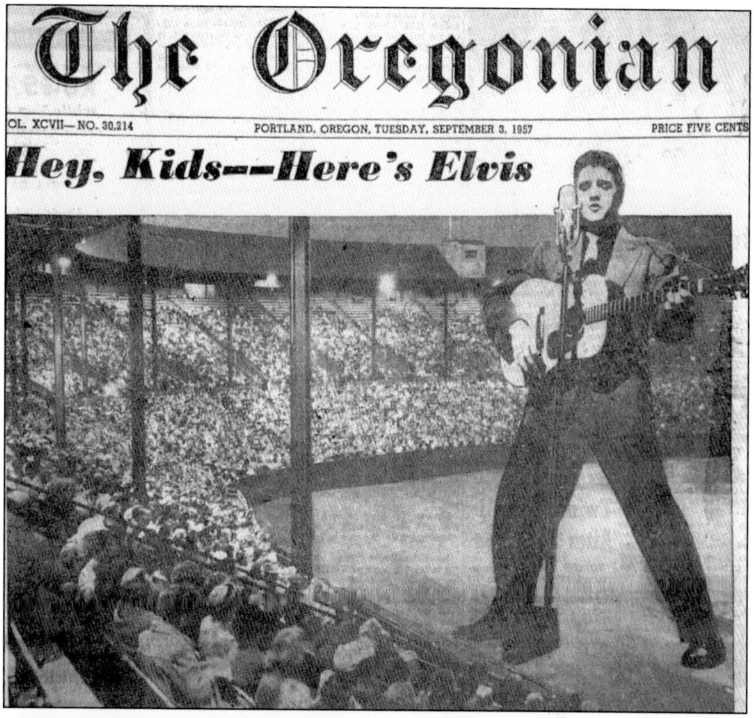

The Oregonian

OL. XCVII—NO. 30,214 | PORTLAND, OREGON, TUESDAY, SEPTEMBER 3, 1957 | PRICE FIVE CENTS

ey, Kids--Here's Elvis

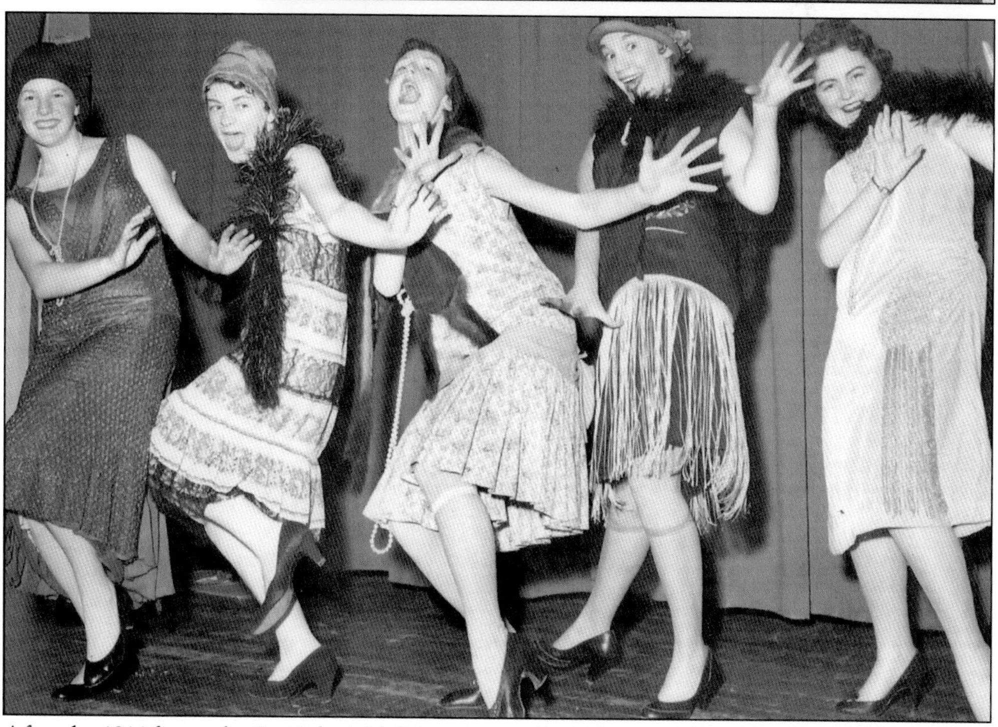

After the 1914 fire at the St. Helen's Hall location on Park Place and Vista Avenue, where the Vista St. Clair Apartments are today, the school moved to Thirteenth Avenue and Hall Street. This site was demolished in 1964 when the Interstate 405 freeway was cut through. This 1957 photograph is from happier days, as students perform in a chorus line of flappers for a skit. (OrHi-bb007406.)

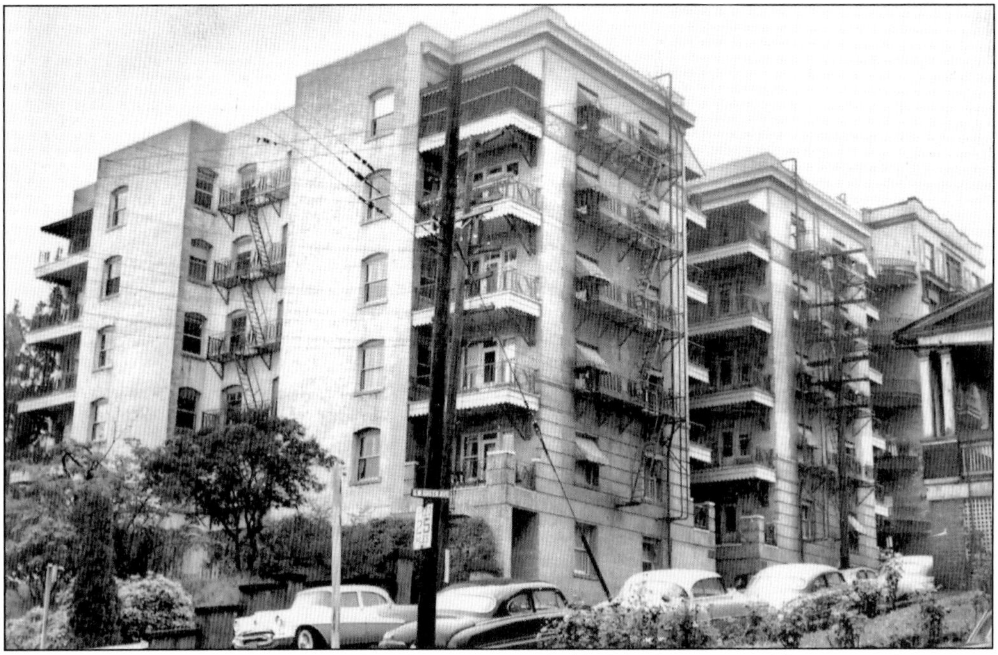

Many residents move to Goose Hollow for a more walkable life than is possible in most American cities. The neighborhood is also fortunate that such a varied and interesting combination of houses and mid- and high-rise apartments and condominiums were built over the decades. Vista Avenue boasts many gracious historic apartments like the Fordham Apartments, pictured here in 1956 at 742 Southwest Vista Avenue. (OrHi-bb007398.)

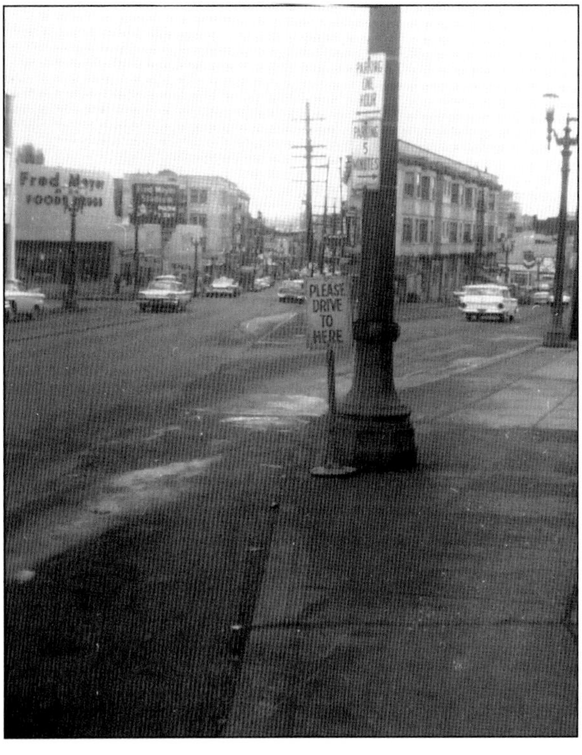

This interesting triangular building, photographed here in 1960, sits between Burnside Street and Morrison Street. (CoPA.)

A 1960 view looks east towards downtown on Burnside Street near King Street. (CoPA.)

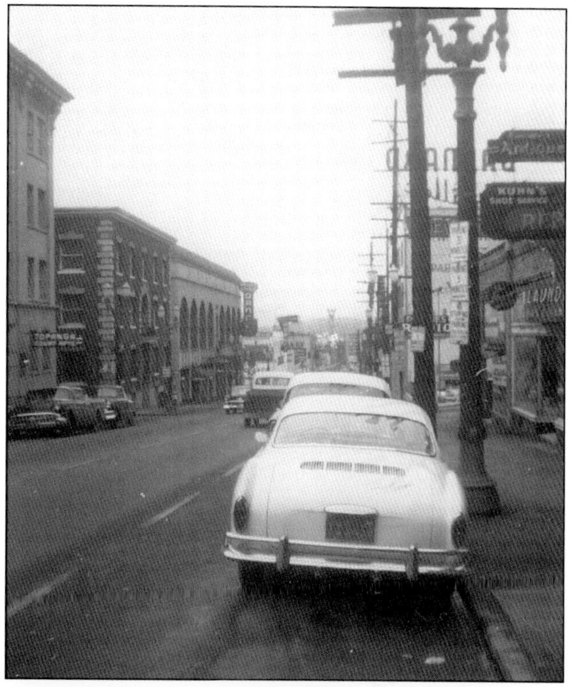

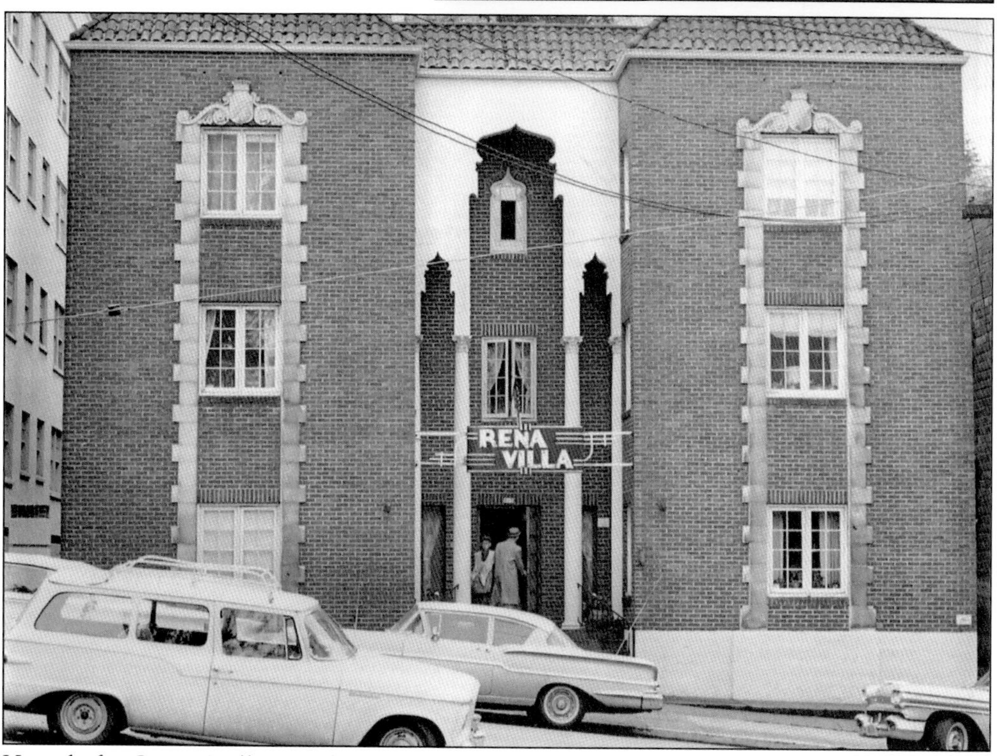

Happily for Goose Hollow, such lavish, ornate, and unique apartment buildings as the Rena Villa were built along streetcar lines such as on Vista Avenue, pictured here in 1962. Built in the 1930s, the design embraces the same Moorish Revival aesthetic that led to such wondrous architectural creations as Portland's Bagdad Theater. (OrHi-bb007416.)

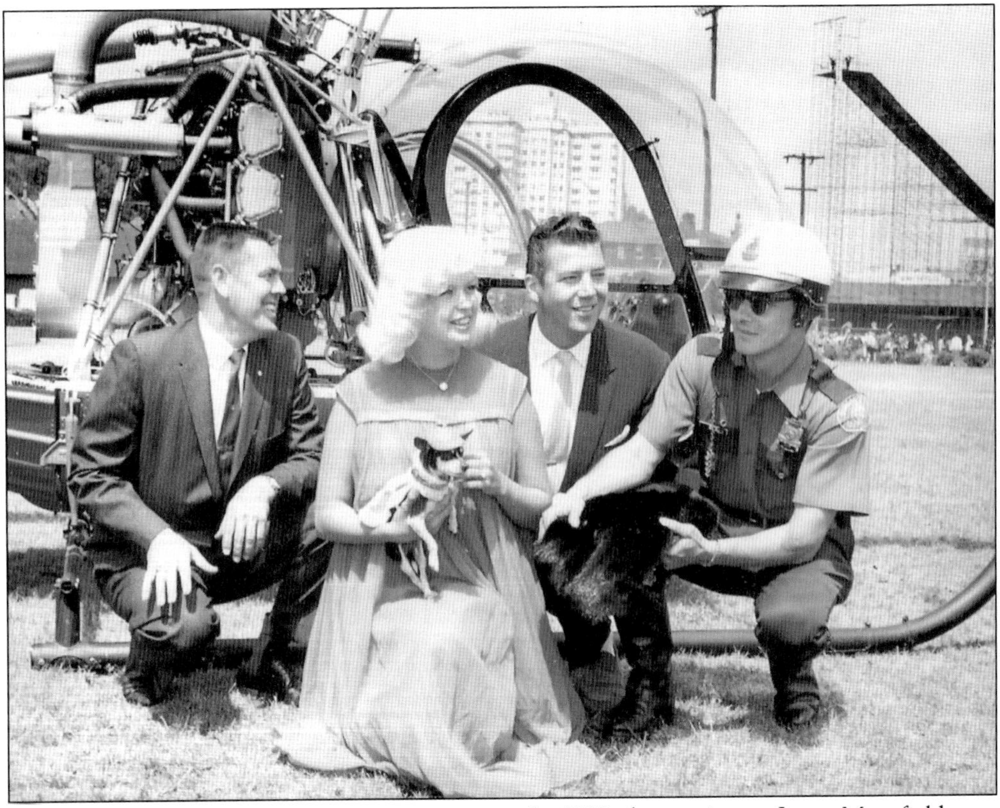

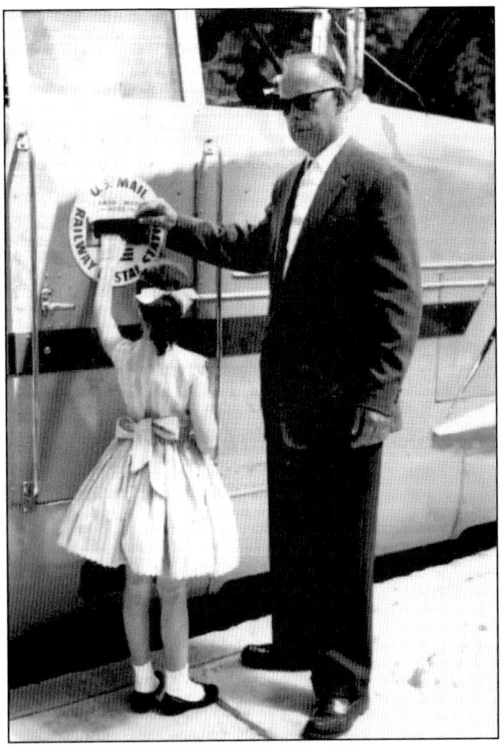

In 1960, the movie star Jayne Mansfield and her husband, Mickey Hargitay, who was 1955's Mr. Universe, were flown in to ride on a float in the Rose Festival. Behind them, to the right, is the ski jump built in the stadium by the Cascade Ski Club and covered with 200 tons of snow—in June. The ski club demonstrated ski jumping and alpine slalom for 40,000 spectators throughout the festival. (OrHi-bb007382.)

In 1958, the Zooliner began service in Washington Park, taking children around the park hills and over to the zoo. On this day in 1961, the train station acquired its own postal cancellation stamp and is today one of the last railroads offering mail service. (Norm Gholston.)

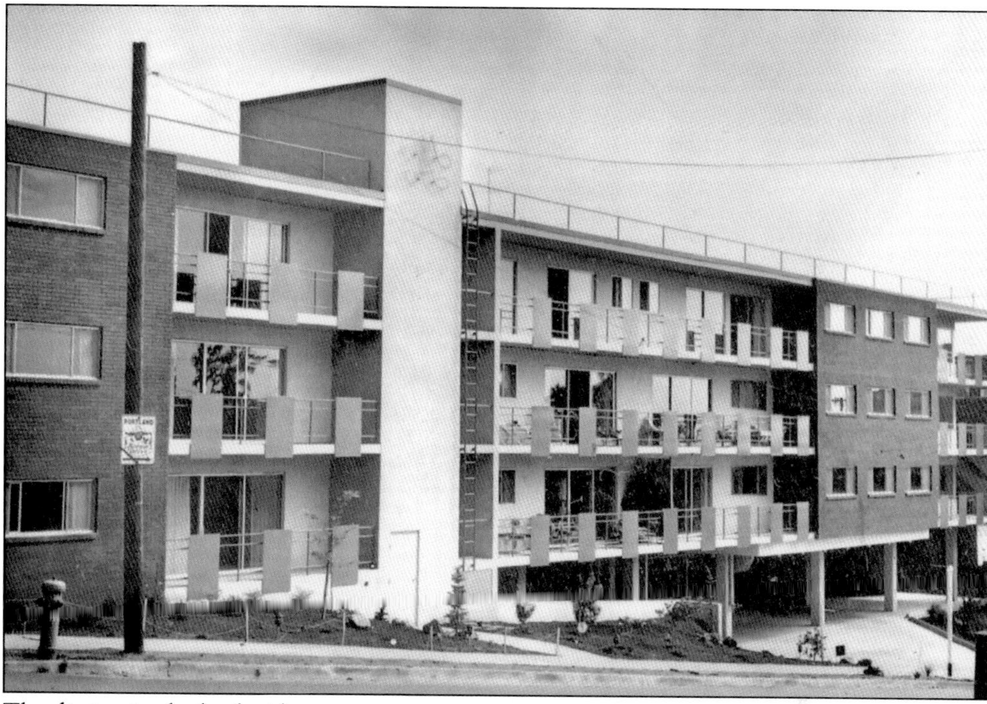

The distinctive look of mid-century modern architecture can be found sprinkled around Goose Hollow. Pictured here in 1964, these apartments are now condominiums at 2393 Southwest Park Place, the former site of the Julius Loewenberg house. (OrHi-bb007432.)

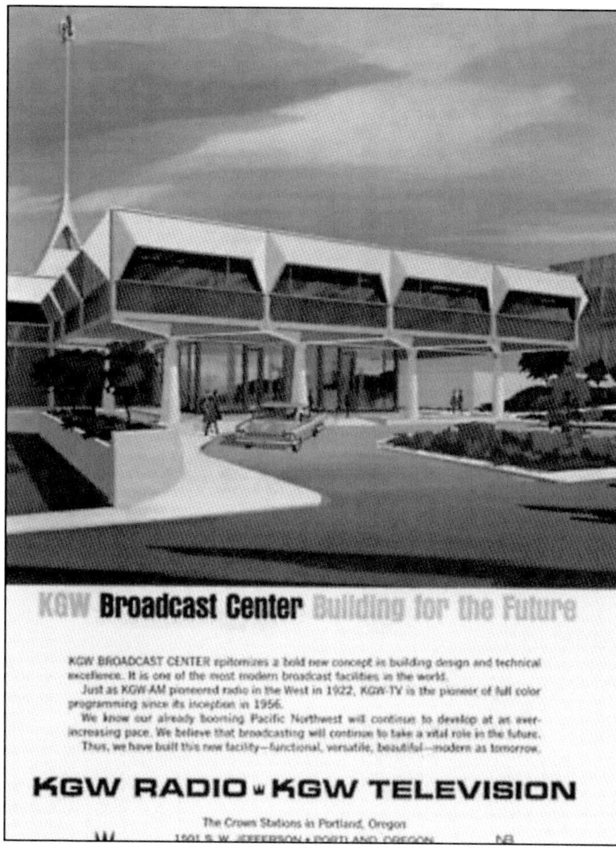

The groovy KGW building is now somewhat obscured by trees. But as depicted in this advertisement, the building is an exuberant display of 1960s quirkiness in architecture. For the building's dedication, View-Master created a commemorative viewer in the shape of the building. The KGW building evokes the spirit of its time, the space-age, the modern age—the future as envisioned by *The Jetsons*. (KGW.)

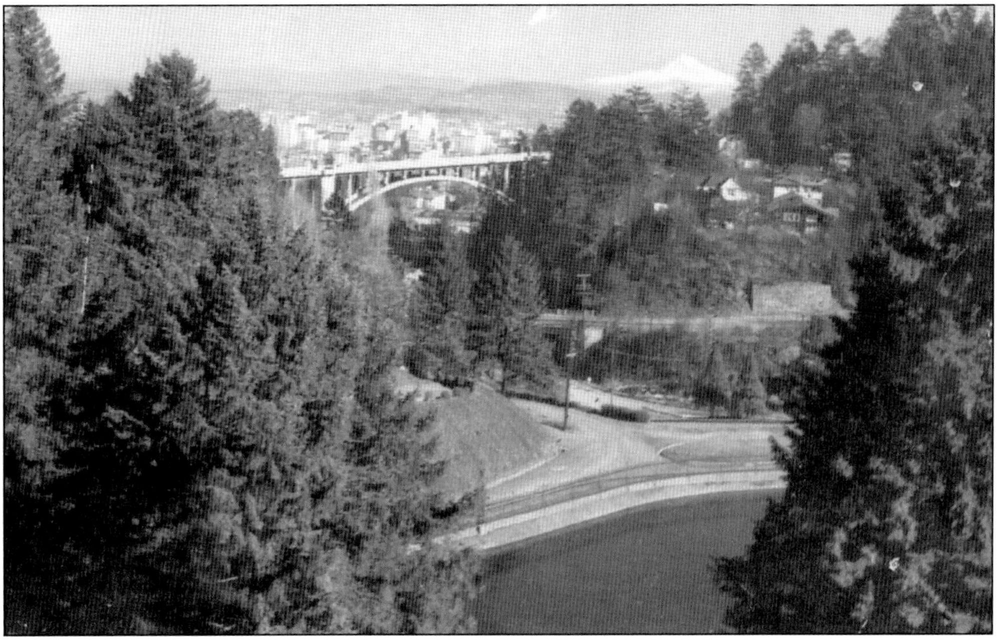

A 1960s view of the Portland skyline, Mount Hood, and the Vista Bridge was taken from Washington Park with Market Street Drive visible on the right. (George and Phyllis Johanson.)

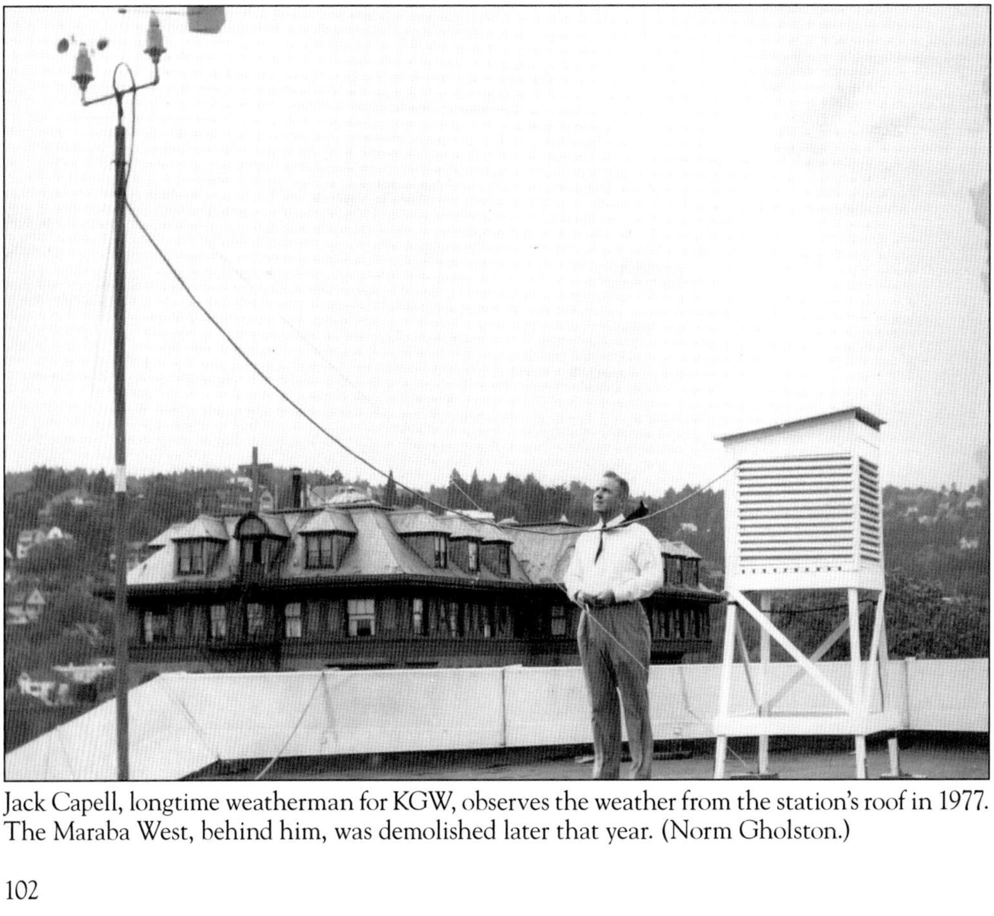

Jack Capell, longtime weatherman for KGW, observes the weather from the station's roof in 1977. The Maraba West, behind him, was demolished later that year. (Norm Gholston.)

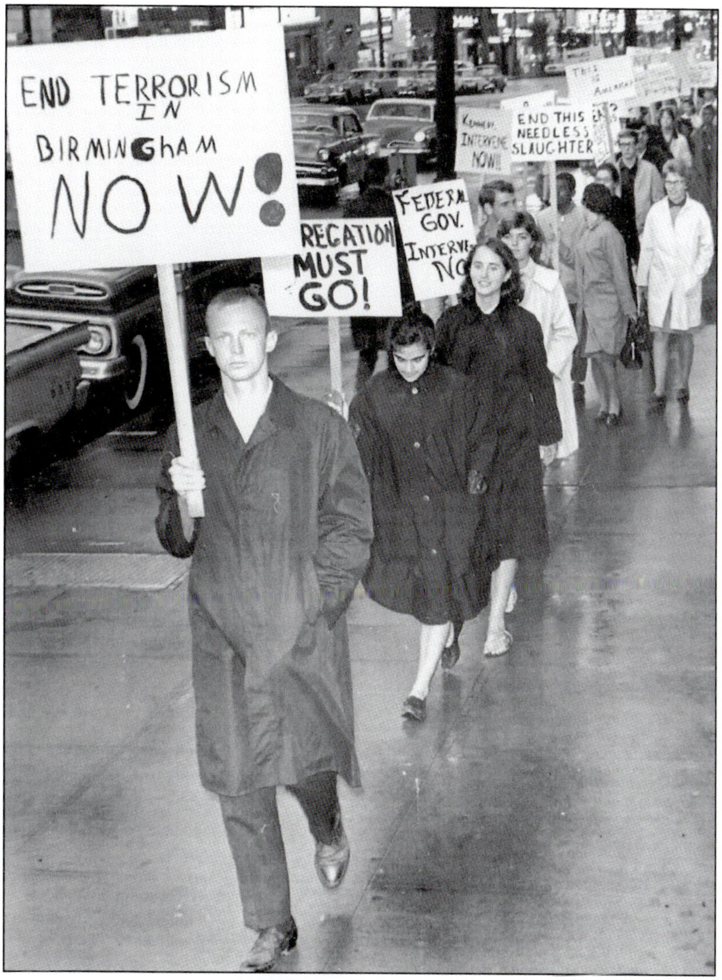

A sign of the turbulent social times in America, these students march, possibly along Burnside or Broadway Street, to protest the September 15, 1963, racially motivated bombing of a Birmingham Alabama church in which four little girls died. This catalyzed students to become more involved in the civil rights movement. These students march as Friends of the Student Non-Violent Coordinating Committee, commonly referred to by the acronym SNCC (pronounced *snick*). (OrHi-bb007423.)

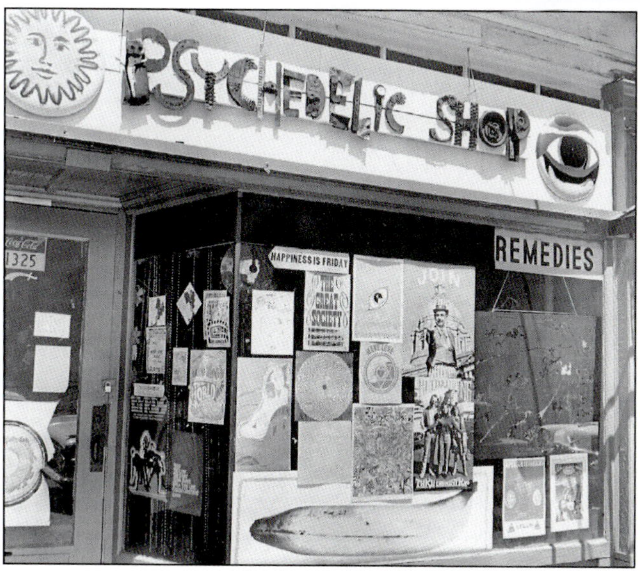

Just outside of Goose Hollow, the Psychedelic Shop, located at 1325 Southwest Washington Street and pictured here in 1967, sums up an era when Goose Hollow was known as a bohemian place where low rents attracted hippies, students, folk musicians, and artists. Author and one-time Goose Hollow resident Chuck Palahniuk lampooned the "trustafarians" who hung out at such establishments, whom he described as would-be hippies and activists "who wear hemp and patchouli and pretend to be poor." (OrHi-bb002266.)

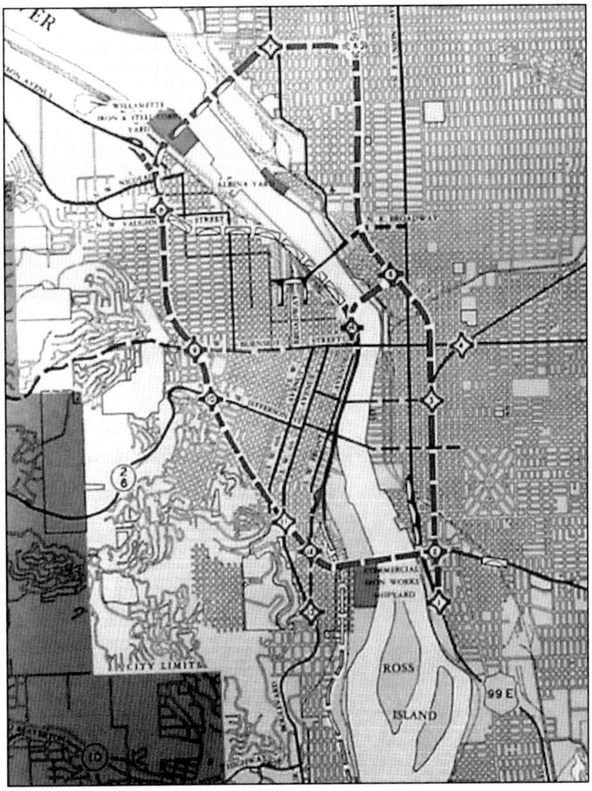

In 1943, Portland hired infamous New York City planner Robert Moses to create a transit plan. Interstate 405 exists where it is today because of this plan depicted at left. Goose Hollow residents who feel that the neighborhood has been made an island by automobile infrastructure can pin the blame on Moses. He was well known for his penchant for highways and dissecting neighborhoods with little regard for the impact of grime, noise, and lost housing. (CoPA.)

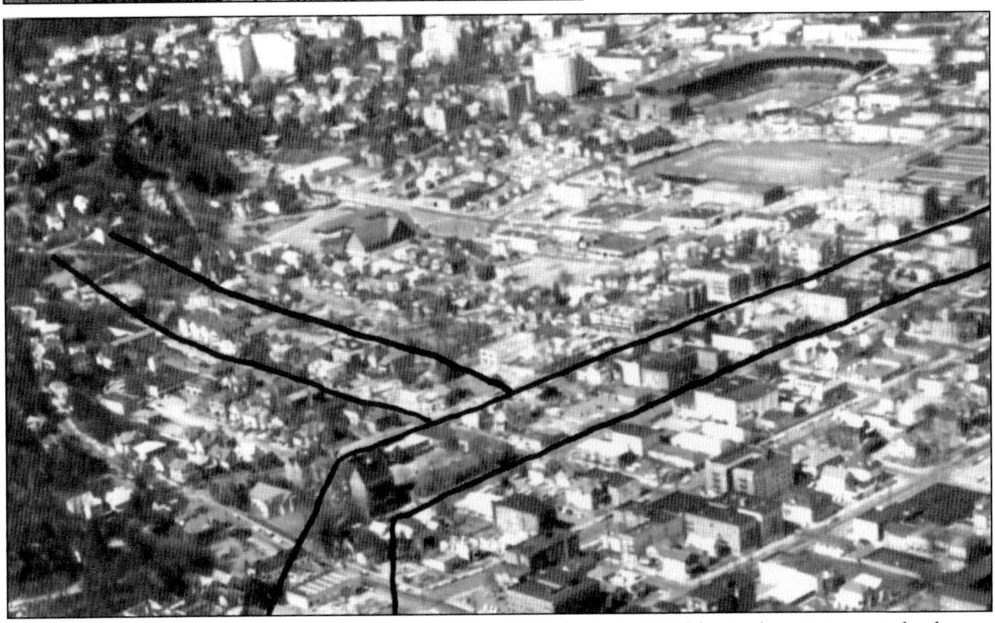

A 1967 aerial view indicates the path of Interstate 405 as planned by Robert Moses, which was sometimes called the Stadium Freeway. It intersected with Highway 26. The connector was called the Foothills Freeway, connecting to the Sunset Freeway. Note the enormous loss of housing and the incredible chasm carved through Goose Hollow. All of Mill Street in Goose Hollow was destroyed. (CoPA.)

Some residents and business owners tried to stop the freeway from ripping through their neighborhood. However, unlike the neighborhoods that were able to stop the Mount Hood Freeway, Goose Hollow did not have the political firepower to stop the Stadium Freeway or Foothills Freeway. In this 1964 image, the Vista Ridge Tunnels are being cut through the hillside. (Don Nelson.)

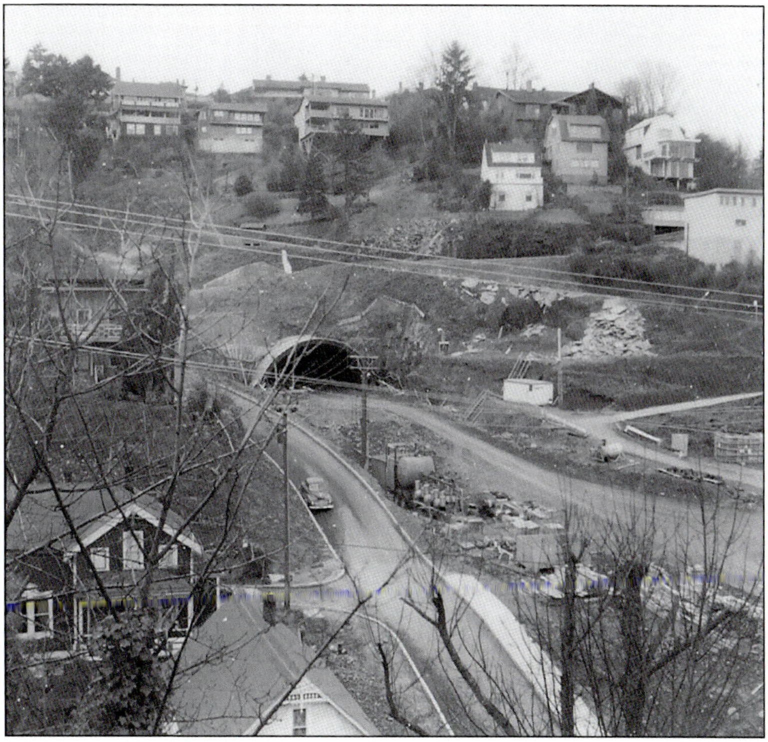

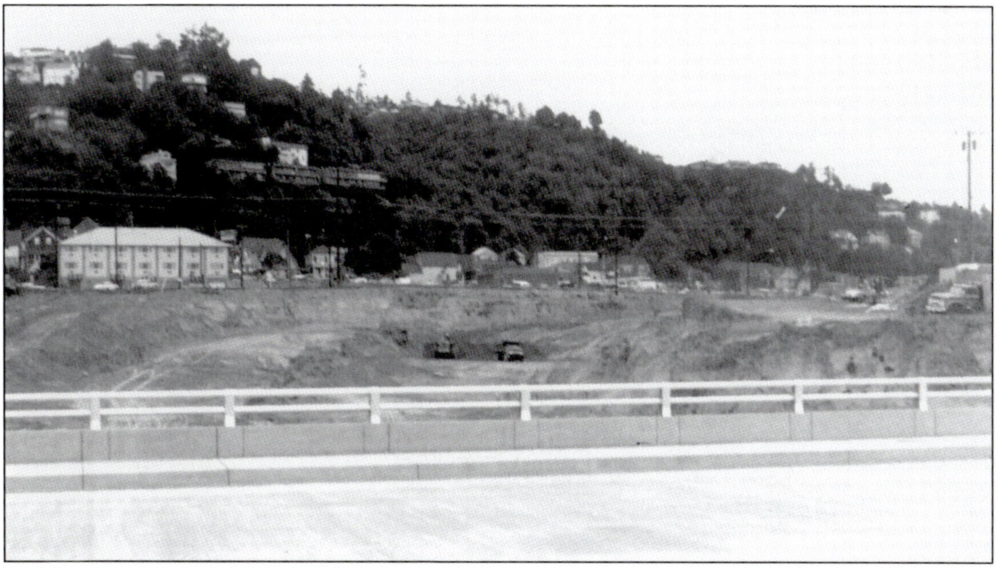

Unlike the South Portland Italian and Jewish neighborhoods displaced by urban "renewal," whose plight is known and grieved over, Goose Hollow's mutilation is rarely discussed. Many Goose Hollow residents would like to see those scars healed with a park, pedestrian path, or other strategies to bridge the freeway chasm. This 1964 view is on the south end of Interstate 405, looking west toward Gander Ridge. (CoPA.)

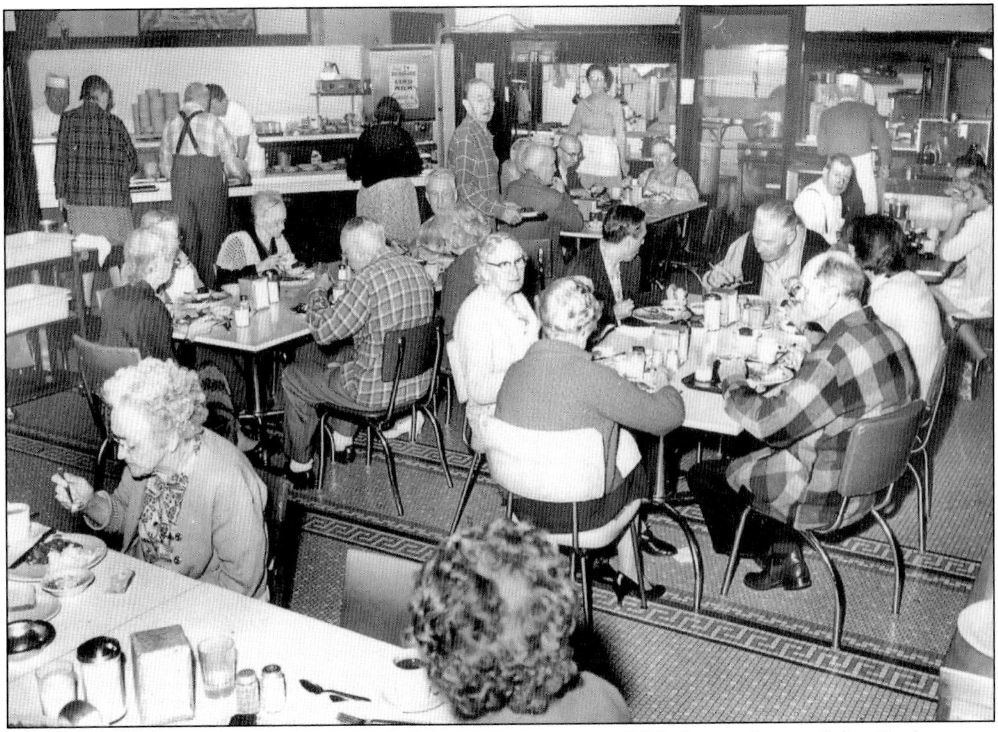

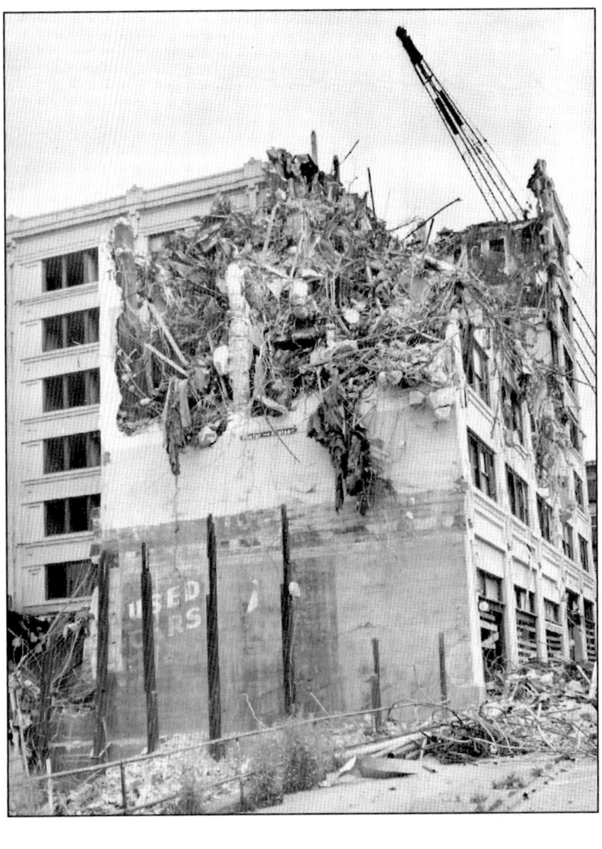

Elderly residents of the Carlton Hotel have a meal together in their dining room in 1964. All were later evicted when the hotel was condemned to clear the route for Interstate 405. The hotel was at Fourteenth Avenue and Burnside Street. (OrHi-bb007377.)

In this 1965 photograph, the Carlton Hotel is demolished to make way for the Interstate 405 freeway. (OrHi-bb007376.)

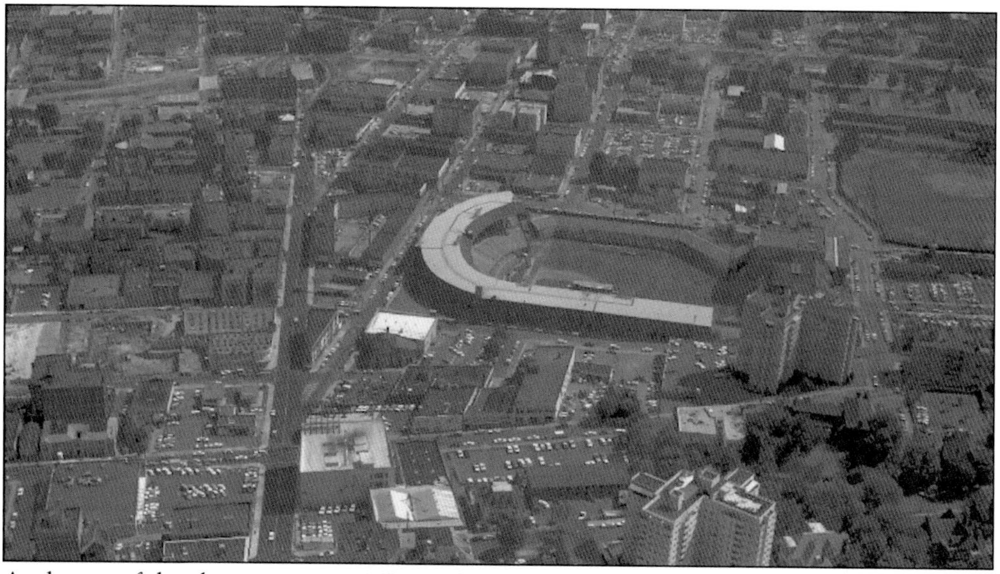

At the top of the above image, a 1967 aerial view shows digging for Interstate 405 around what is now the Burnside Street and the Taylor Street overpasses. On the bottom, a 1980s aerial photograph demonstrates the harsh reality of Robert Moses's now realized freeway plan. Mill Street Terrace now rides atop the Vista Ridge Tunnel. Mill Street no longer exists. Homes on Gander Ridge, in the Cable Car Canyon, on Market Street, and buildings on Fourteenth Avenue now front a freeway. Gander Ridge is now completely cut off from neighboring streets to the north and west in Goose Hollow, only accessible by a pedestrian and bike path grimly nicknamed by locals as the Ho Chi Minh Trail, which runs alongside the Foothills Freeway. (Above, CoPA; below, Mike Ryerson.)

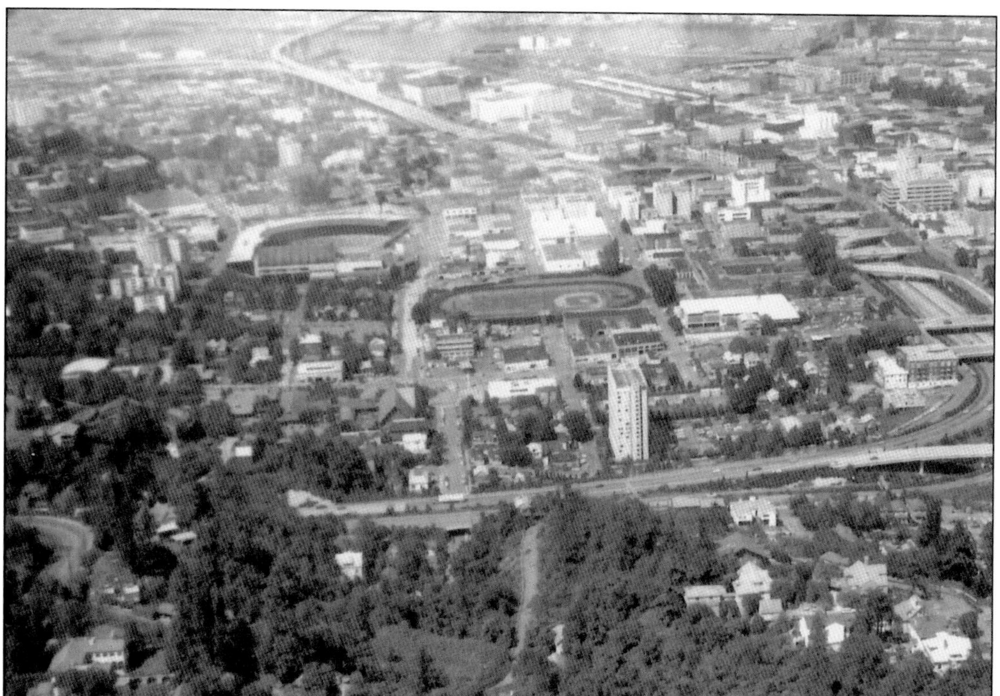

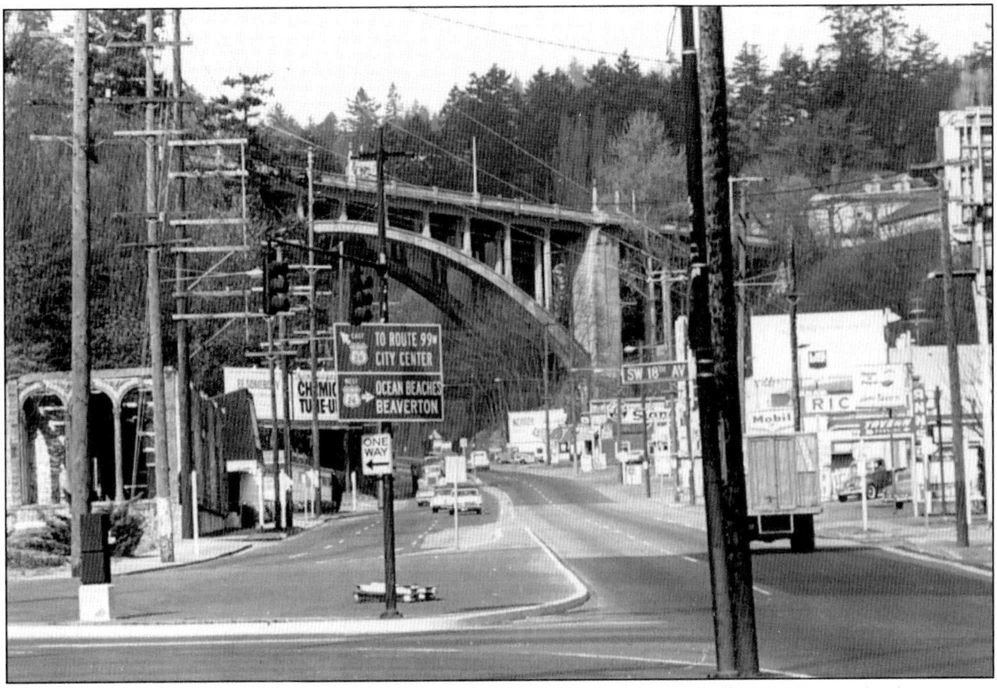

The above photograph hangs in the Goose Hollow Inn. It depicts Jefferson Street looking west toward the Vista Bridge in the 1960s. The colonnades at left were architectural salvage erected there by Eric Ladd for a never completed project. Ladd was ahead of his time with his commitment to saving Portland's historical treasures, but he struggled with a life-long affliction of too much vision and not enough follow through. Bud Clark remembers when Jefferson Street provided the only access to Highway 26, so there were many service stations here as travelers took advantage of the last stop for gasoline heading out of town. The bottom image is of the Imperial Arms Apartments, still standing at 1429 Southwest Fourteenth Avenue, where Bud Clark's family lived during his childhood in Goose Hollow. (Above, Bud Clark; below, OrHi-bb007402.)

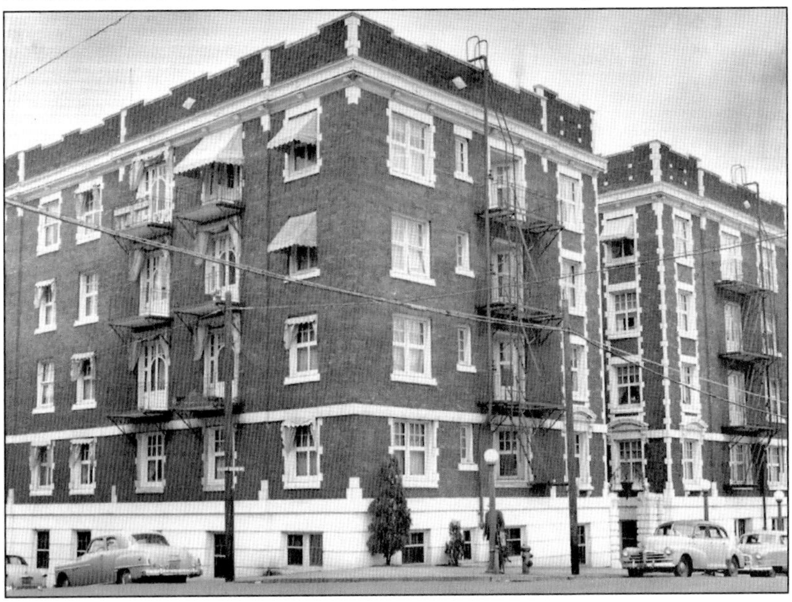

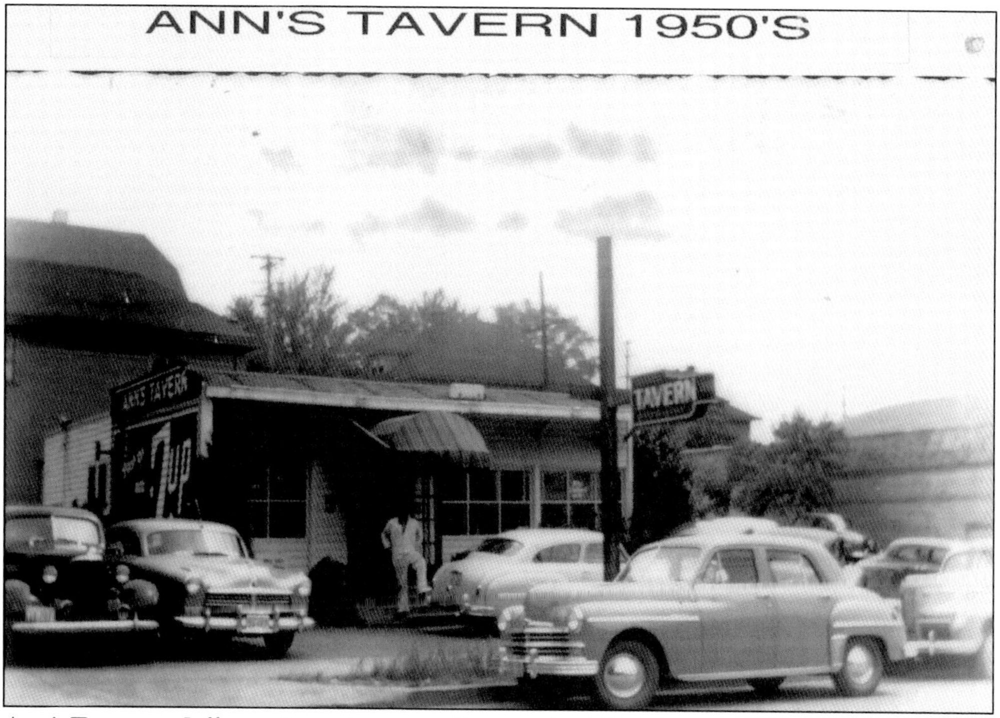

Ann's Tavern on Jefferson Street is pictured here in the 1950s. It was purchased by Bud Clark in 1967 and renamed the Goose Hollow Inn in an attempt to jog the neighborhood's memory and rekindle civic regard for the Goose Hollow neighborhood identity. Without Bud Clark's efforts, the whimsical neighborhood name of Goose Hollow may have faded from Portland's collective memory. (Bud Clark.)

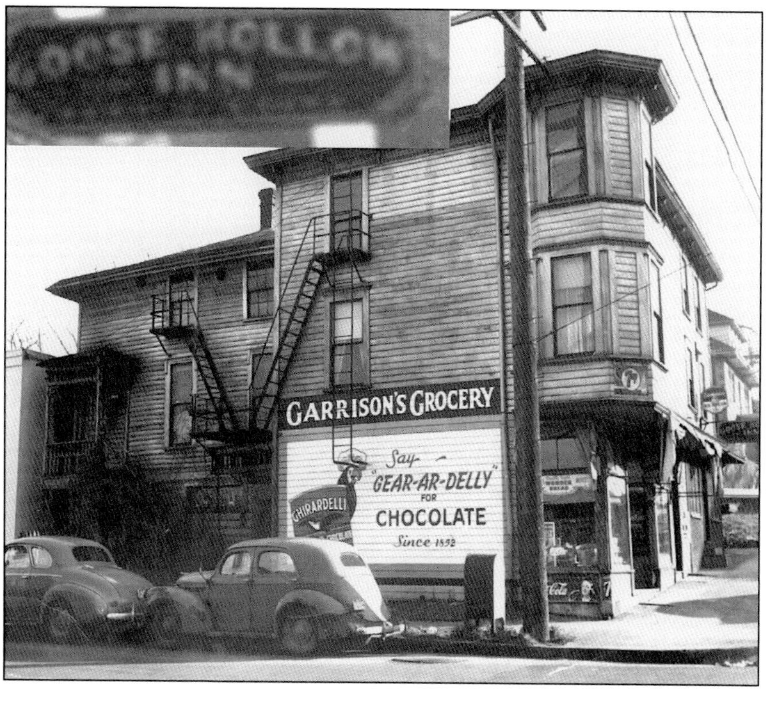

This is the original Goose Hollow Inn that Bud Clark remembered from his childhood (sign enlarged, inset). It was condemned in 1948 as a fire hazard and demolished. Located on the north side of Jefferson Street at Sixteenth Avenue for 67 years, the old Goose Hollow Inn housed a store, "housekeeping rooms," and a bar. (Bud Clark.)

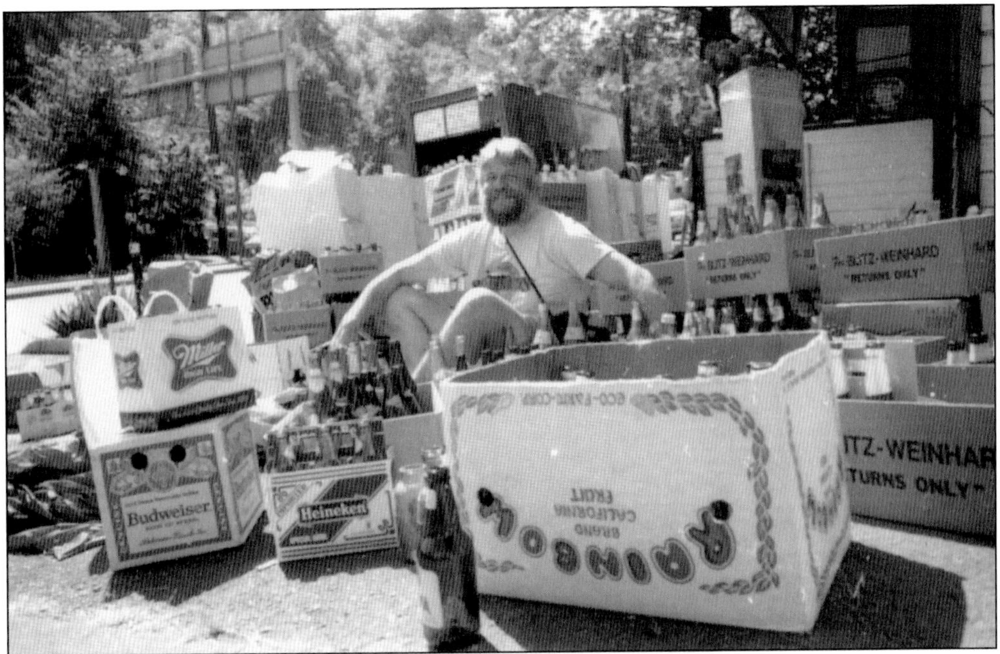

A photograph taken outside of the Goose Hollow Inn in 1983 shows Bud Clark surrounded by recyclable glass for Portland's Recycle Sunday. He was elected mayor of Portland the following year. (Mike Ryerson.)

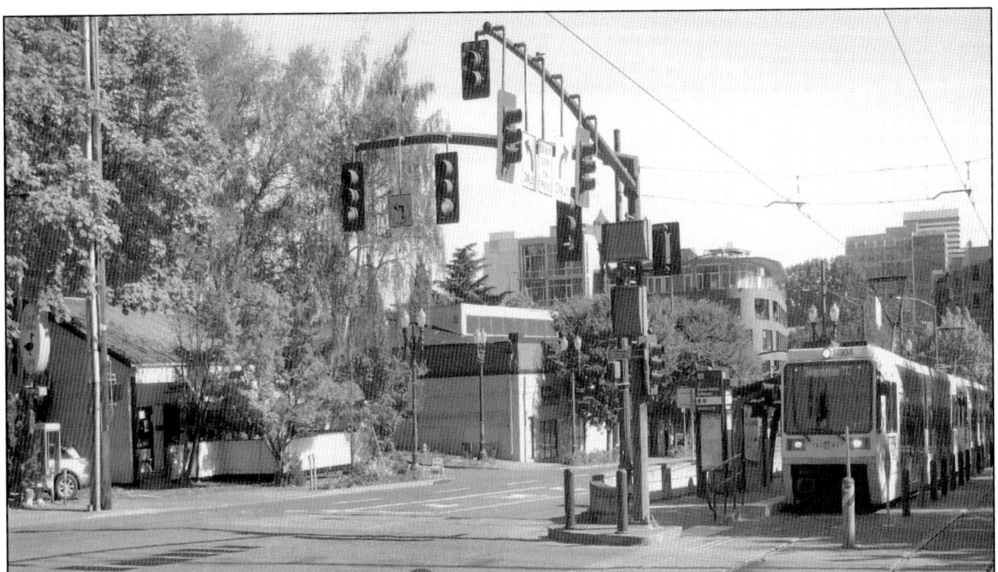

The Goose Hollow Inn, as it appears today, is perfectly situated across Jefferson Street from the Goose Hollow MAX Station. Note the iconic sign to the left featuring a goose. As the MAX train rolls by, patrons sit on the deck, enjoying a summer day.

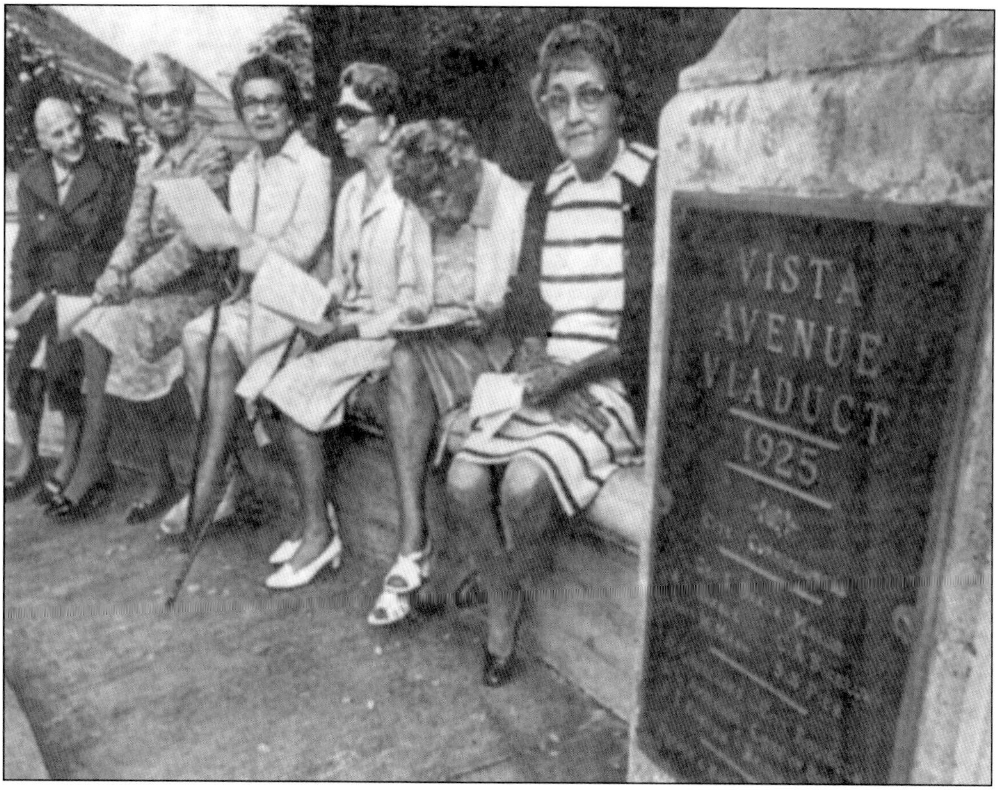

As Bud Clark had hoped, the winds of neighborhood pride were blowing. In 1975, the *Oregonian* featured Goose Hollow residents who threw a big party to celebrate the Vista Bridge's 50th anniversary. (*Oregonian*.)

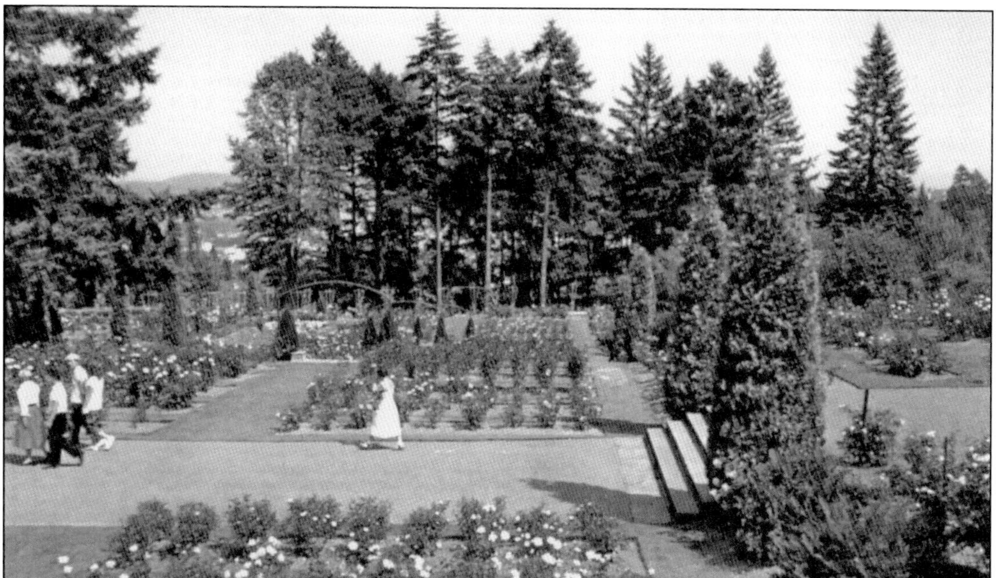

Up at Washington Park's International Rose Test Garden in the late 1960s, the garden was gathering steam and gaining international recognition. (Norm Gholston.)

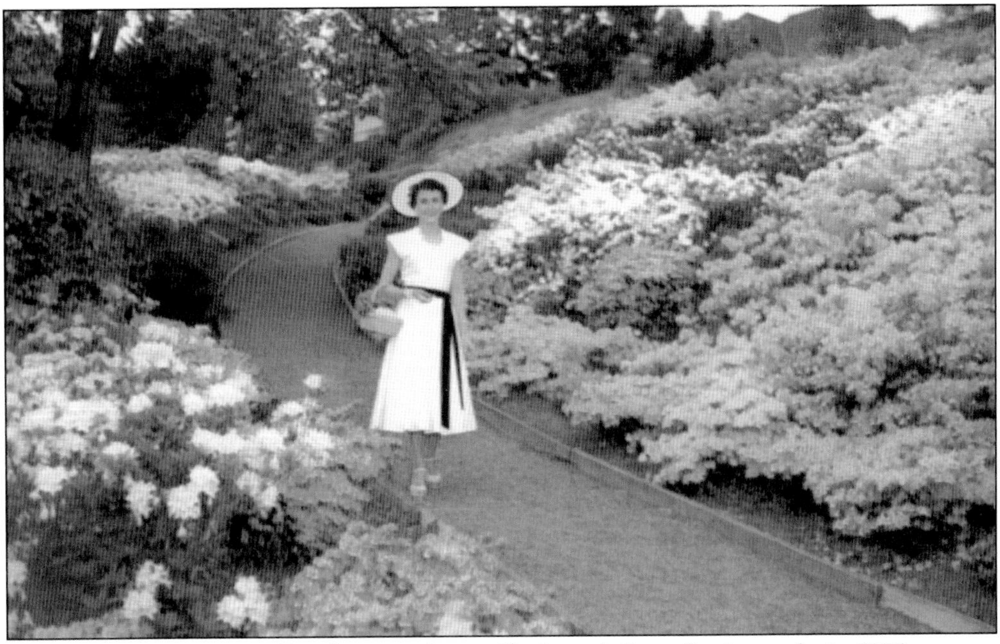

This woman is a picture of loveliness as she strolls through Rose Garden paths in 1965. (Norm Gholston.)

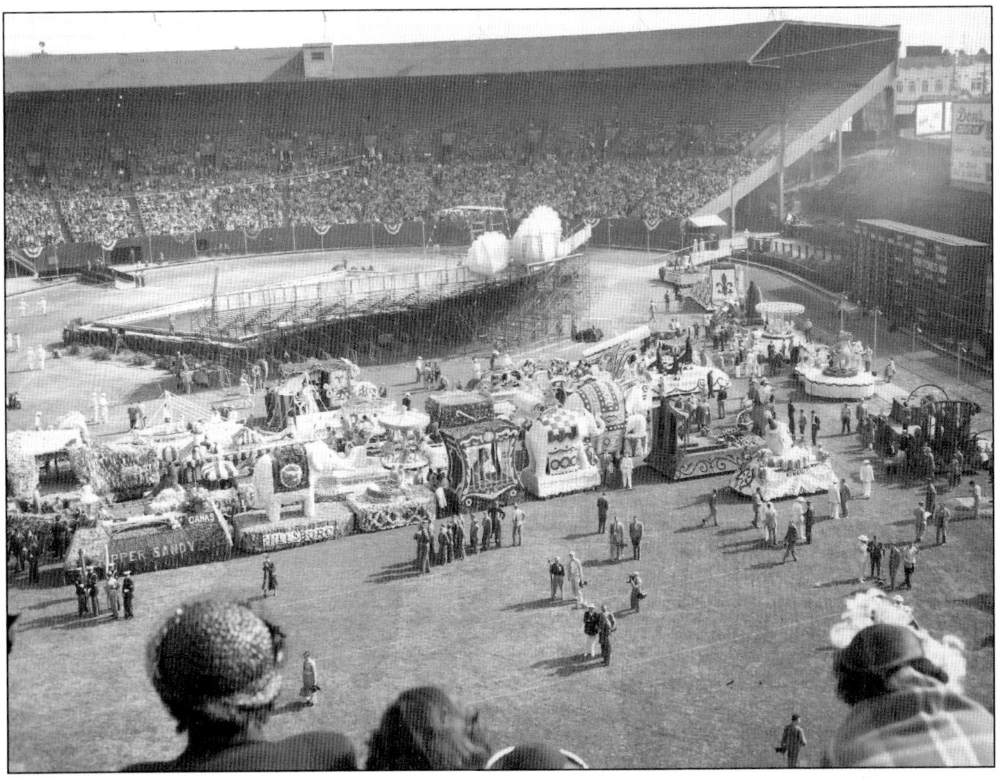

A 1950s Rose Festival parade passes through Multnomah Stadium. (Mike Ryerson.)

These young ladies were part of the Jantzen Knitting Mills float. The famed Portland swimsuit maker won first place for its float in the 1953 Rose Parade. (OrHi-bb007404.)

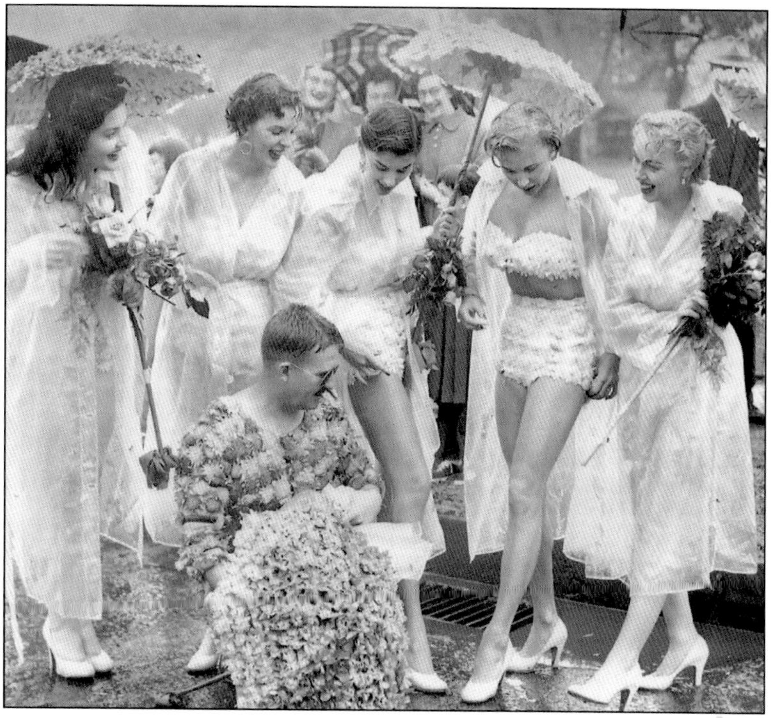

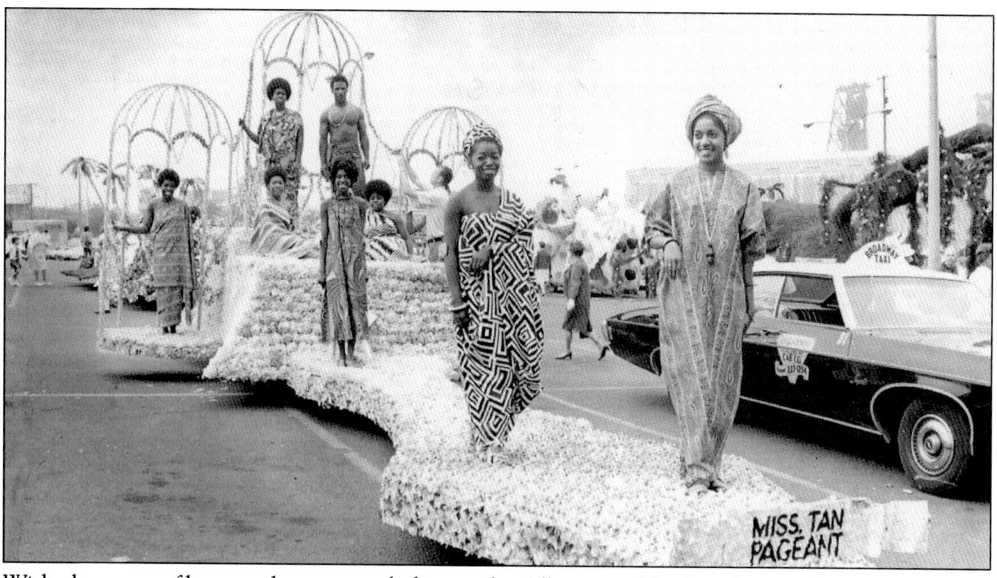

With clever use of humor, these young ladies on the Albina neighborhood's 1969 float made a larger cultural point. The first African American Rose Festival princess was elected in 1967 and the first African American queen in 1980. In 1960, floats began passing through Memorial Coliseum so by the time of this picture were no longer passing through Goose Hollow and Multnomah Stadium. In 1966, the stadium was sold to the city and renamed Civic Stadium. (OrHi-bboo7405.)

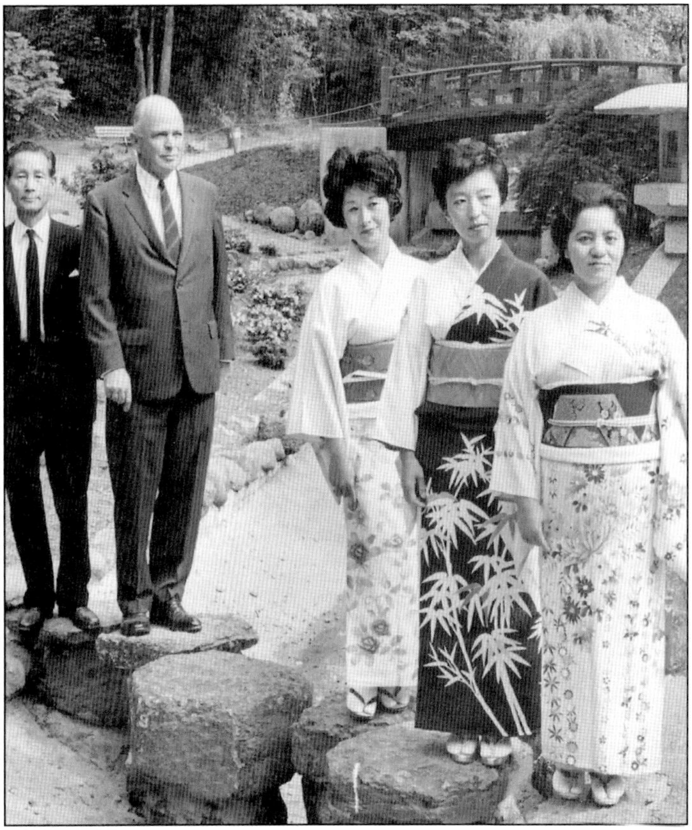

The Japanese Garden in Washington Park is a quick walk from Goose Hollow and is well loved by its residents. In the image at left, Japan's Consul General visits the Japanese Garden in 1967. He is joined by the president of the Japanese Garden Society, while three ladies from Portland lead the way in kimonos. In the bottom image, four young ladies from Portland perform a dance at the Japanese Garden for *Tanabata*, the Star Festival, in 1978. As part of the Star Festival, wishes are written on colorful strips of paper that are hung on fresh cut bamboo branches in hope that the dreams will come true. (Left, OrHi-bb007407; below, OrHi-bb007422.)

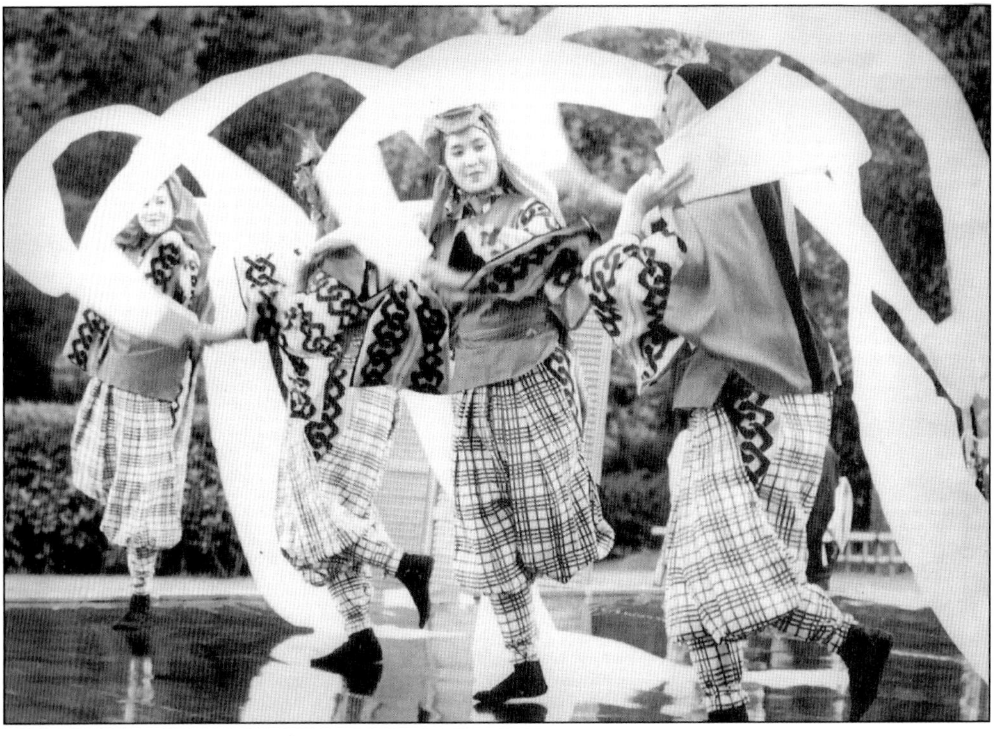

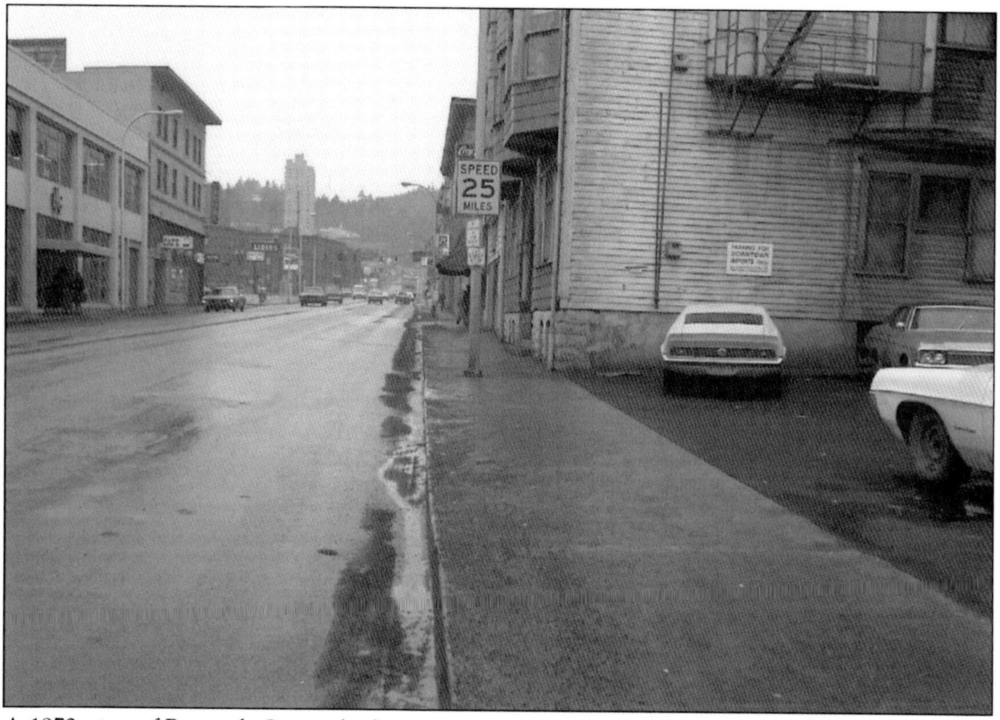

A 1972 view of Burnside Street, looking west, is near Sixteenth Avenue. (CoPA.)

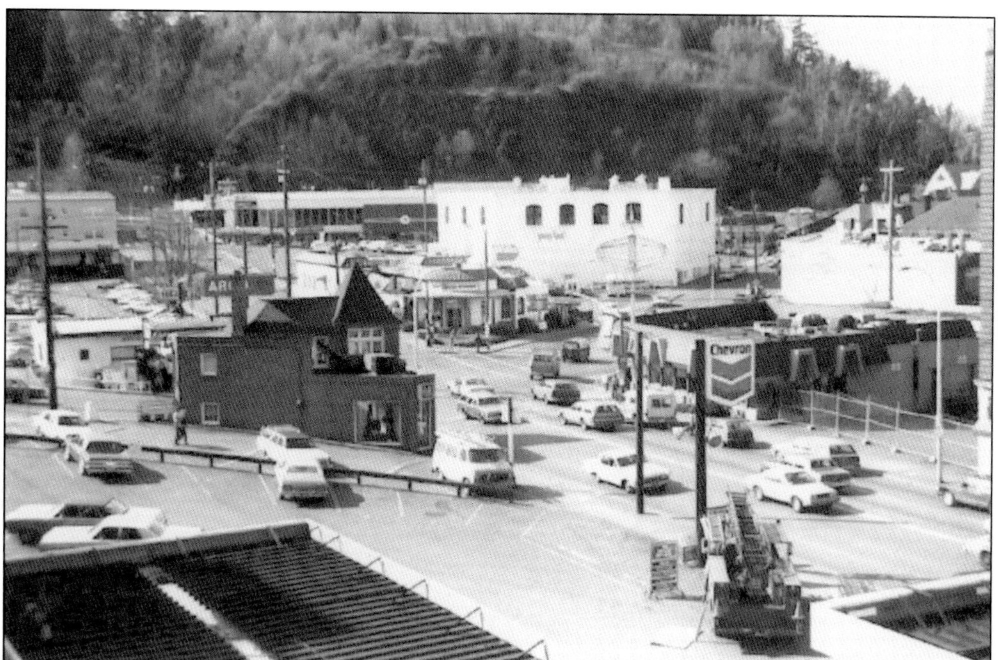

In this 1975 photograph of the corner of Burnside Street and Vista Avenue is the historic triangular building that was once home to Burkhardt's Flowers. (CoPA.)

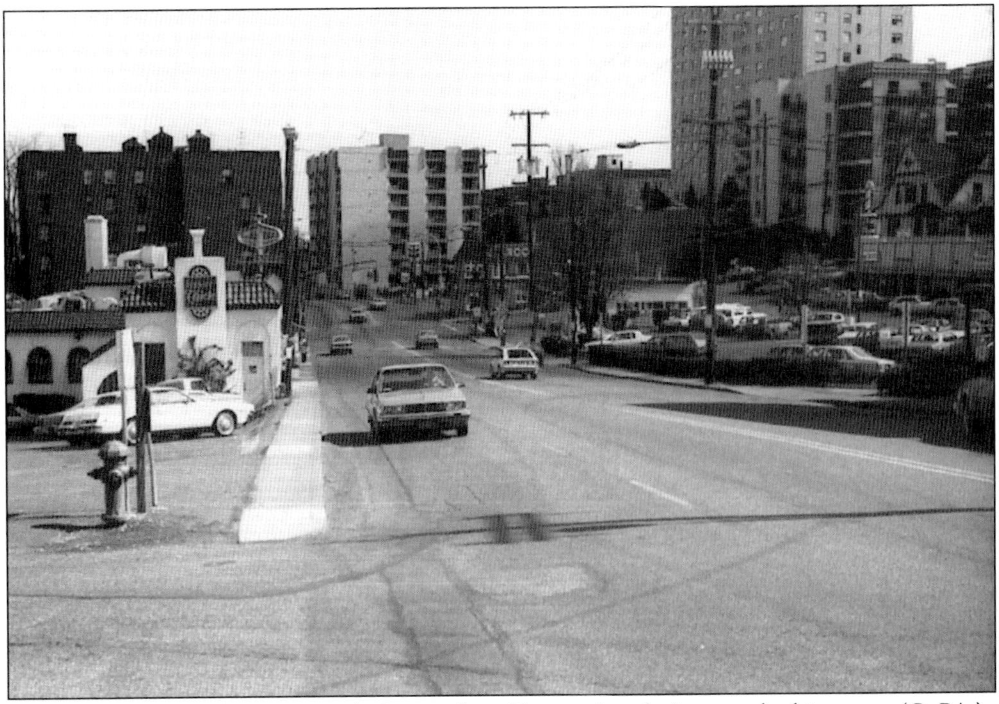

A 1975 photograph shows Burnside Street, from Twenty-fourth Avenue, looking east. (CoPA.)

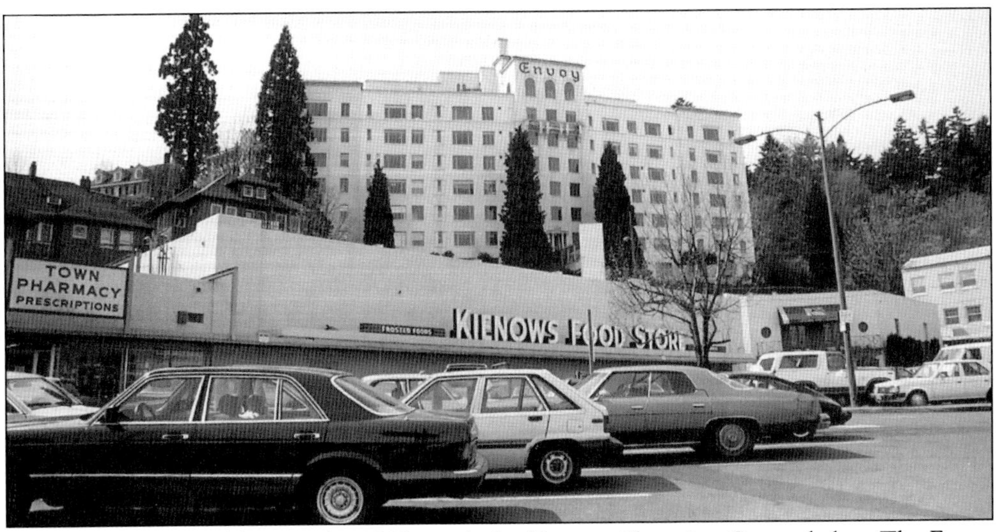

The Envoy is pictured here in the 1980s, with the Uptown Shopping Center below. The Envoy faces north, providing many units with a spectacular view of Mount St. Helens. This section of the shopping center was built in 1940 and the section to the northwest in 1950. (Mike Ryerson.)

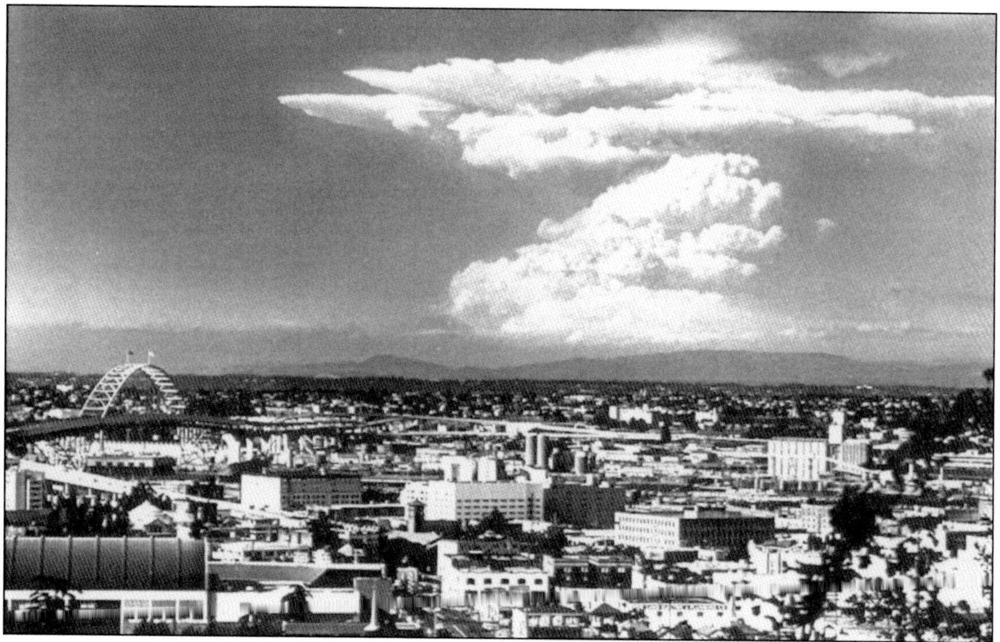

On May 18, 1980, Mount St. Helens erupted and a mountain that had loomed over the Portland skyline blew its top. The mountain's elevation dropped by 1,312 feet, and its once symmetrical cone was flattened. The next day, the *Oregonian*'s headline read: "Eruption decapitates St. Helens." In this photograph, Goose Hollow is in the foreground as the volcano is erupting. The round domed building to the right is the contemporary version of the Multnomah Athletic Club, with the stadium to the north behind it. (*Oregonian*.)

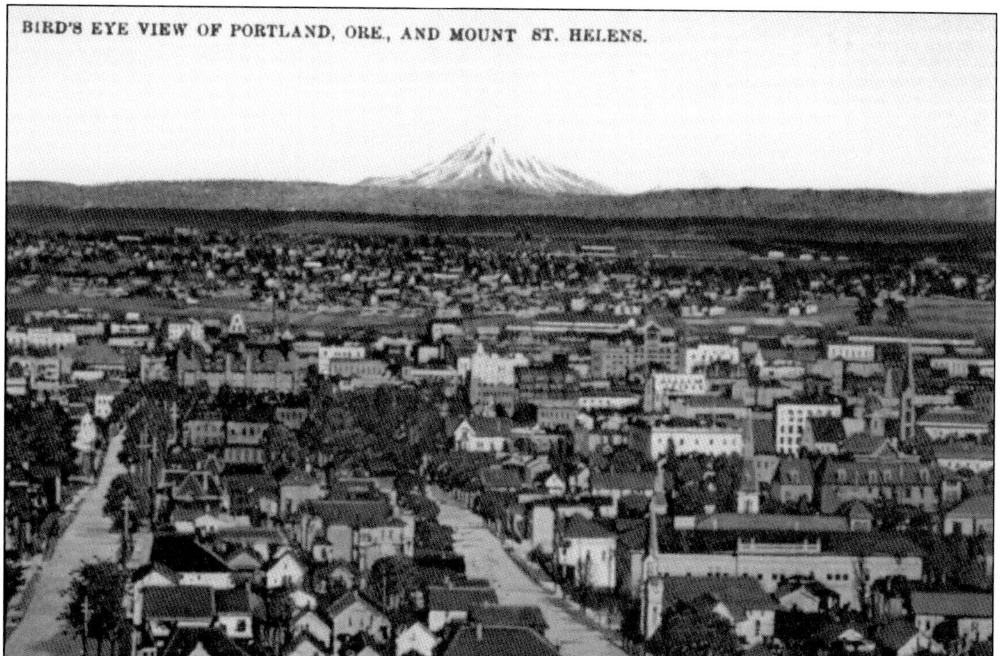

A c. 1919 postcard captures a spectacular views of Mount St. Helens from Goose Hollow. The entire street on the right was destroyed when Interstate 405 was created. (Margaret Parypa.)

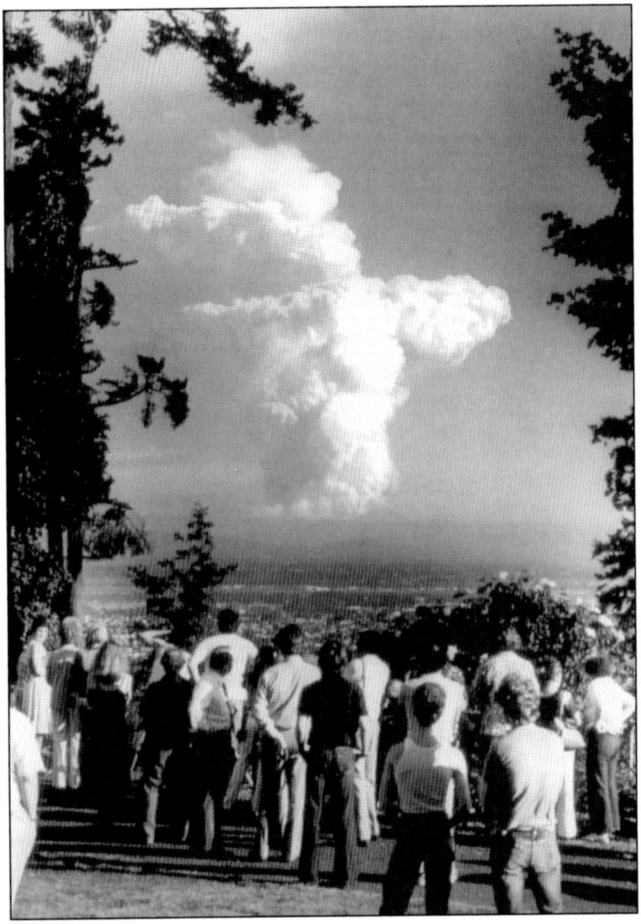

Sixty-five miles from Mount St. Helens, Portlanders watched the nine-hour-long eruption in shock. This photograph was likely taken at the historic Pittock Mansion in the West Hills. Today the volcano continues to steam and rumble, as a new dome is growing within the more than 1-mile-wide crater left by the 1980 eruption. (*Oregonian*.)

Fifty-seven people were killed, and vegetation and buildings were destroyed for 230 square miles. The morning after the 1980 eruption, ash was reported as far away as Edmonton, Alberta. This photograph, taken on Interstate 405 looking south toward Goose Hollow, shows ash hanging in the air the next day. (*Oregonian*.)

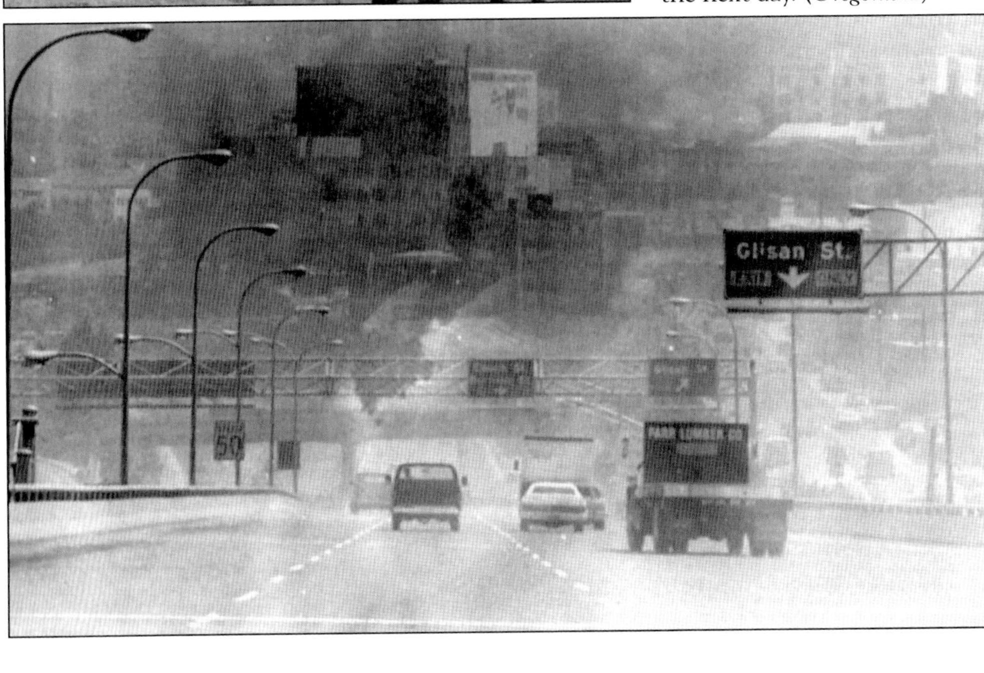

Five

Notable Residents and Conteporary Landmarks 1845–Present

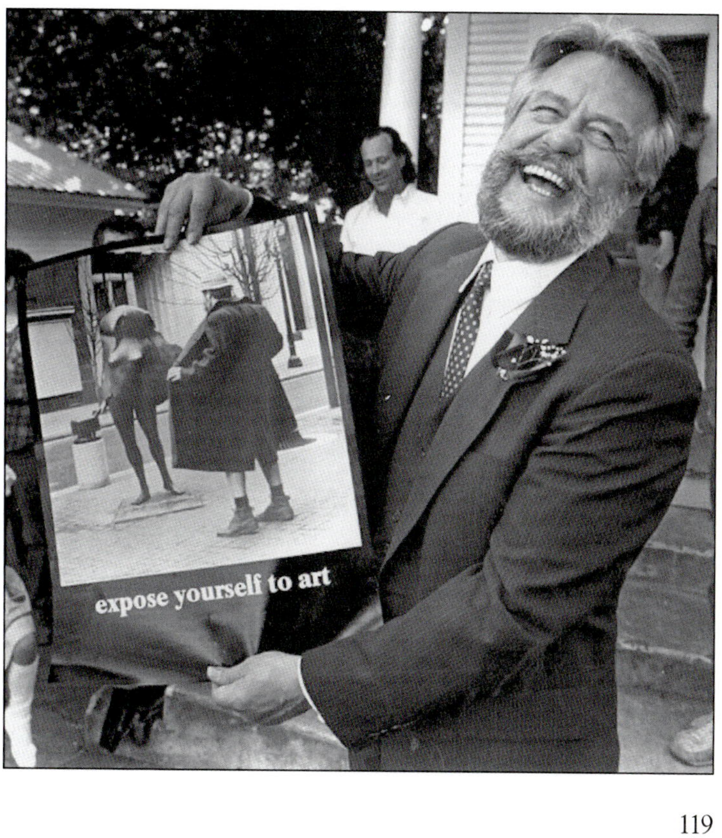

An advocate who kept the Goose Hollow name from fading away, Bud Clark made news when the "expose yourself to art" posters he posed for in 1978 started flying off the shelves. Clark's friend Mike Ryerson took the infamous photograph. But it became a national sensation when the fellow from that poster was elected mayor from 1985 to 1992. He is pictured here in 1984 outside the Goose Hollow Inn after winning the election. (Photograph, *Oregonian*; poster, Michael Beard, errolgraphics.com.)

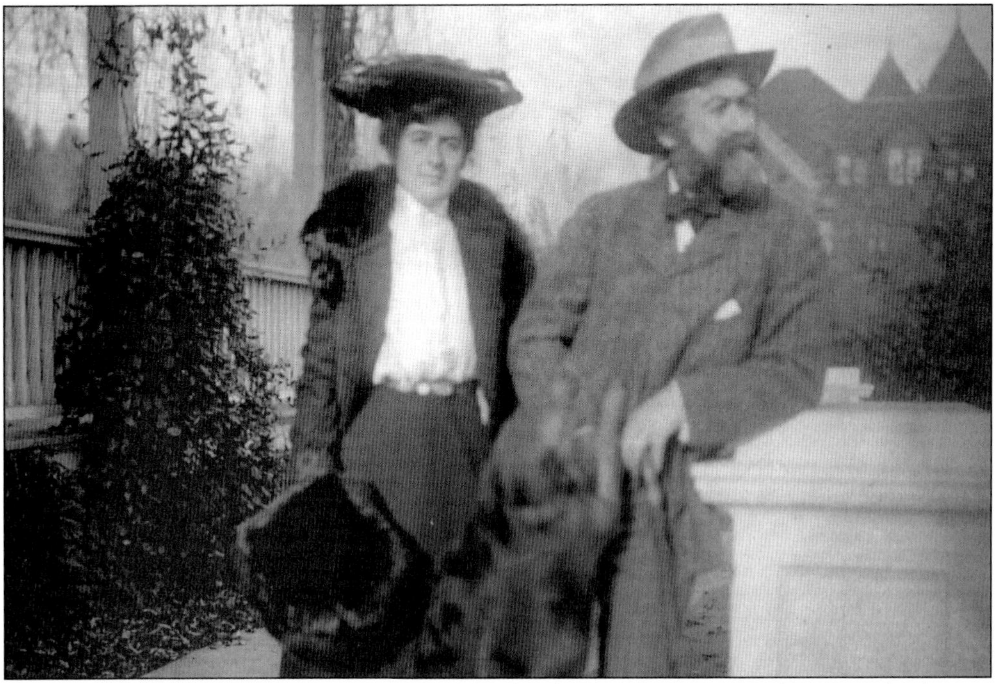

Charles Erskine Scott Wood (1852–1944) and his daughter Nan Honeyman (1881–1970), who was Oregon's first congresswoman, pose at the Wood house with St. Helen's Hall in the background. At Vista Bridge's north end, pictured below in 1992, the site of the Wood home at 1132 Southwest Vista Avenue is now the Portland Garden Club. Wood was a colonel, lawyer, and civic leader. He resigned from the bar association when it refused to admit a black attorney, was a noted suffragist, and advocated for the Nez Perce Native American tribe. A self-described "philosophical anarchist," he mentored John Reed, even funding his neighbor and friend's final trip to Russia. He founded the Portland Art Museum. Artists Ansel Adams and Childe Hassam and writers Langston Hughes, Mark Twain, and John Steinbeck were friends. The Rose Festival was his idea, and his words "good citizens are the riches of the city" are on the Skidmore Fountain. (Above, Lewis & Clark College, Special Collections; below, photographer Aaron Johanson.)

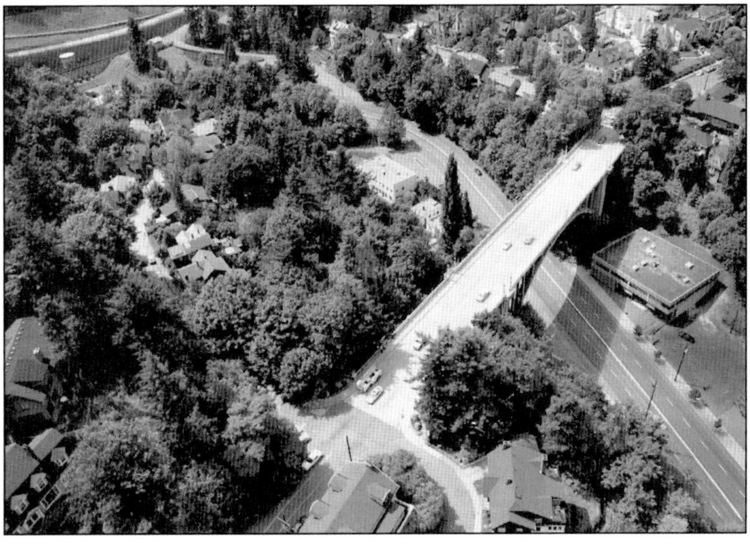

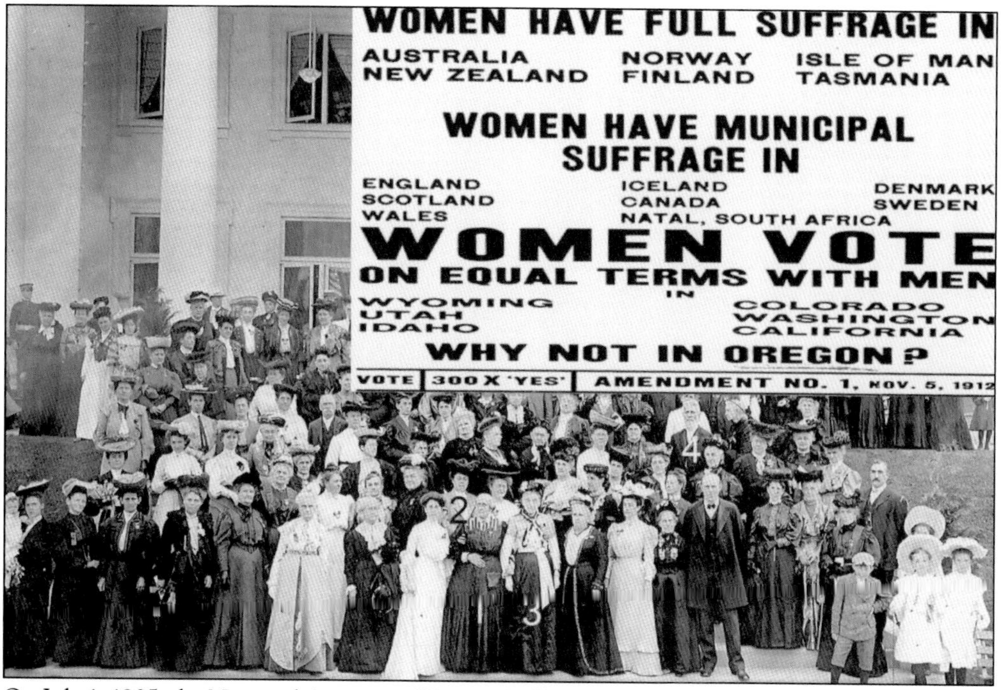

On July 1, 1905, the National American Woman Suffrage Association Convention led by suffrage leader Susan B. Anthony (identified below as No. 1) unveiled the Sacajawea statue at the Lewis and Clark Exposition. Three Goose Hollow residents were important suffragists. Dr. Marie Equi (No. 2), 1872–1952, lived from 1926 to 1936 at 1423 Southwest Hall with Elizabeth Gurley Flynn, who was the "Rebel Girl" in Joe Hill's Wobbly song. Equi was a birth control advocate, an abortionist, a labor advocate, a lesbian in what was called a "Boston marriage," and a pacifist who served time in San Quentin for an antiwar speech at Portland's IWW Hall in 1918. Important suffrage leader Abigail Scott Duniway (No. 3), 1834–1915, lived at the Fordham Apartments in her later years (see page 98). C. E. S. Wood (No. 4), a suffragist, provided legal representation to Equi, Margaret Sanger, and Emma Goldman. Women's voting rights were not obtained in Oregon until 1912 (note the handbill overlay). (Both, OrHibb003476; handbill, OrHi-mss1534.)

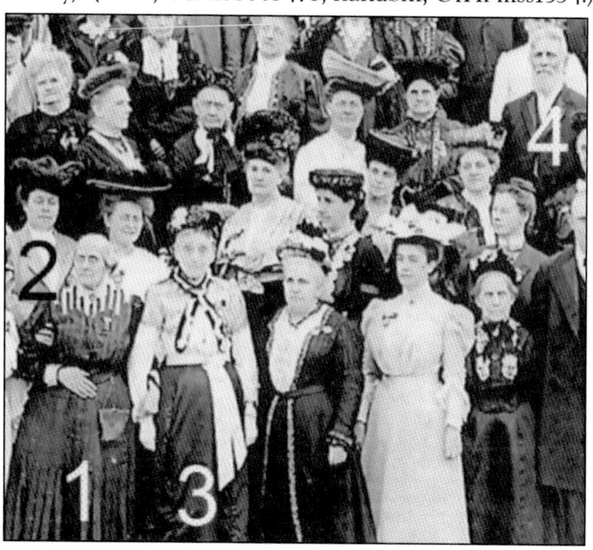

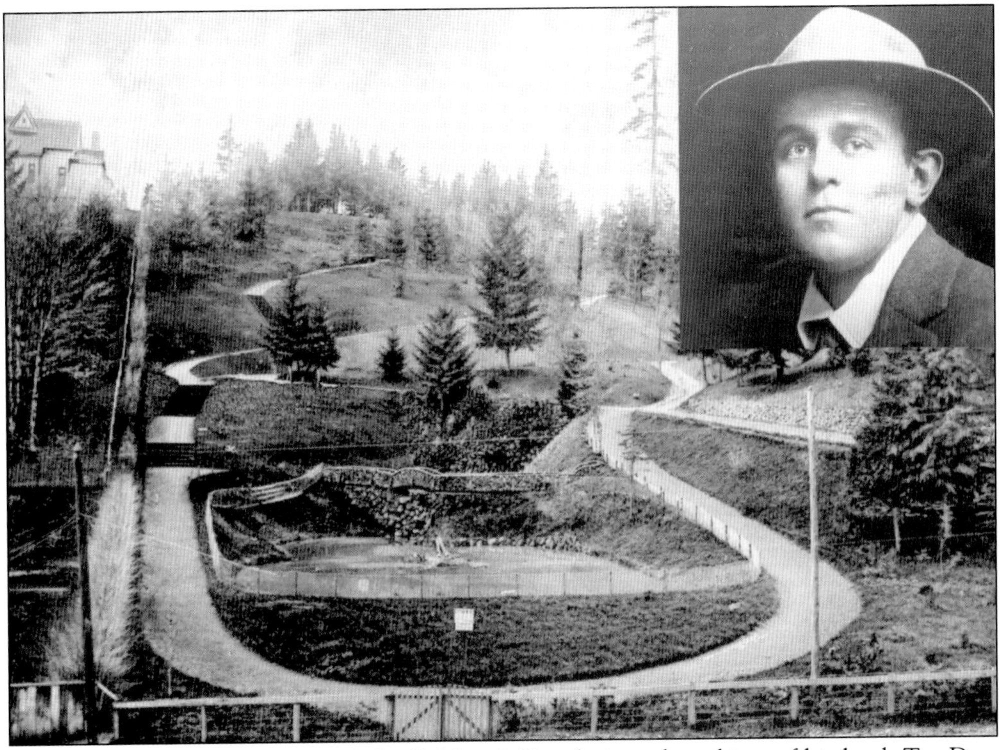

John Reed (1887–1920) witnessed the Bolshevik Revolution, the subject of his book *Ten Days That Shook the World*, and was buried in Russia at the Kremlin. Warren Beatty played Reed in the movie *Reds*. Reed was born in his grandfather Henry Green's mansion, pictured at the upper left (built 1880s, demolished 1910). Cedar Street was the original estate driveway, and the grand staircase at Cedar Street and Cactus Drive, pictured in 2010, led to the carriage house. After Green died, the estate was sold and Reed's family moved to Northwest Portland in 1890. In 1896, his family moved to a Goose Hollow apartment (see page 89), then bought a house at 2020 Southwest Salmon Street. He remembered brutal boys in the Montgomery Street Gang and once paid a "Goose Hollowite" a nickel to keep from being hit. A memorial bench in Washington Park overlooks the site of Reed's birthplace. (Above, Norm Gholston; inset, Mike Ryerson.)

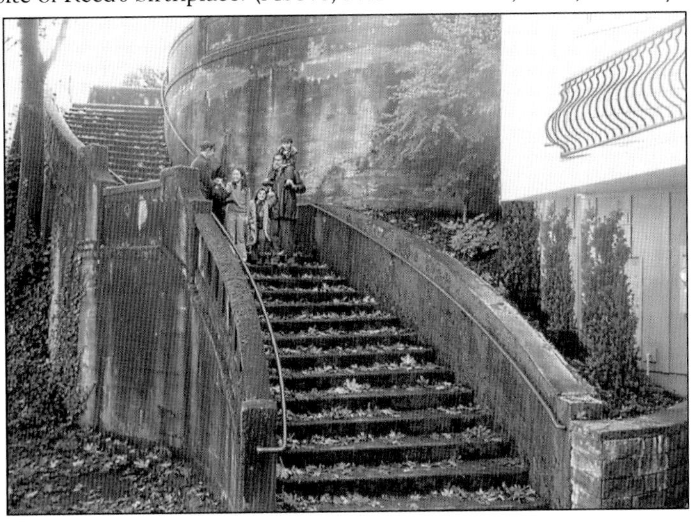

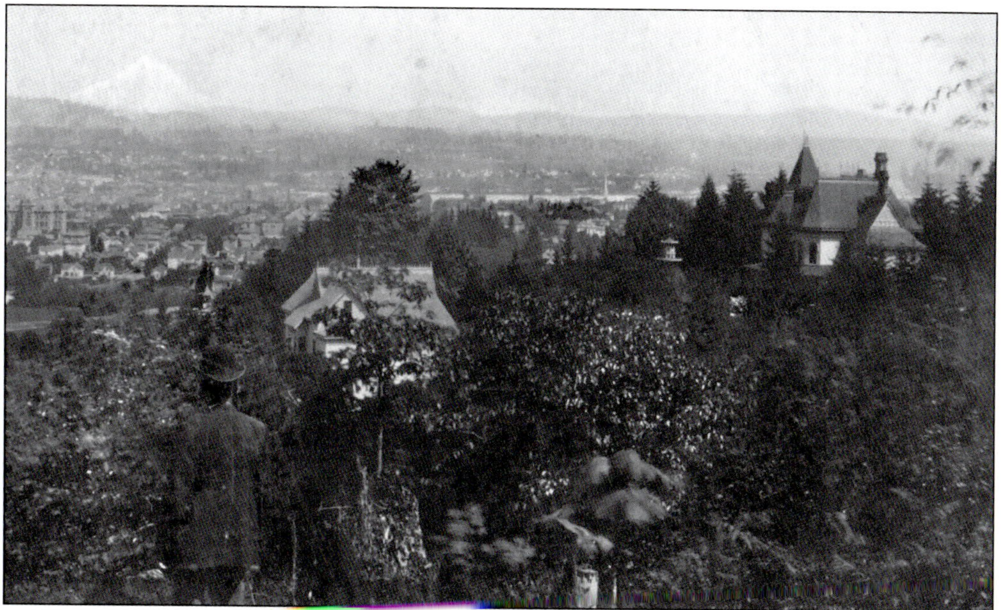

Named after landowner Amos King, King's Hill has been home to many prominent residents: Gen. Charles Beebe (1848–1922), Robert Livingstone (1853–1927), Theodore Wilcox (1856–1918), Hardy C. Wortman (1859–1934), Isaac Lipman (1864–1927), Percy Blyth (1866–1941), Charles J. Schnabel (1867–1921), Julius Meier (1874–1937), Erskine Wood (1879–1983), Aaron Holtz (1879–1953), Dent Mowrey (1888–1959), Aaron Frank (1891–1968), and Thomas H. Banfield (1885–1950), among many others. Famous pediatrician Dr. Lendon Smith (1921–2001) lived nearby on Vista Ridge. Pictured above is a rare photograph of the mansion and carriage house of Henry Green, John Reed's grandfather—both famous King's Hill residents. Mount Hood is in the distance. (Above, Norm Gholston.)

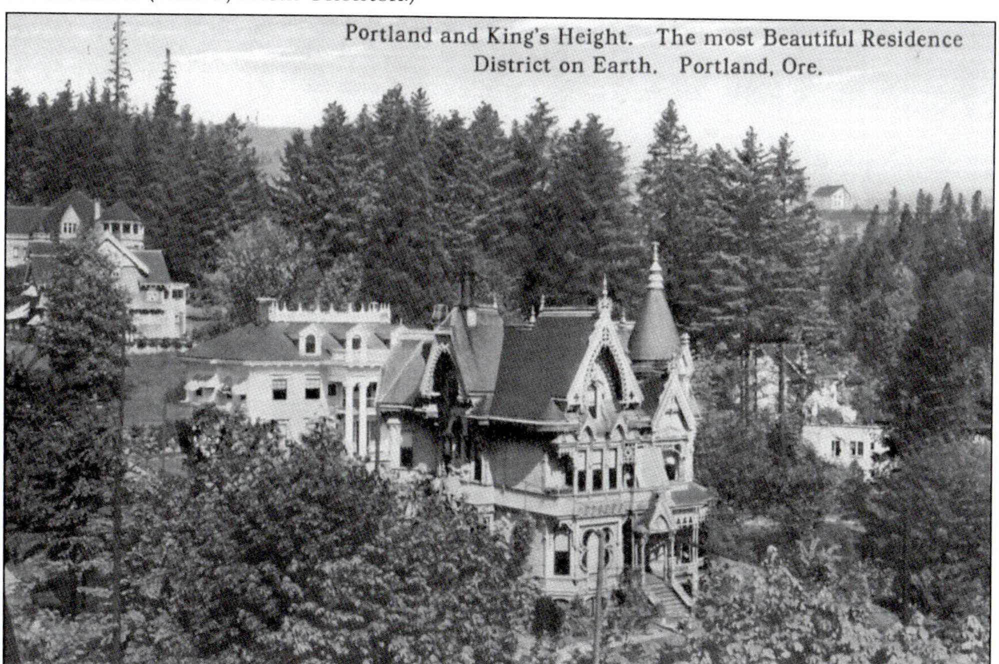

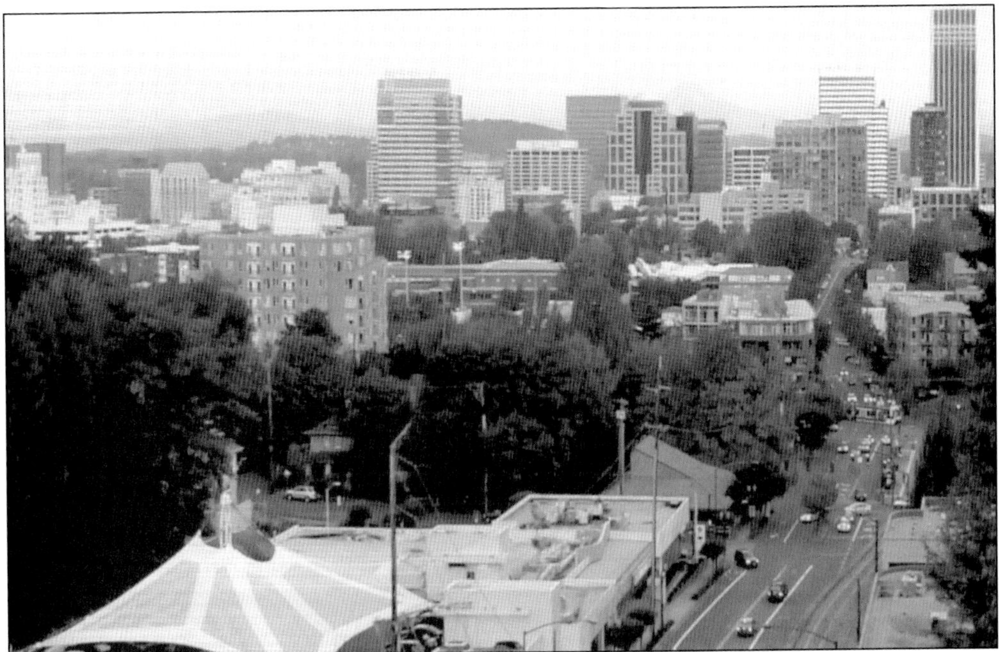

Looking east from the Vista Bridge onto Jefferson Street in 2010, Mount Hood is visible behind the downtown skyline. The MAX train rolls toward the Goose Hollow Station. During light rail construction, workers uncovered old trolley tracks, original slabs from the Great Plank Road, and the bed of Tanner Creek.

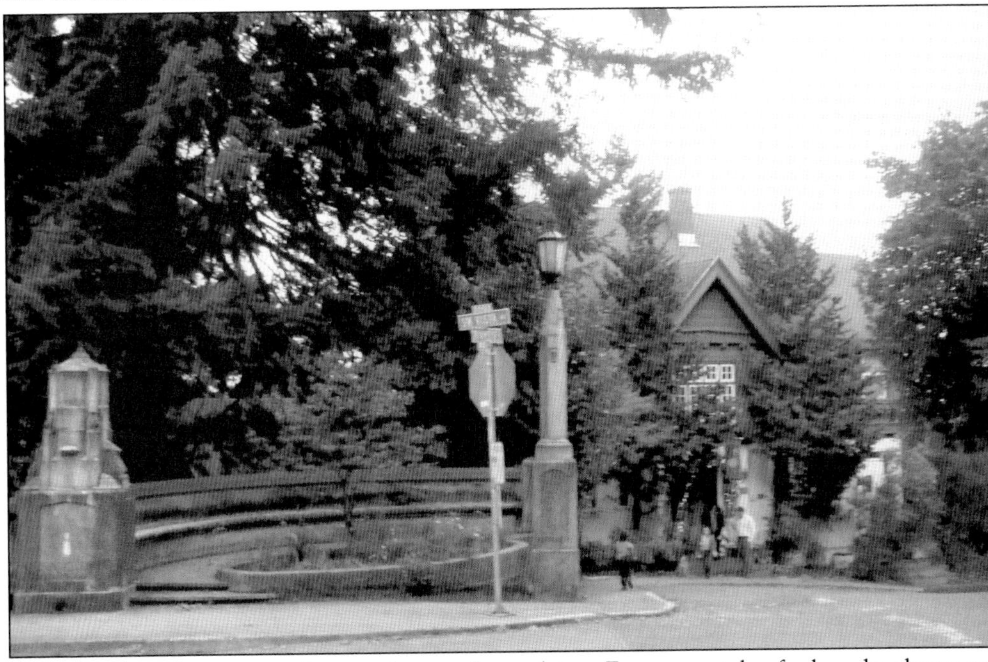

Goose Hollow's houses are often set close to the curb in a European style of urban development, encouraging neighborly interaction. The neighborhood also features many original iron horse rings set into sidewalks, including here at Market Street Drive by the Vista Bridge. Contemporary artist Scott Wayne Indiana uses the rings to tie up toy ponies, to the delight of neighborhood children.

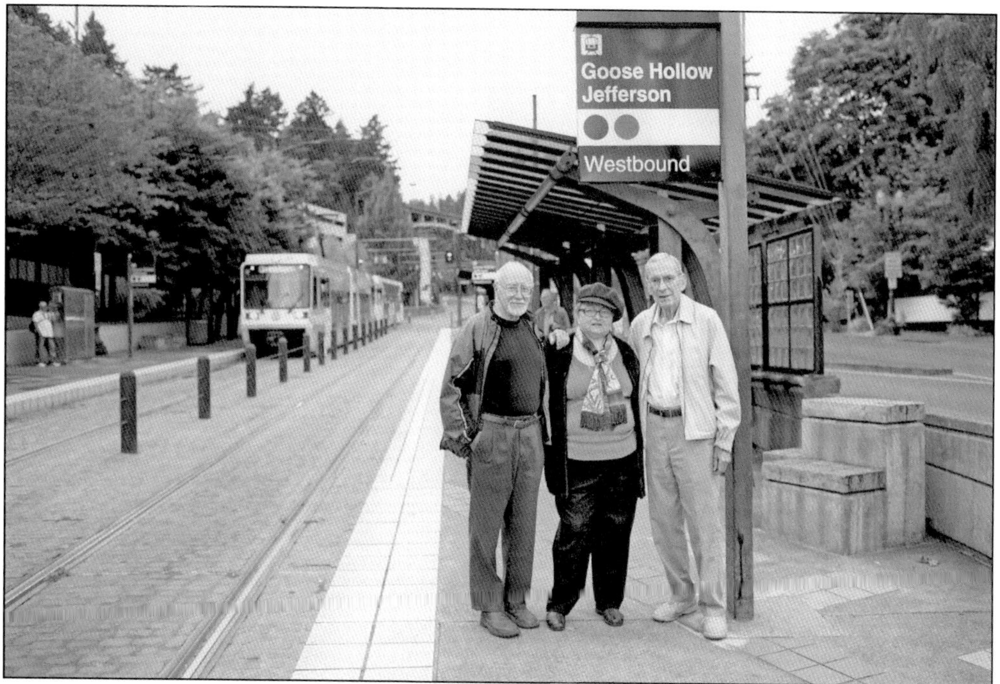

Goose Hollow has a reputation for attracting creative neighbors. Pictured are Goose Hollow residents and important Oregon artists George Johanson, left, and Ken Shores, right, with world-renowned author Jean Auel at the Goose Hollow MAX Station. Vista Bridge is in the distance, and the Goose Hollow Inn is tucked into the trees on the right. Artist Clara Jane Stephens (1877–1952); architect Pietro Belluschi (1899–1994); Works Progress Administration photographer Minor White (1908–1976), who lived on Cable Street from 1938 to 1945; artist Milton Wilson (1923–2004); and writer Chuck Palahniuk have all lived in Goose Hollow. (Photograph by Aaron Johnson.)

Pictured at right in 2010 is the incorrectly punctuated "Kings Hill" MAX station in front of Civic Stadium. The goose sculpture is by artist Rip Caswell. In 2001, naming rights were sold for Civic Stadium, which then became PGE Park, now converted to a Major League Soccer venue for the Portland Timbers. In nearby Civic Plaza are quotes about labor leaders Dr. Marie Equi, John Reed, Beatrice Morrow Cannady, and Harry Bridges.

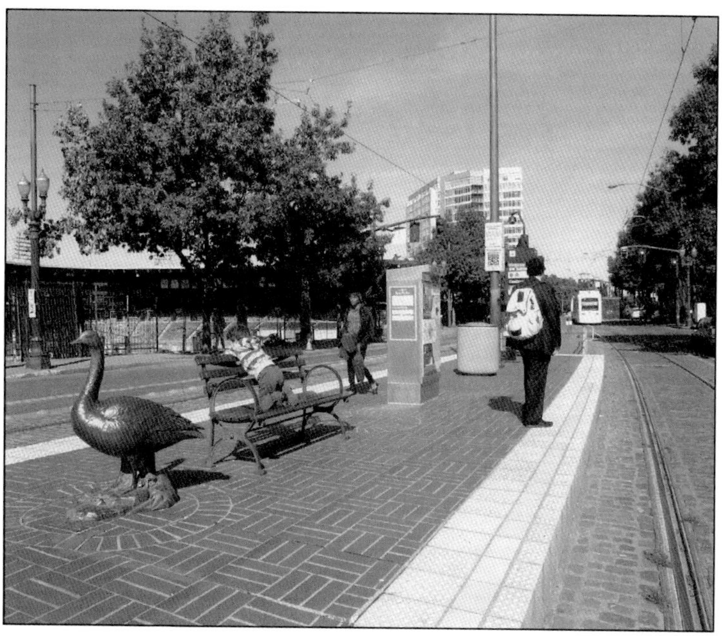

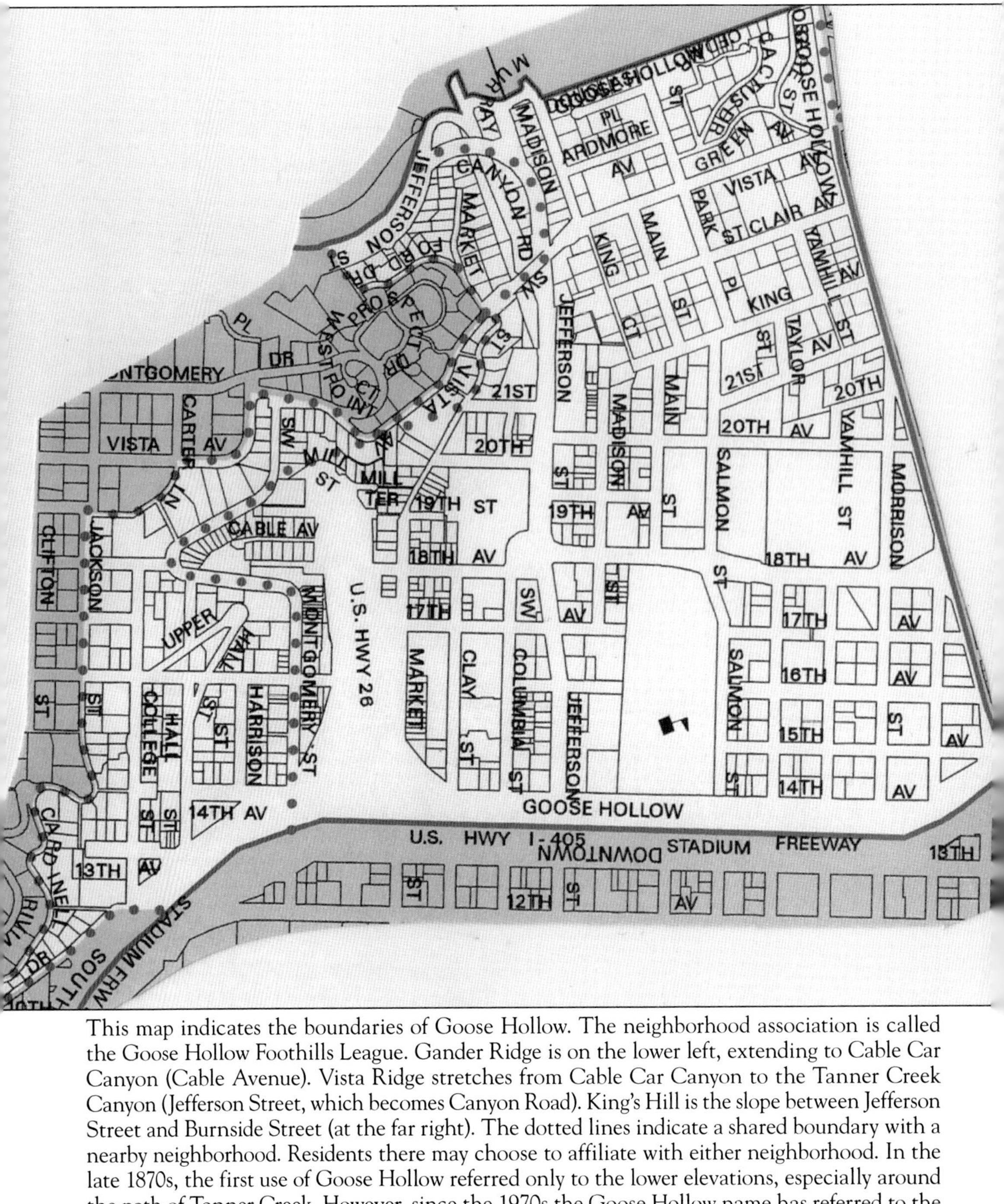

This map indicates the boundaries of Goose Hollow. The neighborhood association is called the Goose Hollow Foothills League. Gander Ridge is on the lower left, extending to Cable Car Canyon (Cable Avenue). Vista Ridge stretches from Cable Car Canyon to the Tanner Creek Canyon (Jefferson Street, which becomes Canyon Road). King's Hill is the slope between Jefferson Street and Burnside Street (at the far right). The dotted lines indicate a shared boundary with a nearby neighborhood. Residents there may choose to affiliate with either neighborhood. In the late 1870s, the first use of Goose Hollow referred only to the lower elevations, especially around the path of Tanner Creek. However, since the 1970s the Goose Hollow name has referred to the entire neighborhood as depicted. (goosehollow.org.)

Thank you to Ian Boyd at the Leaky Roof, Portland's first gastropub, for underwriting the Oregon Historical Society image usage fees.

Consistent with our mission to preserve history on a local level, this book was printed in South Carolina on American-made paper and manufactured entirely in the United States. Products carrying the accredited Forest Stewardship Council (FSC) label are printed on 100 percent FSC-certified paper.

MADE IN THE USA